# Business
# Bankruptcy
# Essentials

Hon. Stan Bernstein
Susan H. Seabury
Jack F. Williams

Cover design by ABA Publishing

The materials contained herein represent the opinions and views of the authors and/or the editors, and should not be construed to be the views or opinions of the law firms or companies with whom such persons are in partnership with, associated with, or employed by, nor of the American Bar Association unless adopted pursuant to the bylaws of the Association.

Nothing contained in this book is to be considered as the rendering of legal advice for specific cases, and readers are responsible for obtaining such advice from their own legal counsel. This book and any forms and agreements herein are intended for educational and informational purposes only.

© 2009 American Bar Association. All rights reserved. No part of this publication may be reproduced, stored in a retrieval system, or transmitted in any form or by any means, electronic, mechanical, photocopying, recording, or otherwise, without the prior written permission of the publisher. For permission contact the ABA Copyrights & Contracts Department, copyright@abanet.org or via fax at (312) 988-6030.

13 12 11 10 09   5 4 3 2 1

Cataloging-in-Publication data is on file with the Library of Congress

Business Bankruptcy Essentials. Bernstein, Stan, Seabury, Susan H., and Williams, Jack F., eds.

Discounts are available for books ordered in bulk. Special consideration is given to state bars, CLE programs, and other bar-related organizations. Inquire at Book Publishing, ABA Publishing, American Bar Association, 321 North Clark Street, Chicago, Illinois 60654-7598.

www.ababooks.org

# Contents

Introduction .................................................................................... ix

**Chapter 1**
**Bankruptcy from Your Client's Perspective** ..................................... 1
   1.1   Single-Asset Real Estate (Undeveloped Land) ........................ 2
   1.2   Real Estate Developer ................................................................ 4
   1.3   Retail (Mom-and-Pop) LLC ........................................................ 6
   1.4   National Retailer ........................................................................ 8
   1.5   Manufacturer .............................................................................. 8
   1.6   Professional Firm ....................................................................... 9
   1.7   Your Firm ..................................................................................... 9

**Chapter 2**
**Sources of Information** ................................................................... 15
   2.1   Notices to Creditors .................................................................. 16
   2.2   The Section 341 Meeting of Creditors ..................................... 17
   2.3   Schedules and Statements Filed with the Court ..................... 18
   2.4   Rule 2004 Examinations ........................................................... 19
   2.5   The Plan and Disclosure Statement ........................................ 20

**Chapter 3**
**Introduction to Bankruptcy Law** .................................................... 21
   3.1   History of Bankruptcy Law ....................................................... 22
   3.2   Policies Embodied in the Bankruptcy Code ............................ 25
   3.3   Individual Debtors ..................................................................... 25
   3.4   Business Debtors ...................................................................... 25

**Chapter 4**
**Types of Bankruptcies** ..................................................................... 27
   4.1   Chapter 7 .................................................................................. 27
   4.2   Chapter 9 .................................................................................. 28
   4.3   Chapter 11 ................................................................................ 28
   4.4   Chapter 12 ................................................................................ 29
   4.5   Chapter 13 ................................................................................ 30
   4.6   Chapter 15 ................................................................................ 30

## Chapter 5
**Bankruptcy as a Financial Tool** .................................................. 33

## Chapter 6
**Jurisdiction and Commencement of a Bankruptcy Case** ............ 35
- 6.1 Core v. Non-Core .................................................................. 35
- 6.2 Filing the Petition .................................................................. 37
- 6.3 Eligibility ................................................................................ 37
- 6.4 Voluntary Cases .................................................................... 38
- 6.5 Involuntary Cases ................................................................. 38
- 6.6 Dismissal or Conversion to Other Chapters ......................... 45

## Chapter 7
**Who May Be a Debtor in Bankruptcy?** ...................................... 49
- 7.1 Chapter 7 .............................................................................. 49
- 7.2 Under Chapter 11 ................................................................. 50
- 7.3 Under Chapter 13 ................................................................. 50
- 7.4 Debtor's Duties ..................................................................... 50

## Chapter 8
**Getting Paid: Professionals in Bankruptcy Cases** ...................... 53
- 8.1 Who Must Be Retained ........................................................ 53
  - 8.1.1 Section 327(a) Professionals ................................... 54
  - 8.1.2 Section 327(e) Special Counsel .............................. 55
  - 8.1.3 Ordinary Course Professionals ................................ 56
- 8.2 The Conflict/Contact Check ................................................. 57
- 8.3 The Application Process ...................................................... 58
  - 8.3.1 The Application ........................................................ 59
  - 8.3.2 The Verified Statement ............................................ 61
  - 8.3.3 Timing ...................................................................... 62
- 8.4 Billing in Bankruptcy ............................................................. 62
- 8.5 The Fee Application ............................................................. 64
  - 8.5.1 Frequency ................................................................ 64
  - 8.5.2 Fee Application Contents ........................................ 65
  - 8.5.3 Fee Considerations ................................................. 66

## Chapter 9
**The Automatic Stay** ..................................................................... 71
- 9.1 The Scope of the Automatic Stay ........................................ 71
- 9.2 Acts in Violation of the Automatic Stay ................................ 72
- 9.3 Exceptions to the Automatic Stay ........................................ 73
- 9.4 Relief from the Automatic Stay ............................................ 73
- 9.5 Filing Requirements ............................................................. 74

| | | |
|---|---|---|
| 9.6 | Why Seek Relief from the Automatic Stay | 74 |
| 9.7 | Criteria for Obtaining Relief from the Automatic Stay | 75 |
| 9.8 | Termination of the Automatic Stay | 77 |

## Chapter 10
## The Bankruptcy Estate ............................................................................. 79

| | | |
|---|---|---|
| 10.1 | Scope of the Bankruptcy Estate | 79 |
| 10.2 | Limits to Property of the Estate | 81 |

## Chapter 11
## The Chapter 11 Case .................................................................................. 83

| | | | |
|---|---|---|---|
| 11.1 | The Debtor in Possession | | 83 |
| 11.2 | Other Players | | 84 |
| 11.3 | First-Day Motions | | 85 |
| | 11.3.1 | Types of Motions | 85 |
| | 11.3.2 | Rule 6003 | 89 |
| 11.4 | Filing a Plan of Reorganization | | 92 |
| 11.5 | Contents of a Plan and Disclosure Statement | | 93 |
| 11.6 | Classification of Claims | | 94 |
| 11.7 | Funding Alternatives for Plans of Reorganization | | 95 |
| | 11.7.1 | Sale of Assets | 95 |
| | 11.7.2 | Avoidance Powers | 95 |
| | 11.7.3 | Post-petition Financing | 96 |
| | 11.7.4 | Equity-for-Debt Swaps | 97 |
| | 11.7.5 | Equity Infusions | 97 |
| | 11.7.6 | Future Operations | 97 |
| 11.8 | Acceptance and Confirmation of a Reorganization Plan | | 97 |
| 11.9 | Plan Confirmation | | 99 |
| | 11.9.1 | Confirmation under Section 1129(a) | 99 |
| | 11.9.2 | Tax Claims and Issues | 101 |
| | 11.9.3 | Cram-down | 103 |
| | 11.9.4 | Competing Plans | 104 |
| 11.10 | Effect of Confirmation | | 104 |
| 11.11 | Modification of the Plan | | 105 |
| 11.12 | Discharge under Chapter 11 | | 106 |

## Chapter 12
## Cash Collateral and Debtor Transactions ........................................ 109

| | | | |
|---|---|---|---|
| 12.1 | Cash Collateral | | 109 |
| | 12.1.1 | Definition of Cash Collateral | 110 |
| | 12.1.2 | The Debtor's Use of Cash Collateral | 110 |
| 12.2 | Transactions with the Debtor | | 111 |

## Chapter 13
## Executory Contracts and Unexpired Leases ............................. 113
13.1 What Is an Executory Contract or Unexpired Lease? ........... 113
13.2 When Must the Trustee Assume or Reject? ......................... 114
13.3 Assume or Reject? ............................................................... 115
13.4 Consequences of Rejection .................................................. 115
13.5 The Standard for Assumption ............................................... 116
13.6 Assignment ........................................................................... 116
13.7 The Special Cases of Real Property ..................................... 117
    13.7.1 Unexpired Lease of Real Property Where the Debtor Is the Lessor ............................................... 117
    13.7.2 Unexpired Lease of Non-residential Real Property Where the Debtor Is the Lessee ............... 118
        13.7.2.1 Time Periods ............................................ 118
        13.7.2.2 Additional Restrictions for Commercial Leases in Shopping Centers .................... 119
13.8 Special Contract Types ........................................................ 119
    13.8.1 Franchisees ............................................................ 120
    13.8.2 Assignments of Interests in Intellectual Property .... 122
    13.8.3 Equipment Leases .................................................. 123
        13.8.3.1 Preliminary Issues ................................... 123
        13.8.3.2 Under BAPCPA ....................................... 124

## Chapter 14
## Avoidance Powers .................................................................... 125
14.1 Trustee's Strong-Arm Powers under Section 544(a) ............... 126
14.2 Trustee's Powers under Section 544(b) ................................. 128
14.3 Avoidable Preferences under Section 547(b) ......................... 129
    14.3.1 Elements ................................................................. 130
        14.3.1.1 A Transfer of the Debtor's Property ......... 130
        14.3.1.2 To or For the Benefit of a Creditor ........... 131
        14.3.1.3 For or on Account of an Antecedent Debt ......................................................... 131
        14.3.1.4 Made Within 90 Days Before Bankruptcy, or, if the Transferee Is an Insider, Within One Year of Bankruptcy .. 132
        14.3.1.5 The Debtor Is Insolvent ............................ 133
        14.3.1.6 Preferential Effect .................................... 133
    14.3.2 Defenses ................................................................. 137
        14.3.2.1 Contemporaneous Exchange .................. 137
        14.3.2.2 Payment Made in the Ordinary Course of Business ............................................. 139

- 14.3.2.3 Enabling Loans ......................................... 143
- 14.3.2.4 Subsequent Advancement of Unsecured Credit ...................................................... 143
- 14.3.2.5 Floating Liens ............................................ 144
- 14.3.2.6 Statutory Liens .......................................... 145
- 14.3.2.7 Payment of Debt for Domestic Support Obligations ............................................... 145
- 14.3.2.8 Small Consumer Debt Payments ........... 145
- 14.3.2.9 Small Business Debt Payments ............. 146
- 14.3.2.10 BAPCPA Changes ................................. 146
- 14.4 Statutory Lien Avoidance under Section 545 ......................... 150
- 14.5 Fraudulent Transfers under Section 548(a) ........................... 150
  - 14.5.1 Constructively Fraudulent Transfers ....................... 153
    - 14.5.1.1 Lack of Reasonably Equivalent Value ..... 159
    - 14.5.1.2 Statutorily Defined Financial Distress ..... 165
    - 14.5.1.3 Insolvent or Rendered Insolvent ............... 165
    - 14.5.1.4 Left with Unreasonably Small Capital ...... 167
    - 14.5.1.5 Left with an Inability to Pay Debts as They Become Due ................................... 171
- 14.6 Changes to Fraudulent Transfer Law ...................................... 171
  - 14.6.1 Two-Year Reach-Back Period .................................. 171
  - 14.6.2 Insider Employment Contracts ................................. 172
  - 14.6.3 Condemnation of Certain Asset-Protection Strategies .................................................................. 173
- 14.7 Post-petition Transfers under Section 549(b) ......................... 175
- 14.8 Setoff under Section 553 ........................................................ 175
  - 14.8.1 Right to Setoff ......................................................... 175
  - 14.8.2 Limitations on a Creditor's Right to Setoff ............... 177
    - 14.8.2.1 Calculation of Possible Recovery ............ 178
    - 14.8.2.2 Additional Analysis and Illustrations ....... 179
- 14.9 Avoidance Power Liability under Section 550 ........................ 181

# Chapter 15
# Claims and Distribution ............................................................... 183
- 15.1 Chapter 7 Case ..................................................................... 184
- 15.2 Chapter 11 Case ................................................................... 184
- 15.3 Chapter 13 Case ................................................................... 185
- 15.4 Claims and Distribution ......................................................... 186
- 15.5 Suppliers of Goods Leading Up to the Bankruptcy ............... 187
  - 15.5.1 Reclamation Rights ................................................. 187
  - 15.5.2 503(b)(9) Administrative Expenses ......................... 188

15.6. Secured Claims ................................................................. 192
15.7 Unsecured Claims ............................................................. 193
15.8 Claims for Unexpired Non-residential Real Property Leases .................................................................................. 194
    15.8.1 Known Factors ..................................................... 195
    15.8.2 Questioned Factor ................................................ 196
    15.8.3 Applying 502(b)(6)(A) ........................................... 197
15.9. Priorities under the Bankruptcy Code ................................ 197
15.10 Distribution to Creditors in a Chapter 11 Case .................... 199
15.11 Distribution to Creditors in a Chapter 13 Case .................... 200
15.12 Subordination of Claims ................................................... 201
15.13 Establishing and Protecting Claims ................................... 202
15.14 Why Not File a Proof of Claim? ........................................ 203

## Chapter 16
## The Discharge ............................................................................ 205
16.1 Discharge in General ........................................................ 205
16.2 Effect of Discharge ........................................................... 206
16.3 Non-discrimination Provision ............................................ 206
16.4 Section 1141 Discharge .................................................... 207
16.5 Tax Claims ....................................................................... 207

## Chapter 17
## Substantive Consolidation .......................................................... 211

## Chapter 18
## Post-confirmation Issues ............................................................ 215

## Chapter 19
## Conclusion: Alternatives to Bankruptcy Relief ............................ 221

**Table of Cases** ......................................................................... 227

**Index** ........................................................................................ 235

**About the Authors** ................................................................... 245

# Introduction

We intend this book to be an overall introduction to the world of business bankruptcy for the non-bankruptcy practitioner, rather than a source book for the bankruptcy practitioner. This book should provide general guidelines for those who encounter bankruptcy cases from time to time in the scope of their normal practice. Many lawyers get through law school and pass the bar without even an introduction to the structure of a business bankruptcy case.

Over the past few years, certain "mega cases" with assets in the billions have garnered much of the media's attention. It is impossible not to have heard at least something about the cases of *Enron, WorldCom,* and *Lehman Brothers.* However, these cases are only a small subset of the cases filed under chapter 11 of the Bankruptcy Code[1] in any given year. In fact, the non-bankruptcy practitioner is much more likely to encounter cases filed by middle-market or small businesses.

Middle-market bankruptcy cases arise from the filing by companies with annual (but declining) revenues prior to their filing ranging from $25 million to $100 million. Many middle-market filings are by larger car and truck dealerships, agricultural implement manufacturers and dealerships, furniture-manufacturing firms, inner-city public hospitals, nursing homes, home health care or long-term care facilities, general contractors or construction industry participants, suburban housing developers, and regional or local grocery store chains.

Toward the bottom rungs of the economy are the privately held small businesses, from the mom-and-pop grocery store, independent pharmacy, or local car-repair garage to small businesses de-

---

1. We use the term "Bankruptcy Code" to describe the statutory law found in Title 11 of the U.S. Code.

fined under the Bankruptcy Abuse Prevention and Consumer Protection Act of 2005 (BAPCPA) as firms with total liquidated debts of slightly over $2 million and reaching toward $10 million to $25 million in declining annual revenues. Some of these debtors are larger suburban restaurants, commercial printing companies, and chains of two or three retail establishments.

The Bankruptcy Code gives formal recognition to chapter 11 cases filed by individual persons, but the structure of these cases is grounded in a modification of the chapter 13 consumer payment plans that run three to five years. Thus, a sole proprietorship filing as an individual or an individual with numerous partnership or limited liability company interests may become a common chapter 11 occurrence.

Congress has also created a separate category for single-asset real estate cases (SAREs), which before BAPCPA were subject to a debt ceiling of $4 million but after BAPCPA are no longer subject to any debt ceiling. SAREs are chapter 11 cases filed by commercial developers of failed or failing single-site projects like apartment buildings, shopping centers, partially unsold condominium complexes, uncompleted suburban housing tracts, strip malls, motels, and hotels. These cases will be discussed separately herein because they represent a significant number of annual filings in virtually every district of the bankruptcy court, and they have their own peculiar footprints in bankruptcy law and practice.

Considerable thought went into the structure of this book. Authors include a former bankruptcy judge and practitioner who presently teaches law, a practitioner and special counsel to a large consulting firm specializing in business restructuring, and a law teacher who occasionally serves as a resident scholar to two think tanks devoted to a better understanding of bankruptcy law and policy. Our collective experience flavors the structure of the book. We recognize that the intended reader is intelligent and may be an expert, but not an expert in bankruptcy law. That is where this book comes in. The book begins with a chapter on approaching bankruptcy issues from your client's perspective. By introducing bankruptcy issues in the context of common debtor scenarios, the book provides a cultural space in which to learn bankruptcy substance and procedure. The signposts identified and mapped to various categories of debtors provide a road map for the non-bankruptcy specialist to consider in representing his or her client.

Chapter 2 provides an introduction to sources of vital information in a business bankruptcy case. Although taken for granted by many bankruptcy practitioners, it is imperative to understand what information is present in a bankruptcy case and how one goes about harvesting that information. Information is power.

Chapters 3 and 4 introduce the history and structure of the Bankruptcy Code. One will quickly learn that many of the most difficult bankruptcy issues are not crisply resolved by reference to crystal-clear code sections; rather, code language, policy, and history inform process and illuminate result.

The remaining chapters introduce fundamental tenets of bankruptcy law. These chapters regularly refer back to chapter 1 in order to relate subject matter concept to its cultural space. Thus, in a sense, the book is designed as a feedback loop that links the fundamental concepts, such as the stay, claims process, and plan process, with the types of cases in which these concepts regularly percolate.

# CHAPTER 1

# BANKRUPTCY FROM YOUR CLIENT'S PERSPECTIVE

For the nonspecialist in bankruptcy, discovering that your client finds itself on the other end of a relationship influenced by a participant that has sought relief under the Bankruptcy Code could be daunting. As one will soon discover, bankruptcy law has both a substantive and procedural dimension. The law borrows heavily from applicable non-bankruptcy law; thus, it resembles more an open code than its does a closed code, such as Article 3 of the Uniform Commercial Code. However, when bankruptcy law borrows from applicable non-bankruptcy law, it does so on its terms and in a manner consistent with bankruptcy law and policy. Of course, hidden throughout the Bankruptcy Code are traps for the unwary; just as you become comfortable traversing the interconnectedness of bankruptcy law and, for example, state real property law, a provision of the Bankruptcy Code pulls the carpet out from under you. That is where this book comes in.

We did not choose to write yet another book surveying the bankruptcy waterfront. There are several small books that already provide that service. Instead, we have endeavored to provide you with a look at bankruptcy from the perspective of the client who is dealing with a customer, borrower, etc., in bankruptcy. The idea is that a book that structures itself in a way in which a non-bankruptcy specialist may approach a bankruptcy issue may ultimately be more useful than a traditional approach. In the remainder of this chapter, we discuss a number of typical relationships that may arise. Within each of these relationships, we identify recurring issues and bankruptcy milestones. The remainder of this book provides the substantive and procedural flesh to those milestones and issues we have identified in an appropriate context.

## 1.1 SINGLE-ASSET REAL ESTATE (UNDEVELOPED LAND)

For many, the scourge of bankruptcy is the single-asset real estate case where the focus is on a parcel or several parcels of undeveloped land. Much ink has been spilled on how irregular single-asset real estate cases are, and how difficult it is to fit them in the overall themes embodied in the Bankruptcy Code. The base case is a borrower who owes money to a lender. The funds were borrowed to acquire the property. The borrower has secured repayment by granting a lien in the undeveloped land. The borrower seeks to either develop the land or flip it as the market goes up. It does not. The value of the land falls precipitously. Soon, the borrower finds that it has no equity in the property; that is, the debt on the property exceeds its value. We say that the property is *under water* or *upside down*. Usually, aside from the lender, there are very few (if any) other creditors. Normally, any additional creditors possess relatively small, unsecured claims. There may be a taxing authority owed some tax—such as a county that is owed an ad valorem property tax—but all parties expect that the tax will be paid. Typically, the insiders of the borrower have guaranteed the debt. The loan is in default. The lender has posted the property for foreclosure (or is close to judgment in a judicial foreclosure state). The facts reek of a two-party dispute: not the type of case that you would generally have in mind when considering the bankruptcy process.

More often, you would see a case like this from the perspective of lender's counsel. On behalf of your client, you have already exercised any rights existing under state law, sued on the note and guaranties, and commenced a foreclosure action. As you approach judgment, you are met with a last-ditch effort by the borrower to keep the property and protect against the adverse tax consequences of a foreclosure sale by commencing a chapter 11 case under the Bankruptcy Code. For your client, the plan of attack is rather straightforward. Your client will generally seek relief from the automatic stay under section 362(d) to permit foreclosure. In the interim, you may ask the court at the preliminary hearing to modify the stay to let you send out the appropriate notices and post the property for foreclosure, if the property happens to be in a nonjudicial foreclosure state and your documents give your client a power of sale. If the property is declining in value, you may also seek adequate protection under section 361. Your client may also seek to dismiss the case under an implied duty of good faith in filing a bankruptcy petition. The argument goes that the case was not commenced in good faith. Courts have developed a panoply of factors indicating bad faith. These factors are discussed in a subsequent chapter. Your client may also seek dismissal of the case or conversion of the chapter 11 case to a case under chapter 7 for one of the delineated grounds found in section 1112(b). Your client may also consider the appointment of a chapter 11 trustee to displace the debtor in possession and liquidate the property in an orderly fashion. All along, your client may be pursuing litigation against the insider guarantors who may seek to extend the stay in the underlying debtor's bankruptcy case through an injunction, a tactic often threatened but seldom successful. Finally, your client may actually consider the possibility of the debtor moving forward with some limited breathing room in bankruptcy if your client thinks that the debtor and its insiders may be in a better position in marketing and selling the property. In sum, although your client has a well-equipped arsenal to launch in a case involving a single-asset real estate debtor whose asset is undeveloped land (and usually interpersonal tensions run very high in these types of cases), once in a while the better course is to allow a short play of the bankruptcy process closely monitored by you on behalf of your client. The rest of this book will provide the legal context to the course we have charted for a relationship like this.

As mentioned, the single-asset real estate debtor with no income-producing property is our base case, but it is not our only case. One can imagine a spectrum of single-asset or near single-asset real estate cases that do house income-producing properties that do look like traditional businesses worthy of a spin at the reorganizational wheel. These cases could include hotels, spas, marinas, apartment complexes, strip malls, and the like. In these cases, often special bankruptcy provisions directed to single-asset real estate cases may be triggered, adding another layer of complexity. These cases also bring with them a range of issues common to most any business bankruptcy, including the authority to use cash collateral, post-petition financing, the treatment of leases and executory contracts, claims adjudication, and access to utilities and post-petition credit. The rest of this book will also provide the legal context to address these issues.

## 1.2 REAL ESTATE DEVELOPER

If cash is king, then dirt is lord. Real estate runs the economy. Distressed real estate drags down the economy. Nowhere is this more true than in real estate development, be it commercial or residential. These types of bankruptcy cases pose a unique nest of bankruptcy issues. Take, for example, a residential real estate developer. In financing its projections, it may have obtained one or more term loans *and* a revolver from several banks or several bank groups, depending on size of the credit. This debtor may be dealing with various subcontractors, suppliers, construction workers, a sales staff, advertising and marketing agencies, purchasers asserting warranty claims, regulatory authorities, and taxing authorities. The debtor may also have some properties housed in land banks. Properties may be generating cash flow (income-producing or investment properties) or may be in various stages of construction or development (developmental properties). Your client may be any one of these interested parties.

With a case like this, the bankruptcy signposts differ depending on your client. If your client is a secured lender, then you will generally focus on protecting its secured position. In doing so, you will negotiate with the debtor over the use of your client's cash collateral, implicating sections 363 and 361. Your client is also interested in whether it is entitled to post-petition interest, and if so, at what rate, and whether it is entitled to recover your fees if the documents so permit. These issues are resolved by reference to sections 506(a) and (b) and the facts and circumstances of your case. Your client may decide to roll over its debt into a tidy post-petition lending facility, implicating section 364. If a new lender is coming into the picture to provide post-petition financing, then your client may seek to protect its relative priority position or insist that it be taken out by the new lender. Although your client may have the right to seek relief from the automatic stay under section 362, that is most likely not the right thing to do, at least not early in the case. If the value of the bankruptcy estate is such that the secured creditors will not be made whole, then you should expect the unsecured creditors, usually through their official committee, to scrutinize closely your client's relationship with the debtor and possibly seek to assert an avoidance action against your client, usually in the nature of a constructively fraudulent transfer action.

If you represent an unsecured creditor with a relatively large claim, your client's first bankruptcy issue may be whether to accept the appointment by the U.S. trustee to become a member of the Official Committee of Unsecured Creditors. The committee is the counterpart to the debtor in possession, is influential in the chapter 11 process, and is privy to virtually all relevant information. However, the committee acts as a collective body and owes a fiduciary duty to the bankruptcy estate. As counsel to a member, you will work closely with the committee's own counsel in mapping out a strategy in the chapter 11 process, investigate pre-petition transfers, and closely scrutinize all insider transactions, among other things. As counsel to your client, you will also act to protect its best interests, timely file proofs of claim, review other claims that have been filed that rank your clients, and ensure that your client has the opportunity to be heard when its interests are at issue.

If you represent a relatively small unsecured creditor, your client may determine it is not in its best interests to participate actively in the case. It may ask you to file a proof of claim and loosely monitor the case to ensure that nothing unexpected happens to its interests. You will learn that this request is fraught with risk for you and your client. Although your client should usually file a proof of claim under section 501, it does not follow that it should always do so, especially if doing so waives certain jurisdictional protections, and the projected distribution is nominal. Moreover, loosely monitoring anything is difficult. Generally, you are either in the case or you are not. If you are in the case, you will file a notice of appearance and request for service of all papers filed with the court, including any copies of the disclosure statement or plan of reorganization under Bankruptcy Rule 2002. Once in, you must be diligent on behalf of your client and regularly monitor the docket.

Thus, even in a simple real estate development bankruptcy case, one may confront a myriad of issues and a multitude of parties. The rest of this book will provide the legal context to handle these issues and to anticipate the motivation of the parties involved.

## 1.3 RETAIL (MOM-AND-POP) LLC

Seventy percent of our economy is driven by consumer demand. One extremely important area where consumers interface with business is the retail sector. The retail sector ranges from very large national department stores (so-called "category killers") to very small ones to a few store operations. This section is about the latter.

Small retailers are the heart and soul of the retail sector. They provide a disproportionate number of jobs and keep a number of vendors and service providers in business. The range of relationships includes a lender who provides both a term loan (for capital expenditures, etc.) and a "revolver" or line of credit (for financing inventory purchases, etc.) secured by various categories of collateral, trade creditors that provide goods and services on open account according to credit terms, the landlord that provides the premises, transportation and shipping providers, advertising, and taxes. The secured lenders confront substantially the same issues as those previously identified in discussions above. Trade creditors are generally unsecured creditors who may possess a general unsecured claim against the estate or a possible administrative expense grounded on reclamation rights or the new priority under section 503(b)(9). Trade creditors often make up the bulk of the seats on the official committee of unsecured creditors. They are also often the recipients of preferential transfers, although they may have certain defenses that may limit or even eliminate any potential preference exposure. Landlords also possess claims against the estate. The extent and priority of those lease claims depend, in large part, on how the lease is treated in bankruptcy. This is a complex issue that is discussed in a later chapter. Transportation and shipping creditors are generally unsecured creditors but must be kept relatively happy, for they provide the essential lifeline between goods and sales. Advertising and insurance providers also possess unsecured claims, although the insurance company may have been prepaid and may owe the estate any unused prepayment if the contract is canceled. Taxes may be in arrears, including certain trust fund taxes like federal payroll taxes. This may expose insiders who are responsible persons under the Internal

Revenue Code to personal liability. All of these issues are further discussed throughout the book.

## 1.4 NATIONAL RETAILER

National retailers pose many of the same issues we just covered in the small retail case, just on a grander scale. In addition to the claims identified above, national retailers may also have international relationships, often purchasing through brokers, factors who are financing receivables by buying or factoring accounts, debt held by bondholders (including public debt), potentially thousands of vendors representing a broad array of goods and services, an impressively large number of nonresidential real property leases, and various classes of equity. Committee composition is important in these cases, especially where the trade creditors are squaring off against the holders of bond debt. In these cases, the going-concern value of the company is of particular importance, as are the relative rights, priorities, and obligations of the parties in interest. If your client finds itself in one of these bankruptcy cases, then, in addition to the issues we have previously discussed concerning creditors, you should add a careful consideration of section 363 sales of assets, including substantially all the assets of the debtor, disclosure-statement issues regarding adequate disclosure, plan-confirmation issues, potential cram down[1] absent unanimous consent by classes, and attempts by old equity to retain an interest in the reorganized debtor under the new value exception to the absolute priority rule.

## 1.5 MANUFACTURER

Manufacturers are part of the bread and butter of bankruptcy practice. These types of debtors bring issues substantially similar to national retailers in regard to secured creditors and general unsecured creditors. In these types of cases, you regularly see section 503(b)(9) claimants, reclamation

---

1. Cram down is the ability of a plan proponent to confirm a plan over the objection of a dissenting class of creditors, assuming certain requirements are met. *See* Section 11.9, *infra*.

claimants, and so-called critical vendor lists that seek to elevate what is a pre-petition unsecured claim to an administrative expense priority. In these cases, you may also represent a union that has a collective bargaining agreement with the debtor manufacturer. Moreover, these cases also regularly expose an underfunded pension, often making the Pension Benefits Guaranty Corporation (PBGC) a big player in the bankruptcy case.

Like the national retailer counterpart, manufacturer bankruptcy cases pose interesting disclosure and plan confirmation issues. The Official Committee is generally very active. Parties often resort to section 363 to sell all or substantially all of the assets without relying on the plan process. Debtors and the committee also often rely on a liquidating or litigation trust to pursue various actions for the benefit of the unsecured creditors once the sales of assets under section 363 have been approved.

## 1.6 PROFESSIONAL FIRM

Law firms and medical practices are not immune from financial distress. These practices are often in the form of some type of limited liability entity vehicle, such as a limited liability company (LLC). The filing of a bankruptcy petition by an LLC poses its own unique bankruptcy issues regarding eligibility, scope of the estate, governance, and claims issues. In these cases, creditors possessing claims face many of the same challenges as discussed above. However, some recurring issues unique to professional firms include insider transfers that must be scrutinized, existence of trust accounts that should not be included as property of the estate, and invasion or commingling of such trust accounts, thus making these funds property of the estate. These issues will be discussed in other chapters of this book

## 1.7 YOUR FIRM

Your firm may find itself a creditor in a bankruptcy case for unpaid billable work or may find itself a defendant in a preference action brought by one of its clients. In these circumstances, it is imperative that you develop all of the facts and circumstances so as to have the information necessary to make a timely and informed decision on how best to proceed. In most instances, you will file a proof of claim; however, in some important instances you may refrain, especially if the projected distribution is nominal and the likelihood of drawing a defense based on malpractice is great. It is also important not to make any demand for payment—informal or formal, express or implied, verbal or nonverbal. Any demand may constitute a violation of the automatic stay and may expose your firm to sanctions.

It is not unusual to possess a retainer to secure payment by your client. Once your client files a bankruptcy petition, you may no longer draw on the retainer to cover any outstanding pre-petition debt. However, you may have a right to setoff and a secured claim to the extent of the retainer funds pursuant to section 506(a). You should return any retainer in excess of amounts billed but unpaid. This overage is property of the estate under section 541 and should be returned in an expeditious fashion to avoid a stay violation under section 362(a)(3).

A recurring issue occurs where your client files for bankruptcy relief and then demands that your firm turn over your files and work product without paying for services rendered in full. This particular issue will require a more detailed response.

A law firm or an accounting firm that had been engaged by a client who later files for relief under the Bankruptcy Code may demand the turning over under section 542 of all of the client files and the professional's work product relating to those files for pre-petition professional services. The attorney or accountant may, however, be quite unwilling to comply with this demand unless it is paid on every outstanding account receivable and any accrued but unbilled time charges; depending upon the jurisdiction in which the professional services were rendered, the attorney or accountant may argue that it holds a charging or retention lien, which is a secured claim, and that it is entitled to be paid in full as a condition for releasing its lien and complying with the demand.

The legislative history of the Bankruptcy Code asserts the proposition that the professional firm must turn over its files to the debtor in possession or to the trustee. There is absolutely no sympathy for the professional firm's insistence upon being paid as a condition for turning over its files to the chapter 11 debtor in possession or to the chapter 7 (or chapter 11) trustee. The policy justification is that these files are likely to be necessary for the orderly administration of the bankruptcy estate, and that policy trumps the rights or interests of the professional firm. To some extent, this is consistent with section 541, which defines property of the debtor or the bankruptcy estate very broadly. Surely the documents or records of the client that have been sent to the professional firm are property of the debtor or of the estate, but it is a stretch to infer that any of the work product of the professional firm is also property of the debtor or of the estate. Section 542(e) governs the protection of the debtor's client-attorney privilege of confidentiality in cases in which turnover of professional files is required. This subsection also extends to the protection of the debtor's client-accountant privilege if that privilege is recognized by the jurisdiction in which the professional services are substantially performed. Subsection 542(e) has been read very liberally by some courts to extend the scope of property of the debtor or of the estate to work product on the rather shaky premise that the work product is prepared for the benefit of the debtor and, therefore, becomes property of the estate. As such, work product is subject to turnover, whether paid for or not.[2]

---

2. For a comprehensive discussion of all of these issues that disfavor the claims of attorneys, *see In re* Am. Metrocomm Corp., 274 B.R. 641 (Bankr. D. Del. 2002).

Many courts have conceded that whether a professional firm is entitled to claim a charging or a retention lien on the client files and especially on the work product files is governed by applicable state law. In fact, there are several jurisdictions that clearly recognize under their common law decisions or under explicit statute that charging or retention liens are valid and enforceable for professional services by attorneys and, in a lesser number, by accountants. So if the applicable state law recognizes the lien of the professionals, then they may treat their claim for unpaid professional services as a secured claim, and may condition the release and delivery of those files to the debtor or debtor in possession upon payment of reasonable professional compensation and reimbursement of expenses. That request is not likely to be supported by the Official Committee of Unsecured Creditors or by the United States trustee. Those firms that have provided professional services during the pre-petition period in a jurisdiction that does not recognize a retaining lien for law firms or accountants are out of luck, and they must deliver the client files and probably their work product to the debtor in possession or the chapter 7 trustee, subject to the claim of confidential privilege held by the debtor with respect to communications with its former attorney or accountant (assuming the jurisdiction recognizes such a privilege for accounting firms), and further subject to the professional's claim of the work product privilege.

Rather than complicate this brief discussion with the complex issue of the confidential privilege, it is settled law that the debtor in possession succeeds to the debtor's privilege, and a chapter 7 trustee succeeds by operation of law to a corporate debtor's privilege. The law is far less settled when a chapter 7 trustee purports to assert the privilege held by a debtor who is a natural person.

Since, in almost all instances, the enforceability of the lien requires continuous possession of the files, the concept of adequate protection under section 361 would seem not to apply. If the files are to be turned over, possession is lost, and the lien fails unless the court enters an order purporting to recognize the lien as valid and enforceable notwithstanding the turnover. But even as a secured claim, it makes no practical sense to offer periodic payments for the use of the files by the debtor in possession, or in certain cases the chapter 7 trustee, and it is difficult to conceive of some treatment of the secured claim based upon an indubitable equivalent.

In a majority of the circuits, the professional law or accounting firm may not collect its pre-petition secured or unsecured claim by agreeing to continue performing services for the chapter 11 debtor in possession under a "general retainer." That is because a professional firm cannot be retained by the debtor in possession or by an operating chapter 11 trustee as long as it is not disinterested.[3] Holding a secured or unsecured claim for unpaid pre-petition professional services owed by the estate is per se disqualifying under the very broad definition of a lack of disinterestedness.

Many pragmatic courts have held that if the professional firm unqualifiedly waives its pre-petition claim, that waiver will remove this disqualification. If the claim is substantial and there is a reasonable probability that the chapter 11 estate will be in a position to pay a decent percentage of the unsecured claims, then the firm may agree to waive the claim, but that is quite a risky bet for the great majority of chapter 11 cases. There is a little more latitude for the retention of special counsel with a pre-petition claim for unpaid legal services under section 327(e) to perform specific functions, usually the prosecution of pending actions for which the general counsel for the debtor in possession has no expertise or is unwilling to do personal injury or other work on a contingent-fee basis.

---

3. *See* section 101(14) for the definition of "disinterested person."

# Chapter 2

# Sources of Information

As you may have gathered, bankruptcy from a creditor's perspective can be quite different from bankruptcy from a debtor's perspective. To the creditor, reorganization is a legitimate goal only because creditors will receive more through the plan of reorganization than they would through chapter 7 liquidation.[1] Moreover, although the creditor may recognize the debtor's dilemmas (the fact that the debtor is unable—not refusing—to pay creditors, and the hardship a bankruptcy case may be for a debtor), the creditor's primary concern is to satisfy as much of its claim as possible.

Although, under a chapter 11 case, the exclusivity period ensures that the bankruptcy case is the debtor's show at least in the first instance, the creditor does have many parts to play. Informally, a creditor can and often does negotiate terms of the plan of reorganization. Formally, a creditor can take numerous steps to protect its interest, to defeat the debtor's proposed plan, to propose its own plan, to seek the appointment of a chapter 11 trustee, to obtain relief from the stay or adequate protection, or to convert the case to a case under chapter 7.

---

1. *See* 11 U.S.C. § 1129(a)(7) (2006).

However, the fuel that turns these creditor-protection gears is information about the debtor, about the debtor's transfers before bankruptcy, and about the debtor's financial condition. Debtors usually know when they are about to file a petition in bankruptcy. Sometimes creditors know when their debtor is about to file a bankruptcy petition, but most often the creditor is caught off guard, at least as to current information on the debtor. Thus, from a creditor's perspective, the first concern is to obtain as much relevant information as practicable so as to allow it to traverse the bankruptcy maze without blinders.

Since much contact with the debtor may be essentially halted by the operation of the automatic stay, readily available sources of information must be identified by creditors to find out what is going on, how and when they will be repaid, and when, if ever, they will be able to pursue their rights and remedies under state law. Typical sources of information include notice to creditors, the first meeting of creditors, schedule and statements filed with the court, and Rule 2004 examinations. Bear in mind it is the wise creditor who reaps as much benefit as possible from these sources.

## 2.1 NOTICES TO CREDITORS

The first and most readily available source of information is the notice to creditors served by the bankruptcy court clerk. Creditors who receive the notice are those who are listed by the debtor in the schedules filed with the bankruptcy court. The notice generally includes the following information:

- The date of filing of the bankruptcy petition.
- The chapter under which the petition was filed.
- The date and time of the first meeting of creditors.
- The bar date for filing proofs of claim, and time periods for objections to discharge of the debts or indebtedness of the debtor.
- Notification of the automatic stay.

If a creditor does not receive a notice from the bankruptcy clerk's office, it may have been incorrectly excluded from the petition filed by the debtor, or the address stated therein may be incorrect. Creditors who do not receive notification of the bankruptcy case and do not have actual knowledge of the case in time for filing a proof of claim may not have their claims discharged in a bankruptcy proceeding. Discharge of the debtor's liability in bankruptcy extends only to those claims that are properly scheduled and not excepted from discharge under section 523 of the Bankruptcy Code.

However, if a creditor is aware of the bankruptcy case and has not formally received any notification from the clerk's office, the creditor should contact the debtor's counsel. It is generally in the creditor's best interest to determine the status of the case and the disposition of any collateral securing the creditor's claim during the bankruptcy case.

## 2.2 THE SECTION 341 MEETING OF CREDITORS

The Bankruptcy Code establishes a forum for creditors to obtain information from the debtor or its representative under oath. The Bankruptcy Code provides that within a reasonable time after an order for relief is entered (the date of the voluntary filing of a bankruptcy petition or the date that an involuntary petition is granted), the U.S. trustee shall convene and preside at a meeting of creditors and equity security holders.[2] The bankruptcy court does not preside at or attend the creditors' meeting.

Pursuant to Bankruptcy Rule 2003, the creditors' meeting will be held not less than 20 or more than 40 days after the order for relief is entered. The main purpose of the creditors' meeting is to provide a mechanism for creditors to elect a trustee and to examine the debtor. Generally, the chapter 7 trustee, or in a chapter 11 case, the U.S. trustee, presides over the creditors' meeting unless there are specific objections to the U.S. trustee in a chapter 11 case or the chapter 7

---

2. 11 U.S.C. § 341 (2006).

trustee presiding over the meeting, or the creditors desire to elect their own trustee at the meeting.

The first meeting of creditors under section 341 involves creditors' propounding questions concerning the debtor's affairs, assets, liabilities, transfers, exemptions, reorganization plans, etc., the list of topics can go on and on. The scope of the meeting is broad; in fact, some debtors liken it to the Inquisition. Because of the overwhelming number of bankruptcy cases filed, the trustees in certain districts have limited the questioning and the length of meetings to approximately 15 to 30 minutes. The trustee may reset the creditors' meeting in order to allow for more time for questioning or to allow the debtor to supplement the information provided to creditors. If not, the meeting is adjourned.

The creditors' meeting is one forum for gathering information. However, in-depth examination of the debtor for an extended period of time does not generally occur at the creditors' meeting.

## 2.3 SCHEDULES AND STATEMENTS FILED WITH THE COURT

The debtor is required to file a detailed schedule of all its assets and liabilities and a statement of affairs. There are two types of statements of affairs—one for those engaged in business and a simpler form for those not engaged in business. The statement of affairs provides information concerning the debtor's actions prior to bankruptcy, transfers of property, and the location of the debtor's assets. The statement of affairs and schedule of assets and liabilities are filed with the petition in a voluntary case or, if certain requirements are met, within 15 days after the commencement of the case. Both documents are signed under oath by the debtor. Extensions of the 15-day time period may be allowed by filing a motion and obtaining an order from the bankruptcy court upon cause shown. This is most often the case in large chapter 11 cases.

A creditor should examine the schedule of liabilities to determine if the debtor has listed its claim properly in terms of amount, collateral securing the claim, and the nature of the property in the individual debtor's estate—that is, whether the property is listed as exempt property under state or federal law. Further, the creditor can ascertain whether the debtor listed the claim on its schedules as contingent, unliquidated, or disputed.

## 2.4 RULE 2004 EXAMINATIONS

Bankruptcy Rule 2004 provides that by motion, a party in interest, which is defined to include the debtor, the trustee, creditors and creditors' committee, and/or equity security holders, may request the examination under oath of "any entity." The scope of the examination is broadly defined and generally relates to "the acts, conduct, or property or to the liabilities and financial condition of the debtor, or to any matter which may affect the administration of the debtor's estate, or to the debtor's right to a discharge."[3] Further, the examination may also relate "to the operation of any business and the desirability of its continuance, the source of any money or property acquired or to be acquired by the debtor for purposes of consummating a plan and the consideration given or offered therefore, any other matter relevant to the case or to the formulation of a plan."[4] The motion for the examination may include the production of documents by the witness. A creditor's attorney can then conduct an extensive examination of the debtor and fully develop facts. This type of examination may take place without a pending action of any kind. Because the 2004 examination is broader in scope than a typical deposition, the sworn testimony may be used only for impeachment purposes.

---

3. FED. R. BANKR. P. 2004(b).
4. *Id.*

## 2.5 THE PLAN AND DISCLOSURE STATEMENT

The contents of the plan and disclosure statement are discussed in some detail later herein. However, the plan and disclosure statement provide a wealth of detail on how the party proposing the plan anticipates handling each class of claims; whether classes of claims are paid in full; how much the claim holder could anticipate receiving if the debtor were simply liquidated; the tax implications of the plan; anticipated litigation; and the management of any entities remaining after the confirmation of the plan. These documents, along with the order confirming the plan, govern the debtor after confirmation.

# CHAPTER 3

# INTRODUCTION TO BANKRUPTCY LAW

The United States bankruptcy law is a body of rules and standards enacted to facilitate the collection of debts, the distribution of the debtor's assets among its creditors in accordance with the priorities embodied in the Bankruptcy Code, and the preservation of the debtor's ability to start anew.[1] Although courts and commentators differ over the primacy of these principles, they are in general agreement with the importance of these principles to modern bankruptcy law.

Like all debtor/creditor law, bankruptcy law is designed to resolve the various legal problems caused by debtors who are unable or unwilling to pay their debts. A creditor has various alternatives under applicable non-bankruptcy law to attempt to satisfy its claim against the debtor. But the applicable non-bankruptcy law remedies, although potent in the right circumstances, contain two acute deficiencies. First, as a general rule, state law procedures reward the creditor who acts first—the general priority rule of "first in time,

---

1. *See generally* Burlingham v. Crouse, 228 U.S. 459 (1913); *see also* Report of the Commission on the Bankruptcy Laws of the United States, H.R. Doc. No. 93-137, at 75, 68–83 (1973).

first in right" applies with vigor. Creditors facing debtors with insufficient assets to cover their debts often race to the courthouse in an attempt to establish priority, while at the same time dismantling the debtor through piecemeal liquidation. The second acute deficiency found in state law is the lack of its ability to effect a forced discharge of indebtedness. Thus, an honest but unfortunate debtor who happens to be down on his or her luck and can no longer pay creditors can never receive a discharge under state law without the creditors' voluntary consent.

Modern bankruptcy law attempts to address these two acute deficiencies found under state debt-collection law. Bankruptcy law does this by balancing and accommodating a creditor's interest in being paid with the honest, but unfortunate, debtor's interest in paying its creditors what it can, and in receiving a fresh start in its economic life. The Bankruptcy Code attempts to achieve this uneasy alliance by balancing the three principles discussed above: the efficient collection of debts, the distribution of the debtor's assets among its creditors in accordance with bankruptcy priorities, and the preservation of the debtor's right to discharge (or reorganization).

## 3.1 HISTORY OF BANKRUPTCY LAW

Article 1, section 8 of the United States Constitution states: "The Congress shall have the Power to establish uniform Laws on the subject of Bankruptcies throughout the United States." Congress first exercised the power to establish bankruptcy laws in 1800. Congress subsequently enacted bankruptcy statutes in 1841, 1867, 1898, and 1978 with the Bankruptcy Reform Act that created what we now call the Bankruptcy Code. In 2005, Congress enacted substantial amendments to the 1978 Bankruptcy Code through the Bankruptcy Abuse Prevention and Consumer Protection Act of 2005 (BAPCPA). Bankruptcy cases are generally reported in *West's Bankruptcy Reporter* and can also be found on the Internet.

The Bankruptcy Code itself is divided into nine substantive chapters. The chapters are organized as follows:

- Chapter 1: General Provisions
- Chapter 3: Case Administration
- Chapter 5: Creditors, the Debtor and the Estate
- Chapter 7: Liquidation
- Chapter 9: Adjustment of Debts of a Municipality
- Chapter 11: Reorganization
- Chapter 12: Adjustment of Debts of a Family Farmer or Family Fisherman with Regular Annual Income
- Chapter 13: Adjustment of Debts of an Individual with Regular Income
- Chapter 15: Ancillary and Other Cross-Border Cases

Chapters 1, 3, and 5 apply to the general operations of the bankruptcy case and are thus applicable in most instances under chapters 7, 11, and 13.[2] (The even-number chapters have been reserved for amendments and additions to the Bankruptcy Code—for example, chapter 12.) All bankruptcy cases, other than ancillary and other cross-border cases, are commenced under chapter 7, 9, 11, 12, or 13.[3]

The protection of both debtor and creditor was not always the function of bankruptcy law. Not long ago, bankruptcy was designed solely to protect creditors. In England, a debtor unable or unwilling to pay its debts could be thrown in debtors' prison. Contrary to the popular view, the function of debtors' prison was not to punish the debtor but to hold the debtor for ransom. It was believed that the debtor's friends and relatives would combine what free assets they had and pay off the debtors' creditors, thus freeing the debtor from prison.

---

2. *See* 11 U.S.C § 103 (2006).
3. *See* 11 U.S.C. §§ 301, 302(a), 303(b) (2006).

True to its historical roots, English and early American bankruptcy law served purely as a debt collection and equal distribution mechanism. Not until 1841 did American bankruptcy law recognize a debtor's right of discharge of indebtedness. At that time, the dualism of protection, so easily taken for granted today, was established.

In 1978, bankruptcy law underwent a substantial revision. With the enactment of the 1978 Bankruptcy Code and its amendments, bankruptcy law has become a vibrant and challenging area of the law. It is no longer an area of law relegated to the small firm; rather, some of the most prestigious and largest firms in the United States have practice areas in bankruptcy and business reorganization. Furthermore, bankruptcy relief is no longer relegated to the fly-by-night operation. Instead, we have seen great firms such as WorldCom/MCI, Enron, Kmart, Adelphia, Texaco, National Gypsum, the Southland Corporation, Delta, United Airlines, Northwest Airlines, Continental Airlines, and Eastern Airlines seek relief under the Bankruptcy Code. No longer is bankruptcy relief only for low-income individuals who are down on their luck. Instead, doctors, lawyers, bank presidents, governors, congressmen, and sports figures are seeking relief under the Bankruptcy Code. As one commentator has cogently observed, bankruptcy has reached sort of a celebrity status in the United States.[4]

In 2005, Congress revisited bankruptcy law in the form of the BAPCPA. Although most of the press was captured by substantial revisions to consumer bankruptcy law, there were several important changes to business bankruptcy practice. Among these changes were the limitations imposed on the court so that extensions for the debtor to determine whether it will assume or reject an unexpired lease cannot exceed 210 days, an 18-month cap on the period of exclusivity, a relaxing of proof issues on reclamation claims, and the cre-

---

4. *See generally* Donald R. Korobkin, *Rehabilitating Values: A Jurisprudence of Bankruptcy*, 91 COLUM. L. REV. 717 (1991).

ation of a new category of administrative expense—the section 503(b)(9) priority for goods delivered to the debtor within 20 days preceding the filing of the petition in bankruptcy.

## 3.2 POLICIES EMBODIED IN THE BANKRUPTCY CODE

The major purposes of bankruptcy law are to provide for the efficient collection of debts, distribution of the debtor's property in accordance with uniform and national priorities, capture of going-concern value, and establishment of the debtor's right to discharge or to reorganize. However, in identifying what policies are embodied in the Bankruptcy Code, it is helpful to first identify the debtor. The public policy rationales embraced by the Bankruptcy Code often differ based on whether the debtor is an individual or a business.

## 3.3 INDIVIDUAL DEBTORS

The fresh start policy underlies the Bankruptcy Code in the case of individuals as the paramount public policy rationale. Essentially, bankruptcy permits an individual, through the use of exemptions of property, the right to a discharge, and the exclusion of future income from the estate, to begin anew his or her economic life. Thus, the Bankruptcy Code exempts certain property so that it may be put aside by an individual to enable a future economic life. Furthermore, the discharge acts like an injunction forever barring enforceability of a prepetition claim against the debtor. However, there is no constitutional right to obtain a bankruptcy discharge.[5]

## 3.4 BUSINESS DEBTORS

The paramount public policy rationale embraced by the Bankruptcy Code in regard to a debtor business is the real-

---

5. *See generally* United States v. Kras, 409 U.S. 434 (1973).

location of limited and finite economic resources or the reorganization of the debtor. Here the fresh start policy is of little importance. Rather, the Bankruptcy Code provides a mechanism by which the resources of a failed business may be reorganized or redistributed to other businesses that may make a better go of it.

# CHAPTER 4

# TYPES OF BANKRUPTCIES

The following is an overview of the types of bankruptcies that will be discussed in detail. Because of space limitations, chapter 9 bankruptcies (those involving municipalities) and chapter 12 bankruptcies (those involving family farmers) will be mentioned here, but not discussed in detail later in this chapter. However, many of the principles learned will also be applicable to those chapters.

## 4.1 CHAPTER 7

A bankruptcy case under chapter 7 of the Bankruptcy Code is a liquidation. Often, you hear lawyers refer to chapter 7 cases as "straight" bankruptcies. Generally, all of the debtor's non-exempt assets are collected by the chapter 7 trustee (who is always appointed by the U.S. trustee) who identifies, collects, liquidates, and distributes them. The proceeds from non-exempt assets are distributed to the various creditors who have filed a proof of claim before the deadline known as the bar date.[1] The assets claimed as exempt by the debtor are retained by the debtor for a fresh start.[2] The case is closed once the estate is fully administered.

---

1. *See* 11 U.S.C. § 726 (2006).
2. *See* 11 U.S.C. § 522 (2006).

For the individual debtor, the ultimate goal of a chapter 7 case is an order of discharge, which discharges the debts that arose before the order for relief owed by the debtor to the creditors and enjoins the creditors from ever collecting on their discharged claims from the debtor.[3] chapter 7 discharges are reserved for individuals; partnerships and corporations may not receive a chapter 7 discharge.

For the creditors, the ultimate goal of a chapter 7 case is the efficient collection, liquidation, and distribution of estate property in satisfaction of allowed claims. The distribution of estate property to satisfy allowed secured and unsecured claims is made in accordance with the distributional scheme embodied in the Bankruptcy Code.

## 4.2 CHAPTER 9

A bankruptcy case under chapter 9 is reserved solely for insolvent municipalities,[4] which are political subdivisions of a state.[5] chapter 9 provides the insolvent municipality with a means by which to propose a plan to adjust its debts. Recently, the city of Bridgeport, Connecticut, sought relief unsuccessfully under chapter 9 of the Bankruptcy Code.

## 4.3 CHAPTER 11

Through the commencement of a chapter 11 case, a debtor attempts to reorganize itself through either rehabilitation or orderly liquidation. Generally, the debtor keeps all of its assets, exempt and non-exempt, and remains in business.[6] Here, the debtor remains in control of the bankruptcy estate. The debtor may continue to engage in ordinary course transactions without court supervision; however, court approval through an order is necessary to authorize transac-

---

3. *See* 11 U.S.C. §§ 727, 524 (2006).
4. *See* 11 U.S.C. § 109(c) (2006).
5. *See* 11 U.S.C. § 101(40) (2006).
6. *See* 11 U.S.C. §§ 1107, 1108 (2006).

tions outside of the ordinary course of business.[7] A trustee may be appointed to operate the debtor's business if defalcation, fraud, incompetency, or gross mismanagement occurred;[8] however, the typical situation is one in which the debtor itself operates the business as a debtor in possession.

In theory, in a chapter 11 case, the debtor proposes a plan of reorganization in which it attempts to provide a satisfactory schedule of payments and possibly collateral to its creditors. After approval of the disclosure statement, the debtor solicits affirmative votes from its creditors and equity holders in favor of its proposed plan of reorganization. Ultimately, the debtor hopes the plan is confirmed by the court.[9] Plan confirmation may take two paths: (1) by unanimous consent, or (2) by cram-down, as long as one non-insider impaired class of claim has accepted the plan.

The above scenario is no longer the common case, however. In many cases, substantially all of the assets and operating businesses are sold under section 365(b) of the Bankruptcy Code within the first six months of the case. This subsection authorizes sales "not in the ordinary course of the [debtor's] business." Originally this provision was used to dispose of surplus or outmoded assets of the debtor in possession, often to raise operating capital or to begin to build a deposit account to fund a proposed plan of reorganization. However, this is no longer the case. Sales under section 365 are used to dispose of all of the assets, leaving the plan of reorganization or liquidation as little more than a distributional scheme.

## 4.4 CHAPTER 12

Chapter 12 is limited to family farmers and fishermen with annual income.[10] The goal of a chapter 12 case is rehabili-

---

7. *See* 11 U.S.C. § 363(c)(1) (2006).
8. *See* 11 U.S.C. § 1104 (2006).
9. *See* 11 U.S.C. § 1129 (2006).
10. *See* 11 U.S.C. § 109(f) (2006).

tation of the family farmer or fisherman debtor. The debtor retains all assets and attempts to satisfy claims pursuant to a chapter 12 plan. The chapter 12 process borrows heavily from both chapters 11 and 13.

## 4.5 CHAPTER 13

Chapter 13 is limited to individuals with regular income who meet certain debt limits.[11] A chapter 13 case is in some ways similar to a chapter 11 case in that the goal of a chapter 13 case is rehabilitation of the debtor and not liquidation. The debtor keeps all the assets, exempt and non-exempt, and attempts to make payments pursuant to a chapter 13 plan or schedule of payments over three to five years. Further, a chapter 13 trustee operates as the disbursing agent, distributing estate property, including disposable income, in accordance with the terms of the chapter 13 plan. Essentially, the debtor makes one payment to the chapter 13 trustee, who then divides the one payment by the debtor into many small payments to the creditors. The chapter 13 plan is generally funded through the debtor's post-petition disposable income.

## 4.6 CHAPTER 15

Chapter 15 is a new chapter added to the Bankruptcy Code by the Bankruptcy Abuse Prevention and Consumer Protection Act of 2005. It is the U.S. domestic adoption of the Model Law on Cross-Border Insolvency promulgated by the United Nations Commission on International Trade Law (UNCITRAL) in 1997, and it replaces section 304 of the Bankruptcy Code.

The purpose of chapter 15 is to provide effective mechanisms for dealing with insolvency cases involving debtors, assets, claimants, and other parties in interest involving more than one country. There are five objectives actually specified in the statute:

---

11. 11 U.S.C. § 109(e) (2006).

- to promote cooperation between the United States courts and parties in interest and the courts and other competent authorities of foreign countries involved in cross-border insolvency cases;

- to establish greater legal certainty for trade and investment;

- to provide for the fair and efficient administration of cross-border insolvencies that protects the interests of all creditors and other interested entities, including the debtor;

- to afford protection and maximization of the value of the debtor's assets; and

- to facilitate the rescue of financially troubled businesses, thereby protecting investment and preserving employment.[12]

Generally, a chapter 15 case is ancillary to a primary proceeding brought in another country, typically the debtor's home country. As an alternative, the debtor or a creditor may commence a full chapter 7 or chapter 11 case in the United States if the assets in the United States are sufficiently complex to merit a full-blown domestic bankruptcy case.[13] In addition, under chapter 15, a U.S. court may authorize a trustee or other entity (including an examiner) to act in a foreign country on behalf of a U.S. bankruptcy estate.[14]

An ancillary case is commenced under chapter 15 by a "foreign representative" filing a petition for recognition of a "foreign proceeding."[15] Chapter 15 gives the foreign representative the right of direct access to U.S. courts for this purpose.[16] The petition must be accompanied by documents showing the existence of the foreign proceeding and the

---

12. 11 U.S.C. § 1501.
13. 11 U.S.C. § 1520(c).
14. 11 U.S.C. § 1505.
15. 11 U.S.C. § 1504.
16. 11 U.S.C. § 1509.

appointment and authority of the foreign representative.[17] After notice and a hearing, the court is authorized to issue an order recognizing the foreign proceeding as either a "foreign main proceeding" (a proceeding pending in a country where the debtor's center of main interests are located) or a "foreign non-main proceeding" (a proceeding pending in a country where the debtor has an establishment, but not its center of main interests).[18] Immediately upon the recognition of a foreign main proceeding, the automatic stay and selected other provisions of the Bankruptcy Code take effect within the United States.[19] The foreign representative is also authorized to operate the debtor's business in the ordinary course. The U.S. court is authorized to issue preliminary relief as soon as the petition for recognition is filed.[20]

One of the most important goals of chapter 15 is to promote cooperation and communication between U.S. courts and parties in interest with foreign courts and parties in interest in cross-border cases. This goal is accomplished by, among other things, explicitly charging the court and estate representatives to "cooperate to the maximum extent possible" with foreign courts and foreign representatives and authorizing direct communication between the court and authorized estate representatives and the foreign courts and foreign representatives.[21]

---

17. 11 U.S.C. § 1515.
18. 11 U.S.C. § 1517.
19. 11 U.S.C. § 1520.
20. 11 U.S.C. § 1519.
21. 11 U.S.C. §§ 1525–1527.

# CHAPTER 5

# BANKRUPTCY AS A FINANCIAL TOOL

Bankruptcy can be a rigorous process where the most confidential financial information of a debtor is disclosed and held up to public scrutiny. The debtor's assets and liabilities are painstakingly explored.[1] The motives behind gifts and charitable contributions are analyzed in detail. Transactions as far as two to six years back from the filing of the petition are routinely investigated. Under these circumstances, why would a debtor ever want to hold himself or itself up to such scrutiny?

Generally, the decision either to forgo an out-of-court settlement or to seek relief under the Bankruptcy Code turns in part on whether the debtor is an individual or a business. Typically, a prime candidate for bankruptcy relief is an individual who has a relatively large amount of unsecured debt that he cannot pay. Bankruptcy relief affords the individual an opportunity to voluntarily surrender his non-exempt assets ultimately to his creditors in exchange for a discharge of prepetition claims. This discharge, coupled with, among other things, the right to declare exemptions, fuels the debtor's fresh start. Moreover, an individual with a large amount of judgments against him may decide to seek relief under the Bankruptcy Code to prevent creditors from

---

1. *See* 11 U.S.C. § 341 (2006), *see also* FED. R. BANKR. P. 2004.

obtaining a secured claim by reason of a sheriff's levy on the property.

The reasons a business may seek relief under the Bankruptcy Code are as varied as the fish in the sea. Often, the business will seek relief under the Bankruptcy Code because of a distortion in the right side of its balance sheet, that is, its liabilities. Where a business has a very good asset base but substantial liabilities, bankruptcy may afford the business an attractive alternative to a straight liquidation. Furthermore, bankruptcy permits the business to focus on its efforts to reorganize by staying repossessions, litigation, and foreclosures.[2] Moreover, bankruptcy often provides a business with a new opportunity to obtain credit or funds.[3] Finally, bankruptcy relief affords a means by which the debtor can bind certain minority creditors who dissented from any informal workout efforts through the use of the classification process and class voting.[4]

It is a fair statement that bankruptcy has become the repository of the nation's woes. Aside from becoming an acceptable corporate management and acquisition tool,[5] bankruptcy courts find themselves picking up the pieces of a failing tort system, a failed pension system, poor labor relations, and the undercollection of federal, state, and local taxes.

---

2. *See* 11 U.S.C. § 362(a) (2006).
3. *See* 11 U.S.C. § 364 (2006).
4. *See* 11 U.S.C. § 1126 (2006).
5. *See* Kaplan, *Bankruptcy as a Corporate Management Tool*, A.B.A. J., Jan. 1, 1987, at 64.

# CHAPTER 6

# JURISDICTION AND COMMENCEMENT OF A BANKRUPTCY CASE

## 6.1 CORE V. NON-CORE

Bankruptcy jurisdiction rests with the district court under 28 U.S.C. section 1334. District courts, however, may assign cases through reference to the bankruptcy court, which, in fact, all have done pursuant to standing orders in each federal district.[1] The bankruptcy court may hear all core and non-core matters unless specifically limited by statute. However, the bankruptcy court may only render final judgments in core matters. In non-core matters, the bankruptcy court may enter proposed findings of fact and conclusions of law, necessarily reviewable by the district court.

A core matter is generically defined as any matter affecting the restructuring of the debtor-creditor relations in the bankruptcy case, which is defined to include, but is not limited to:

- the authorization and approval of the terms and conditions of the employment of any professional person (counsel, accountants, appraisers, investment bankers,

---

1. *See* 28 U.S.C. § 157.

or financial advisors for any party in interest) when the professional intends to seek compensation from the chapter 11 estate;

- the allowance, disallowance, or reduction of all applications for fees and expenses of the authorized professional persons;

- the allowance or disallowance of any claim against or interest in the debtor or in the property of the estate;

- the authorization and approval (or disapproval) of any assumption and assignment of, or rejection of, any executor contract of unexpired lease;

- the authorization and approval of sales not in the ordinary course of the debtor's business; and

- the approval of the disclosure statement and the confirmation of a plan of reorganization.

The distinction between core and non-core adversary proceedings (the latter also referred to as "related proceedings") is far from clear. A useful general rule, however, is that the bankruptcy court may not enter a final judgment in any adversary proceeding that relates to the bankruptcy case when any non-debtor defendant is sued by a representative of the bankruptcy estate on a claim that arose before the petition date under state law and where the defendant has not filed a proof of claim or interest in the chapter 11 case. In these circumstances, these non-debtor defendants are entitled to stand upon their "rights" to have any adverse final judgments entered by the district court. Under the formal rules of jurisdiction and procedure, without the written consent of the non-debtor defendant, the bankruptcy judge may only try (that is, hear) the adversary proceeding on the merits and is obligated to submit a report and recommendation of proposed findings of fact and proposed conclusions of law. In this case, the bankruptcy judge exercises the limited authority similar to that of a U.S. magistrate judge. The district court, after reviewing the report, may enter a final judgment or order, or may decide to hear the entire proceeding, or any part thereof, de novo.

## 6.2 FILING THE PETITION

A case under the Bankruptcy Code may be commenced by either a voluntary petition filed by the debtor, or, for a chapter 7 or 11 case, by an involuntary petition filed against the debtor by the requisite number of creditors.[2] The petition is filed with the bankruptcy court clerk. The petition should state the chapter under which it is filed. Along with the petition, the debtor must pay the appropriate filing fee. Although the fee may be paid in installments, it cannot be waived entirely. Section 302 of the Bankruptcy Code permits a husband and wife to file a joint petition, thus saving the cost of one filing fee.

The date of the filing of the bankruptcy petition is a critical date in the bankruptcy case because it establishes a line of demarcation. Any payment or satisfaction by the debtor of any claims arising prior to this date is at least temporarily suspended. Generally, these prepetition claims are either satisfied or discharged through a liquidation under chapter 7 or a plan under chapters 11 or 13.[3]

## 6.3 ELIGIBILITY

To establish eligibility, a debtor must meet four requirements. First, the legal status of the potential debtor must be determined—whether the debtor is an individual, partnership, corporation, etc.—because certain entities may be ineligible for relief under specific chapters. Second, the debtor must meet the residency or contact requirements with the United States, a sort of minimum contacts test that betrays the historical in rem foundation to bankruptcy jurisdiction. Third, the bankruptcy court must determine if a categorical exclusion applies. For example, banks, credit unions, and insur-

---

2. *See* 11 U.S.C. §§ 301–303 (2006).
3. 11 U.S.C. § 101(5) (2006) (defining "claim").

ance companies may not file for relief under the Bankruptcy Code. Note, however, that a bank or insurance holding company is a corporation and may seek relief under the Bankruptcy Code. Finally, an individual debtor must have taken an approved counseling session within 180 days before the commencement of the case to be eligible for relief.

## 6.4 VOLUNTARY CASES

A debtor commences a voluntary case by filing a petition under the appropriate chapter of the Bankruptcy Code.[4] Such a filing automatically triggers an order for relief. The petition is simple and basically states that the debtor has sought the particular relief in question, for example, chapter 7 relief. The petition need not show whether the debtor has any assets or is insolvent.[5] Many debtors have no assets; and theoretically, a solvent debtor may voluntarily file for bankruptcy protection.[6]

## 6.5 INVOLUNTARY CASES

An involuntary case is commenced pursuant to 11 U.S.C. section 303 under either chapter 7 or chapter 11; however, involuntary petitions may not be filed under chapters 9, 12, or 13.

An involuntary case is commenced pursuant to 11 U.S.C. section 303 under either chapter 7 or chapter 11, chapters 9, 12, or 13 not being a permitted alternative.[7] An involuntary case cannot be commenced against a railroad, farmer, family farmer, or charitable institution.[8] Additionally, an involuntary petition must be signed by the requisite number

---

4. *See* 11 U.S.C. §§ 301–302 (2006).

5. The sole exception is for municipalities that seek relief under chapter 9. *See* 11 U.S.C. § 109(c) (2006).

6. *But see* 11 U.S.C. § 109(c) (2006).

7. A petitioning creditor may be entitled to reimbursement of its actual and necessary expenses for filing an involuntary case. *See In re* On Tour LLC, 276 B.R. 407, 415 (Bankr. D. Md. 2002).

8. *See* 11 U.S.C. § 303(a).

of creditors. Generally, three petitioning creditors must possess unsecured, bona fide, non-contingent claims totaling at least $13,475[9] in order to validly file an involuntary petition. If the debtor has less than 12 holders of bona fide, non-contingent claims against it, a single creditor with a single unsecured, bona fide, non-contingent claim of $13,475 is sufficient.[10] A single fully secured creditor can waive its secured status as to a limited amount of its debt to satisfy this requirement or may join two others without waiving its claim. Moreover, a general partner may, in his capacity as a partner, file a petition on behalf of the partnership. Such filing is characterized as an involuntary case unless and until all general partners join in the filing.

Upon the filing of an involuntary petition, the debtor is permitted 20 days in which to answer the petition. Only the debtor may respond.[11] The alleged debtor may respond to the involuntary petition by consenting to the entry of an order for relief, converting the pending case to a case under a different chapter, or contesting the involuntary petition. Grounds for a denial of an involuntary petition include:

- lack of jurisdiction;
- improper venue;
- insufficient aggregate debt amounts;
- insufficient number of petitioning creditors;
- non-qualifying petitioning creditors; or
- insufficient facts to prove the substantive grounds under subsection (h).

---

9. Most dollar amounts under the Bankruptcy Code are adjusted automatically for inflation.

10. *See* 11 U.S.C. § 303(b); *see also* Jack F. Williams, *Counting Creditors Under Code § 303(b): The Tale of the Ubiquitous "Such,"* NORTON BANKR. L. ADVISOR 7 (June 1992).

11. *See* 11 U.S.C. § 303(d).

If the debtor contests the involuntary petition, the court generally proceeds to trial on the merits. Parties are entitled to conduct discovery pursuant to the Rules of Bankruptcy Procedure (generally incorporating select rules from the Federal Rules of Civil Procedure with important variations). Parties may also move for summary judgment on the issues raised in the pleadings, if appropriate.[12]

If the debtor does not timely answer the petition, the court will enter an order for relief against the debtor. If the debtor does timely answer the petition, the court can grant relief against the debtor only if the creditors can establish one of two grounds. The petitioning creditors must establish that either (i) the debtor is not generally paying its present debts as they become due unless such debts are subject to a bona fide dispute as to liability or amount, or (ii) within 120 days of the date of petition, a receiver, assignee, or custodian had taken possession of substantially all of the debtor's property.[13]

Sections 303(b)(1) and (b)(2) require that a petitioning creditor possess a claim that is not contingent as to amount or subject to bona fide dispute as to liability or amount. The non-contingent and undisputed claims requirements of the Bankruptcy Code are not jurisdictional. Rather, these requirements go to the merits—an element that must be established to sustain an involuntary case.[14] Petitioning creditors cannot prevail unless they show that their claims are non-contingent and not subject to bona fide disputes.

A claim that is contingent as to liability is a claim where an involuntary debtor's obligation to pay does not arise until the occurrence of some future event, which the parties contemplated at the time their relationship started.[15] In *In re Taylor & Assocs. LP*,[16] the bankruptcy court addressed the

---

12. *See* FED. R. BANKR. P. 7026, 7056.
13. *See* 11 U.S.C. § 303(h).
14. *In re* Rubin, 769 F.2d 611, 615 (9th Cir. 1985).
15. *In re* Sims, 994 F.2d 210, 220 (5th Cir. 1993).
16. 193 B.R. 465 (Bankr. E.D. Tenn. 1996).

phrase "contingent as to liability" and adopted the following standard for determining whether a claim is contingent as to liability under §303(b):

> When all the events have occurred which allow a court to adjudicate a claim and determine whether or not payment should be made, there is no contingency concerning the claim itself, unless "it is apparent, to a legal certainty," that the petitioning creditor would be unable to obtain a judgment against the debtor upon adjudication of its claim.[17]

A petitioning creditor's claim must also not be the subject of a bona fide dispute.[18] The majority of courts have adopted an objective standard to decide whether a claim is subject to a bona fide dispute.[19] "If there is either a genuine issue of material fact that bears upon the debtor's liability, or a meritorious contention as to the application of law to undisputed facts, then the petition must be dismissed."[20] A court need not resolve any issue of fact or law; it must only decide that such issues exist. In determining the existence of a bona fide dispute, courts determine whether "there is either a genuine issue of a material fact that bears upon the debtor's liability, or a meritorious contention as to the application of law to undisputed facts. . . ."[21] The court is not called upon to determine the likely outcome of any controversy; instead, the court simply determines whether there are facts giving rise to a legitimate legal dispute as to liability or amount.

The phrase "generally not paying debts" as they become due is not defined in the code and not subject to ease in interpretation. Courts consistently hold that the question of

---

17. 193 B.R. 465, 475 (Bankr. E.D. Tenn. 1996), *citing Longhorn 1979-11 Drilling Program*, 32 B.R. 923, 927 (Bankr. W.D. Okla. 1983).

18. 11 U.S.C. § 303(1).

19. *See, e.g.,* Key Mech Inc. v. BDC, 330 F.3d 111 (2d Cir. 2003).

20. B.D.W. Assocs. Inc. v. Busy Beaver Bldg. Ctrs. Inc., 865 F.2d 65 (3d Cir. 1989).

21. *In re* Lough, 57 B.R. 933, 996–97 (Bankr. E.D. Mich. 1986); s*ee also In re* Busick, 831 F.2d 745 (7th Cir. 1987).

whether a debtor is generally not paying debts as they become due is a question of fact. In assessing this requirement, courts characteristically consider "the totality of the circumstances existing when the petition is filed."[22] This area of the law is short on doctrine and may more appropriately be characterized as illuminated by clusters of cases. These cases tend to gravitate toward several factors, including:

- the number of debts,
- the amount of the delinquency,
- the character of the debt,
- the nature and relationship of the creditors being paid and those not being paid,
- the materiality of the nonpayment,
- the nature and conduct of the debtor's business,
- the rapid decline in the value of the debtor's assets resulting from asset sales rather than profit-generating activity,
- the amount of the debtor's debts compared to the debtor's yearly income, and
- the debtor's voluntary shutdown of operations.

Between the filing of the petition and the hearing on the involuntary petition (the so-called "gap period"), the debtor is permitted to continue to operate its business much like a debtor in possession in a voluntary chapter 11 case.[23] However, the bankruptcy court may require a bond from the debtor upon a showing of cause by a party in interest.[24] Furthermore, upon motion of any creditor or party in interest, the bankruptcy court can restrict the debtor's use of property or appoint an interim trustee to take possession of the

---

22. *In re* Bishop, Baldwin, Rewald, Dillingham & Wong, 779 F.2d 471, 475 (9th Cir. 1985).
23. 11 U.S.C. § 303(f).
24. *See* 11 U.S.C. § 303(e).

debtor's property and operate the debtor's business if it is established that such action is necessary to prevent loss or destruction of property of the estate.[25]

During the operation of the business during the gap period, the debtor may incur debt in the ordinary course of business—for example, trade credit. Those that deal with the involuntary debtor in the ordinary course are generally entitled to a level 3 priority claim under section 507(a)(3).

If the debtor is successful in establishing that the grounds for involuntary relief have not been satisfied, the court may grant a judgment in favor of the debtor for its costs and attorney fees.[26] Moreover, any petitioning creditor that files an involuntary petition in bad faith may be held liable for compensatory and punitive damages.

As part of the Bankruptcy Abuse Prevention and Consumer Protection Act of 2005 (the 2005 Act), section 303(l)[27] was amended to curb abusive involuntary cases that are improperly filed against, among others, public officials and private individuals. This subsection provides that records of a fraudulent involuntary case may be sealed if certain requirements are met. Thus, if (1) the petition is false or contains fraudulent statements, (2) the debtor is an individual, and (3) the court dismisses the petition, then the court shall, upon motion of the debtor, seal the record of the case and all references to the case. In addition, under subsection (l)(2), if the debtor is an individual and the court dismisses under subsection (l), then a court may enter an order prohibiting consumer credit reporting agencies from making a consumer report that contains information relating to such involuntary petition or the bankruptcy case.

Moreover, as part of the 2005 amendments, Congress amended 18 U.S.C. § 157, now making it a crime to file a

---

25. 11 U.S.C. § 303(g).
26. *See* 11 U.S.C. § 303(i).
27. Although styled as subsection (l), it appears that this subsection should be labeled subsection (k).

fraudulent involuntary case. In an orchestrated press release, Congressman James Sensenbrenner summed up the purpose of the criminalization of fraudulent involuntary petitions:

> Unfortunately, tax protesters and other extremists are now resorting to filing fraudulent involuntary bankruptcy petitions against public officials and other innocent parties. In the case of the Ozaukee County officials, some of the county employees didn't even realize they were the subject of a pending involuntary bankruptcy case until after their lines of credit were terminated, or were charged higher interest rates. In addition, some officials even had their mortgage statuses negatively affected. These filings were subsequently dismissed, but not until after causing financial problems for these folks.[28]

Involuntary bankruptcy cases are relatively rare. In light of the litany of sanctions that a court may impose on an unsuccessful petitioning creditor, coupled with the difficulty in making out the prima facie case, there appears to be little chance of that number increasing. However, the involuntary case is still an important tool in a creditor's toolbox. For example, a creditor should consider commencing an involuntary case where:

- You learn of a large payment to a creditor that diminishes the potential recovery of other creditors;

- You learn that a creditor has converted an unsecured position into a secured one;

- You learn that a secured creditor has grabbed additional collateral;

- You learn that your debtor may be selling assets below fair market value to gin up cash in a distressed situation or to benefit insiders.

Although rare, a creditor must be aware of the application, benefits, and costs of commencing an involuntary case.

---

28. Press Statement, F. James Sensenbrenner, Jr., June 10, 2003.

## 6.6 DISMISSAL OR CONVERSION TO OTHER CHAPTERS

The bankruptcy court may dismiss a bankruptcy case even though all requirements for filing are satisfied. Dismissals may be based on either non-statutory or statutory grounds. Non-statutory grounds for dismissal rest on an implied duty of good faith in filing the petition. Although there is no statutory requirement that a petition be filed in good faith, there is a requirement that any chapter 11 or chapter 13 plan be proposed in good faith. Courts have looked to the good-faith confirmation requirement for a basis to imply a good-faith filing requirement. In determining whether a debtor has filed its petition in good faith, courts consider a number of factors, including:

- whether the case is a single-asset real estate case where there is essentially little or no business to reorganize other than the development of real estate;

- whether the only significant asset of the estate is undeveloped land;

- whether the assets of the estate are encumbered land;

- whether the debtor has no equity in the significant assets of the estate;

- whether the debtor has few to no employees;

- whether the debtor has little or no cash flow from operations;

- whether the estate has a few creditors with small claims and one or two secured creditors with relatively large claims;

- whether secured creditor action, such as a pending foreclosure, forced the filing;

- whether the bankruptcy filing was timed to prevent a foreclosure or judgment;

- whether the insiders of the debtor are involved in parallel litigation, such as a lawsuit on a guaranty; and

- whether a borrower has transferred or exchanged the property in question to a new entity that then filed a bankruptcy petition, that is, the "new debtor syndrome."

Statutory grounds for relief begin with the generally applicable section 305. That section provides that a bankruptcy case may be dismissed at any time if the interests of the creditors and the debtor would best be served by dismissal. Additionally, each chapter has its own conversion section.[29] A chapter 7 case may be dismissed only for cause, including a delay by the debtor that is prejudicial to creditors or failure of the debtor to comply with orders of the court.[30] A chapter 7 debtor can convert its case to a chapter 11 or chapter 13 case if the case had not previously been converted to a chapter 7 case from a chapter 11 or chapter 13 case.[31] The court may convert a chapter 7 case to a chapter 11 case at any time. However, there can be no forced conversion to chapter 13.

Furthermore, through BAPCPA, Congress substantially modified section 707(b) to include a "means test" for relief under chapter 7. The means-testing requirement rests on the perception by Congress that individual debtors were abusing the bankruptcy process by filing chapter 7 petitions when they had sufficient post-petition income to support funding payments under a chapter 13 plan. Thus, section 707(b) now provides that a case may be dismissed for debtor abuse. A presumption of abuse is created where the debtor has sufficient income, after certain deductions are made, to fund a chapter 13 plan sufficiently to provide a meaningful payment to his creditors. If a debtor fails the means test, then he must convert to a chapter 13 case or suffer dismissal. How-

---

29. *See* 11 U.S.C. § 348 (2006) (dealing with the consequences of conversion).
30. *See* 11 U.S.C. § 707(a) (2006).
31. *See* 11 U.S.C. § 706 (2006).

ever, as previously mentioned, the court does not have the authority to force conversion of the case to chapter 13.

A debtor may convert a chapter 11 case to a chapter 7 case at any time, unless the case was originally commenced as an involuntary chapter 11 case.[32] The court may convert a chapter 11 case to a chapter 7 case or dismiss the case for cause, such as the debtor's inability to effectuate a plan, unreasonable delay by the debtor, failure to file income tax returns, or the absence of a reasonable likelihood of rehabilitation.[33] Additionally, by way of answer to an involuntary chapter 7 petition, a debtor may elect to convert the case to chapter 11 and proceed as a debtor in possession. The bankruptcy court may not convert a case from chapter 11 to chapter 7 if the debtor is a farmer or a nonprofit.

Under chapter 13, a case may be dismissed or converted by a debtor at any time (subject to very limited restrictions). A creditor or any other party in interest may seek dismissal or conversion of a chapter 13 case for cause.[34]

---

32. *See* 11 U.S.C. § 1112 (2006).
33. *See* 11 U.S.C. §§ 1112(b)(1), (b)(2), (b)(5); 1129(a)(3) (2006).
34. *See* 11 U.S.C. §§ 1307(b), 1307(c) (2006).

# CHAPTER 7

# WHO MAY BE A DEBTOR IN BANKRUPTCY?

Not everyone or everything may be a debtor in bankruptcy. Certain debtors are categorically excluded from bankruptcy relief, including banks, thrift institutions, and insurance companies.[1] The common attribute that excludes these entities from relief under the Bankruptcy Code is close regulation by the government and their own set of insolvency laws. Aside from general categorical exclusion, some debtors may be eligible for relief under one chapter but not another.[2] Before turning to the requirements under particular chapters, one requirement applicable to all chapters must first be satisfied: "Only a person that resides or has a domicile, a place of business, or property in the United States, or a municipality, may be a debtor" under the Bankruptcy Code.[3]

## 7.1 CHAPTER 7

A debtor under chapter 7 of the Bankruptcy Code is a person (defined as an individual, partnership, or corporation, but not a governmental unit), except that railroads may not

---

1. *See* 11 U.S.C. § 109(b), (d) (2006).
2. An example is a railroad, which may only seek relief under chapter 11 of the Bankruptcy Code. *See* 11 U.S.C. § 109(d) (2006).
3. 11 U.S.C. § 109(a) (2006).

seek relief under chapter 7.[4] A sole proprietorship is not a person and cannot file as an entity separate from the individual under the Bankruptcy Code.

## 7.2 UNDER CHAPTER 11

A debtor under chapter 11 of the Bankruptcy Code may be any person eligible for relief under chapter 7, plus railroads; however, stock and commodity brokers may not seek relief under chapter 11 of the Bankruptcy Code, their choice being limited to chapter 7.[5]

## 7.3 UNDER CHAPTER 13

Recall that a chapter 13 case, unlike chapter 7 or 11 cases, cannot be commenced through an involuntary petition. Under chapter 13, only an individual with regular income whose debts do not exceed $922,975 of secured debt and $307,675 of unsecured debt may file a chapter 13 petition.[6]

## 7.4 DEBTOR'S DUTIES

A quid pro quo exists in bankruptcy. Once the debtor files a petition seeking relief under the Bankruptcy Code, the debtor receives the protection of the automatic stay[7] and ultimately the right to discharge.[8] The disclosure obligations for these bankruptcy protections are outlined at section 521 of the Bankruptcy Code. Section 521 requires the debtor to perform a number of duties: "file a list of creditors, and unless the court orders otherwise, a schedule of assets and liabilities, a schedule of current income and expenditures, and a statement of the debtor's financial affairs."[9] The debtor must also cooperate with any appointed trustee or examiner, including the surrender of property if ordered by the court.

---

4. *See* 11 U.S.C. § 109(b) (2006).
5. *See* 11 U.S.C. § 109(d) (2006).
6. *See* 11 U.S.C. § 109(e) (2006).
7. *See* 11 U.S.C. § 362(a) (2006).
8. *See* 11 U.S.C. § 727(a) (2006).
9. *See* 11 U.S.C. § 521(a) (2006).

This surrender includes turning over the books and records to the trustee. The debtor must additionally appear at the discharge hearing. Furthermore, the debtor will have to appear and submit to an examination under oath at a meeting of creditors under section 341; provide interested parties with notices of amendments to petitions, lists, schedules, and statements; attend and submit to examinations ordered by the bankruptcy court under Bankruptcy Rule 2004; comply with all court orders; and identify and assist in recovery of the property of the estate. Finally, a debtor must file appropriate tax returns. The various lists, schedules, and statements, and the time limits in which they must be filed, are discussed in detail at Bankruptcy Rule 1007.

Bankruptcy Rule 4002 lists other duties of the debtor, which include:

> In addition to performing other duties prescribed by the Code and the Rules, the debtor shall (1) attend and submit to an examination at the times ordered by the court; (2) attend a hearing on a complaint objecting to discharge and testify, if called as a witness; (3) inform the trustee immediately in writing as to the location of real property in which the debtor has an interest and the name and address of every person holding money or property subject to the debtor's withdrawal or order if the schedule of property has not yet been filed pursuant to Rule 1007; (4) cooperate with the trustee in the preparation of an inventory, the examination of proofs of claim, and the administration of the estate; and (5) file a statement of any change of the debtor's address.

Failure by the debtor to abide by his or her duties may result in the court's dismissing the bankruptcy case and prohibiting the refiling of the case for 180 days.

# Chapter 8

# Getting Paid: Professionals in Bankruptcy Cases

Acting as lead counsel or financial advisor to the debtor or an official committee in a business bankruptcy is not for the novice. However, from time to time, non-bankruptcy professionals may be needed as special counsel or additional advisors to the debtor or an official committee. The provisions of this chapter are directed to the occasional professional rather than those engaged in the practice on a regular basis.

## 8.1 WHO MUST BE RETAINED

The minute a debtor enters bankruptcy, all professionals retained by that debtor or any official committee for that debtor that seeks to be paid from the debtor's estate must have its employment approved by the bankruptcy court. In a chapter 11 bankruptcy case of any size, there are generally at least four sets of professionals: counsel for the debtor in possession, financial advisor for the debtor in possession, counsel for the official committee of unsecured creditors, and financial advisors for the official committee of unsecured creditors. Of course, as the size of the case increases, so does the number of creditors. Many cases also have investment bankers, communications professionals, noticing agents, claims administrators, and a whole host of other professionals. However, these professionals can be classified into three basic categories: (1) bankruptcy professionals—those professionals employed by the debtor or other constituencies to provide advice and services related to the administration and activities inherent in the bankruptcy process; (2) special purpose professionals—those professionals hired for a limited purpose, such as prosecuting or defending in specific litigation; and (3) ordinary course professionals—those professionals that the debtor has routinely hired within the day-to-day operations of their business, generally having nothing to do with bankruptcy or the bankruptcy case.

### 8.1.1 *Section 327(a) Professionals*

Section 327(a) of the Bankruptcy Code authorizes the trustee (or the debtor in possession in chapter 11 cases) to:

> [e]mploy one or more attorneys, accountants, appraisers, auctioneers, or other professional persons, that does not hold or represent an interest adverse to the estate, and that are disinterested persons, to represent or assist the trustee in carrying out the trustee's duties under this title.[1]

Professionals employed pursuant to section 327(a) of the Bankruptcy Code must be disinterested as defined by section 101(14), which states:

> The term "disinterested person" means a person that—
>
> (A) is not a creditor, an equity security holder, or an insider;

---

1. 11 U.S.C. § 327(a).

(B) is not and was not, within 2 years before the date of the filing of the petition, a director, officer, or employee of the debtor; and

(C) does not have an interest materially adverse to the interest of the estate or of any class of creditors or equity security holders, by reason of any direct or indirect relationship to, connection with, or interest in, the debtor, or for any other reason.

This standard requires that you not be a creditor; thus, any prepetition arrearage must be waived. This fact, along with the fact that any payments on antecedent debts may lead to preference claims that would render a potential professional not "disinterested," is a serious consideration when representing a potential debtor on the eve of bankruptcy. The easiest way to avoid these issues is to draft the retention letter to require an evergreen retainer and always stay in a prepaid position so that there is no arrearage and no potential preference.[2]

### 8.1.2 *Section 327(e) Special Counsel*

Not all attorneys must meet the standards in section 327(a) of the Bankruptcy Code—only those performing the "bankruptcy-specific" tasks. Section 327(e) allows the trustee to retain attorneys who have previously represented the debtor for specific purposes other than acting as lead counsel in the case as long as "such attorney does not represent or hold any interest adverse to the debtor or the estate with respect to the matter on which such attorney is to be employed."[3] Therefore, under section 327(e) of the Bankruptcy Code, the special-purpose attorney does not need to waive prepetition arrearages and may represent a party potentially adverse to the debtor in an unrelated matter as long as it does not impact the purpose for which the attorney is being employed.

---

2. *See* 11 U.S.C. § 547(b) for the elements of a preferential transfer.
3. 11 U.S.C. § 327(e).

### 8.1.3 *Ordinary Course Professionals*

During the course of its operations, the debtor in possession has likely hired multiple professionals to perform day-to-day tasks such as audit the books, prepare tax returns, prepare trademark and patent applications, etc. If there are a sufficient number of such professionals, the debtor may seek to employ them in the ordinary course.[4] Unlike the professionals retained under section 327 of the Bankruptcy Code, there is no statutory predicate for ordinary course professional retention, though section 363 of the Bankruptcy Code, along with the expansive equitable powers of section 105, are often cited. However, there is significant precedent for such retentions.[5]

Generally, ordinary course professional orders allow such professionals to bill under their normal procedures after filing a certification of disinterestedness, without filing a full application to employ or a fee application. However, most

---

4. There is an overlap in 11 U.S.C. § 327(e) professionals and "ordinary course professionals." Generally, if an ordinary course professional order is in place, the debtor will seek to employ professionals not used in the bankruptcy case itself under that order rather than 11 U.S.C. § 327(e).

5. *In re* Sieling Assocs. Ltd. P'ship, 128 B.R. 721, 723 (Bankr. E.D. Va. 1991) (authorizing the debtor to retain an environmental consultant in the ordinary course of business); *In re* Riker Indus., Inc., 122 B.R. 964, 973 (Bankr. N.D. Ohio 1990) (not requiring section 327 approval of the fees of a management and consulting firm that performed only "routine administrative functions" and whose "services were not central to [the] bankruptcy case"); *In re* Fretheim, 102 B.R. 298, 299 (Bankr. D. Conn. 1989) (only those professionals involved in the actual reorganization effort, rather than the debtor's ongoing business, require approval under section 327); *In re* Johns-Manville Corp., 60 B.R. 612, 619 (Bankr. S.D.N.Y. 1986) (only those professionals involved in the actual reorganization effort, rather than the debtor's ongoing business, require approval under section 327); Elstead v. Nolden (*In re* That's Entmt't Mkt'g Group. Inc.), 168 B.R. 226, 230 (Bankr. N.D. Cal. 1994) (only the retention of professionals whose duties are central to the administration of the estate require prior court approval under section 327); *In re* D'Lites of Am., Inc., 108 B.R. 352, 353 (Bankr. N.D. Ga. 1989) (section 327 approval is not necessary for "one who provides services to debtor that are necessary regardless of whether petition was filed").

such orders generally contain both a monthly and total engagement cap on the amount of fees that can be charged under such an order. Note, however, that who may be retained under an ordinary course professional order varies from jurisdiction to jurisdiction and may be dependent on the U.S. trustee for the jurisdiction. For example, some jurisdictions hold that only those employable under section 327(e) of the Bankruptcy Code can be ordinary course professionals, and, thus, accountants always must be retained under section 327(a).

## 8.2 THE CONFLICT/CONTACT CHECK

Regardless of whether the professional is retained pursuant to section 327(a), section 327(e), or an ordinary course order, a rather extensive check of not only the proposed professional's potential conflicts but also the proposed professional's contacts must be run. For example, if an accounting firm is attempting to be retained as a professional, and that firm prepares the tax returns of one of the creditors, this fact must be disclosed in the verified statement despite the fact that it does not constitute a conflict; it is said to be a disclosure issue rather than a conflict issue.

While there is no set list of parties against whom you should run the check (and the debtor's primary bankruptcy counsel usually can supply the list), minimally, the professional should run a check against:

- the debtor, including names under which it does business or formerly did business;
- the debtor's affiliates, including names under which they do business or formerly did business;
- the debtor's current and former officers and directors;
- the debtor's lenders;
- the debtor's 30 largest unsecured creditors;

- the lessors of any of the debtors' real or personal property;

- any party having a lien on the debtor's property; and

- any entity involved in active or potential litigation with the debtor.

The general rule, rightly or wrongly, is that when in doubt, disclose. Also, remember that the duty to disclose is an ongoing one. Therefore, periodic checks should be run throughout the course of the bankruptcy case. If new contacts are discovered, the verified statement should be supplemented.

The failure to properly disclose or of subsequently being found to not be "disinterested" is severe and spelled out in section 328(c) of the Bankruptcy Code, which provides:

> (c) Except as provided in section 327 (c), 327 (e), or 1107 (b) of this title, the court may *deny allowance of compensation* for services and reimbursement of expenses of a professional person employed under section 327 or 1103 of this title *if, at any time during such professional person's employment under section 327 or 1103 of this title, such professional person is not a disinterested person, or represents or holds an interest adverse to the interest of the estate with respect to the matter on which such professional person is employed* (emphasis added).[6]

## 8.3 THE APPLICATION PROCESS

Bankruptcy professionals and those employed for special purposes in the bankruptcy case must file an application to employ signed by the employing fiduciary—either the debtor in possession, the trustee, or the official committee. Bankruptcy Rule 2014 specifies what must be included in the

---

6. 11 U.S.C. § 328(c).

application, the declaration attached to that application, and the order emanating from that application:

> The application shall state the specific facts showing the necessity for the employment, the name of the person to be employed, the reasons for the selection, the professional services to be rendered, any proposed arrangement for compensation, and, to the best of the applicant's knowledge, all of the person's connections with the debtor, creditors, any other party in interest, their respective attorneys and accountants, the United States trustee, or any person employed in the office of the United States Trustee. The application shall be accompanied by a verified statement of the person to be employed setting forth the person's connections with the debtor, creditors, any other party in interest, their respective attorneys and accountants, the United States trustee, or any person employed in the office of the United States trustee.[7]

### 8.3.1 *The Application*

The application itself is a pleading, much like any other, that should include provisions showing that the jurisdiction and venue are proper and giving the background of the case. Further, if the professional began work prior to filing the application or the application's being approved, the application should seek nunc pro tunc retention as of the later of the date work commenced or the date the petition was filed. To comply with section 327 of the Bankruptcy Code and Bankruptcy Rule 2014, the application should also clearly state:

- the name of the firm/person to be employed;
- the specific facts necessitating the employment;
- the reasons the professional was selected;

---

7. FED. R. BANKR. P. 2014(a).

- the professional services to be provided with some degree of specificity;
- the proposed compensation arrangements; and
- connections with the parties in interest and reference to the detail in the verified statement.

Along with the requirements mentioned above, the application should also state that the proposed retention is in accordance with the fee-splitting prohibition found in section 504 of the Bankruptcy Code, which states:

(a) Except as provided in subsection (b) of this section, a person receiving compensation or reimbursement under section 503 (b)(2) or 503 (b)(4) of this title may not share or agree to share—

(1) any such compensation or reimbursement with another person; or

(2) any compensation or reimbursement received by another person under such sections.

(b) (1) A member, partner, or regular associate in a professional association, corporation, or partnership may share compensation or reimbursement received under section 503 (b)(2) or 503 (b)(4) of this title with another member, partner, or regular associate in such association, corporation, or partnership, and may share in any compensation or reimbursement received under such sections by another member, partner, or regular associate in such association, corporation, or partnership.

(2) An attorney for a creditor that files a petition under section 303 of this title may share compensation and reimbursement received under section 503 (b)(4) of this title with any other attorney contributing to the services rendered or expenses incurred by such creditor's attorney.

(c) This section shall not apply with respect to sharing, or agreeing to share, compensation with a bona fide public service attorney referral program that operates in accordance with non-federal law regulating attorney referral services and with rules of professional responsibility applicable to attorney acceptance of referrals.[8]

This provision allows for the sharing of fees within a firm, but prohibits the sharing of fees between firms unless the exceptions are met.

### 8.3.2 *The Verified Statement*

The requirements for the verified statement are much like those for the application. However, the verified statement is made by a person, under penalty of perjury, on behalf of the entity to be retained, who is authorized to bind the entity. The verified statement should minimally set forth:

- the name of the person making the statement and his/her position with the firm;
- the name and address of the firm;
- the qualifications of the firm and the firm's background in similar cases;
- the compensation to be sought;
- all connections with the parties in interest from the conflict/contacts search (this may be attached as an exhibit);
- a listing of the parties against whom the search was performed;
- the method by which the search was performed;
- the belief that the entity is disinterested;
- any payments made within 90 days of the filing of the bankruptcy case;

---

8. 11 U.S.C. § 504.

- the total of unpaid pre-petition fees and that such fees are waived; and

- compliance with section 504 of the Bankruptcy Code.

If the parties entered into an engagement letter, the engagement letter should be attached as an exhibit.

### 8.3.3 *Timing*

Historically, the debtor in possession's professionals submitted their applications for employment on the first day along with other first-day motions, with notice given to a limited number of parties and such applications approved in relatively short order. However, Bankruptcy Rule 6003 has changed that by providing that:

> Except to the extent that relief is necessary to avoid immediate and irreparable harm, the court shall not, within 20 days after the filing of the petition, grant relief regarding the following:
>
> (a) an application under Rule 2014; . . .[9]

Thus, the order approving the application to employ professionals is generally not entered within the first 20 days of the bankruptcy case.[10]

## 8.4 BILLING IN BANKRUPTCY

The Bankruptcy Code does not specify fee arrangements for professionals. Flat fees, contingent fees, and the like are perfectly acceptable in the bankruptcy context if that is the normal fee arrangement in the industry in question, they are clearly set out in the application, and they are approved by the court. However, most professionals are compensated on an hourly basis utilizing the Lodestar Standard, which requires that a professional:

---

9. FED. R. BANKR. P. 6003(a).

10. *See* Section 11.3, *infra,* on first-day order for more discussion of this rule and its exceptions.

1. properly record all time expended on behalf of the debtor or official committee with the appropriate degree of specificity; and

2. assign the appropriate personnel to the task to be performed.

The level of specificity required is often difficult for the non-bankruptcy professional. For example, a time entry of six hours for the research and drafting of a legal memorandum on a specific issue is too general and is often called "lumping." Rather, the amount of time spent performing the research should be one entry; the amount of time doing the original drafting should be another entry; and the time reviewing and revising should be a third entry. Generally, an entry should not be more than two or three hours in length, and time entries should be in tenths of an hour. The U.S. trustee publishes guidelines on billing and timekeeping, and compliance with those guidelines greatly facilitates the fee process.

Note, however, that the Bankruptcy Code is not mute on the factors that control fees; section 328 speaks to the matter, stating:

> (a) The trustee, or a committee appointed under section 1102 of this title, with the court's approval, may employ or authorize the employment of a professional person under section 327 or 1103 of this title, as the case may be, on any reasonable terms and conditions of employment, including on a retainer, on an hourly basis, on a fixed or percentage fee basis, or on a contingent fee basis. *Notwithstanding such terms and conditions, the court may allow compensation different from the compensation provided under such terms and conditions after the conclusion of such employment, if such terms and conditions prove to have been improvident in light of developments not capable of being anticipated at*

*the time of the fixing of such terms and condition* (emphasis added).[11]

Thus, even if the fee is flat or contingent, the professional is well advised to keep detailed time records in case the court decides that the fee needs to be reviewed under this provision at the end of the engagement.

## 8.5 THE FEE APPLICATION

Any bankruptcy professional will tell you that the only part of bankruptcy practice more tedious than the application for employment is the fee application process. It is, however, a necessary evil, because the bankruptcy professional is being paid from the property of the debtor's estate. Thus, the court is the client reviewing the bill, and it requires details.

There are generally two types of fee applications: interim and final. All fee applications during the pendency of the case are considered interim, and though an order may be entered approving the application, such an order is subject to subsequent revision. Orders on final fee applications are final orders of the court.

### 8.5.1 *Frequency*

The frequency of interim fee applications is generally governed by section 331 of the Bankruptcy Code, which provides:

> A trustee, an examiner, a debtor's attorney, or any professional person employed under section 327 or 1103 of this title may apply to the court not more than once every 120 days after an order for relief in a case under this title, or more often if the court permits, for such compensation for services rendered before the date of such an application or reimbursement for expenses incurred before such

---
11. 11 U.S.C. § 328(a).

date as is provided under section 330 of this title. After notice and a hearing, the court may allow and disburse to such applicant such compensation or reimbursement.[12]

Thus, the default rule is that fee applications cannot be submitted more frequently than once every 120 days. However, often one of the first-day motions is for a procedure for the payment of professionals that will allow for a monthly payment subject to a holdback and a quarterly fee application.

### 8.5.2 Fee Application Contents

The contents of the fee application are governed by Bankruptcy Rule 2016(a), which provides:

> **Application for compensation or reimbursement.** An entity seeking interim or final compensation for services, or reimbursement of necessary expenses, from the estate shall file an application setting forth a detailed statement of (1) the services rendered, time expended and expenses incurred, and (2) the amounts requested. An application for compensation shall include a statement as to what payments have theretofore been made or promised to the applicant for services rendered or to be rendered in any capacity whatsoever in connection with the case, the source of the compensation so paid or promised, whether any compensation previously received has been shared and whether an agreement or understanding exists between the applicant and any other entity for the sharing of compensation received or to be received for services rendered in or in connection with the case, and the particulars of any sharing of compensation or agreement or understanding therefor, except that details of any agreement by the applicant for the sharing of compensation as a member or regular associ-

---

12. 11 U.S.C. § 331.

ate of a firm of lawyers or accountants shall not be required. The requirements of this subdivision shall apply to an application for compensation for services rendered by an attorney or accountant even though the application is filed by a creditor or other entity. Unless the case is a chapter 9 municipality case, the applicant shall transmit to the United States trustee a copy of the application.[13]

Thus, the fee application should include attachments of the detailed billing records and detailed expenses. Further, within the application, the professional should clearly summarize:

- the total number of hours spent during the period covered by the application;
- the total amount requested for compensation;
- the total amount requested for the reimbursement of expenses;
- what services have been provided during the period;
- any previous fees awarded; and
- whether any fees have been shared.

Other exhibits may be required by local rule or the U.S. trustee for the jurisdiction in question. The U.S. trustee should be consulted for such requirements.

### 8.5.3 *Fee Considerations*

When reviewing the fee application, the court looks at the request in light of the provisions of section 330(a) of the Bankruptcy Code, which is quite detailed and provides as follows:

> (1) After notice to the parties in interest and the United States Trustee and a hearing, and subject to sections 326, 328, and 329, the court may award to a trustee,

---

13. FED. R. BANKR. P. 2016(a).

a consumer privacy ombudsman appointed under section 332, an examiner, an ombudsman appointed under section 333, or a professional person employed under section 327 or 1103—

(A) reasonable compensation for actual, necessary services rendered by the trustee, examiner, ombudsman, professional person, or attorney and by any paraprofessional person employed by any such person; and

(B) reimbursement for actual, necessary expenses.

(2) The court may, on its own motion or on the motion of the United States Trustee, the United States Trustee for the District or Region, the trustee for the estate, or any other party in interest, award compensation that is less than the amount of compensation that is requested.

(3) In determining the amount of reasonable compensation to be awarded to an examiner, trustee under chapter 11, or professional person, the court shall consider the nature, the extent, and the value of such services, taking into account all relevant factors, including—

(A) the time spent on such services;

(B) the rates charged for such services;

(C) whether the services were necessary to the administration of, or beneficial at the time at which the service was rendered toward the completion of, a case under this title;

(D) whether the services were performed within a reasonable amount of time commensurate with the complexity, importance, and nature of the problem, issue, or task addressed;

(E) with respect to a professional person, whether the person is board certified or otherwise has demonstrated skill and experience in the bankruptcy field; and

(F) whether the compensation is reasonable based on the customary compensation charged by comparably skilled practitioners in cases other than cases under this title.

(4) (A) Except as provided in subparagraph (B), the court shall not allow compensation for—

(i) unnecessary duplication of services; or

(ii) services that were not—

(I) reasonably likely to benefit the debtor's estate; or

(II) necessary to the administration of the case.

(B) In a chapter 12 or chapter 13 case in which the debtor is an individual, the court may allow reasonable compensation to the debtor's attorney for representing the interests of the debtor in connection with the bankruptcy case based on a consideration of the benefit and necessity of such services to the debtor and the other factors set forth in this section.

(5) The court shall reduce the amount of compensation awarded under this section by the amount of any interim compensation awarded under section 331, and, if the amount of such interim compensation exceeds the amount of compensation awarded under this section, may order the return of the excess to the estate.

(6) Any compensation awarded for the preparation of a fee application shall be based on the level and skill reasonably required to prepare the application.

(7) In determining the amount of reasonable compensation to be awarded to a trustee, the court shall treat such compensation as a commission, based on section 326.[14]

Despite the length and complexity of this provision, it is included in its entirety because it is essential to the bottom line for any professional providing services to a fiduciary in a bankruptcy case—getting paid. Careful consideration of this provision while preparing the fee application is essential to maximizing fee recovery.

---

14. 11 U.S.C. § 330(a).

# CHAPTER 9

# THE AUTOMATIC STAY

One of the most fundamental aspects of the Bankruptcy Code is the creation, scope, effect, and duration of the automatic stay found at section 362 of the Bankruptcy Code. It is the most hotly contested issue in bankruptcy practice.

## 9.1 THE SCOPE OF THE AUTOMATIC STAY

Upon the filing of a voluntary or involuntary petition in bankruptcy, the automatic stay arises under section 362 of the Bankruptcy Code. The automatic stay applies to all entities, including governmental units. The stay is theoretically of infinite duration, continuing until it is terminated by the bankruptcy court under section 362(d) or by the Bankruptcy Code under section 362(c).

The purposes of the automatic stay are to enable the trustee to preserve the estate, to allow the trustee time to marshal the assets of the estate, to allow the trustee time to satisfy the claims of any creditors, and to afford the debtor time to confirm a plan of reorganization in a chapter 11 case.[1] The automatic stay stops the commencement or continuation of

---

1. *See* Interstate Commerce Comm'n v. Holmes Transp., Inc., 931 F.2d 984, 987 (1st Cir. 1991); *see also In re* Richardson Builders, Inc., 123 B.R. 736, 738 (Bankr. W.D. Va. 1990).

almost all civil actions against the debtor and all acts to create liens, collect or enforce claims, recover property, repossess or foreclose, or exercise control over property of the estate. The automatic stay also prevents the enforcement of all judgment, judicial, and consensual liens as well as halting the commencement or continuation of a proceeding before the United States Tax Court.[2] In essence, the automatic stay halts any collection activities worth the effort.

Generally the automatic stay protects only the debtor, the debtor's property, and property of the estate. Further, the more broadly a court defines the estate, the broader the protections of the stay. Third parties, such as guarantors, generally may not reap the benefits of the automatic stay unless they file their own bankruptcy petition.[3] However, certain provisions of the Bankruptcy Code—for example cases brought under chapter 13—may allow for a co-debtor's stay for family members or those closely affiliated with the debtor where the transaction that created the debt was a consumer transaction.[4]

## 9.2 ACTS IN VIOLATION OF THE AUTOMATIC STAY

Any act in violation of the automatic stay is void because the stay is self-enforcing. Thus, a repossession or sale of any property that is property of the estate by a creditor in violation of the stay, irrespective of the knowledge of the stay's existence, is void. Moreover, the creditor may be subject to a litany of sanctions ranging from paying the attorney's fees of the debtor to punitive damages and, ultimately, to contempt of court if the stay violation was willful.[5]

---

2. *See* 11 U.S.C. § 362(a) (2006).
3. Some authorities, however, hold or suggest that the bankruptcy court has the inherent authority under section 105 to issue an injunction to protect insiders of the debtor, such as partners of a debtor partnership, when in the best interests of the estate.
4. *See* 11 U.S.C. § 1301 (2006).
5. *See* 11 U.S.C. § 362(k) (2006).

## 9.3 EXCEPTIONS TO THE AUTOMATIC STAY

Certain narrowly drawn and strictly construed acts, however, are not stayed. For example, the commencement or continuation of a criminal action or proceeding against a debtor, the collection of alimony, maintenance or support from property that is not property of the estate, the commencement or continuation of an action or proceeding by a governmental unit to enforce such governmental unit's police or regulatory power, and the issuance to the debtor by the governmental unit of a notice of tax deficiency, along with several other limited exceptions, are all excepted from the scope of the automatic stay.[6] In accordance with the 1994 amendments, assessments, requests for tax information and filings, and administrative summonses are no longer violations of the automatic stay pursuant to section 362(b)(9) (as amended).

## 9.4 RELIEF FROM THE AUTOMATIC STAY

In an oft-litigated area of bankruptcy law, a secured creditor or other party in interest may file a request with the court seeking relief from the automatic stay.[7] Essentially, for a secured creditor to obtain relief from the automatic stay, it must show either cause for the termination of the automatic stay, including lack of adequate protection,[8] or that the debtor has no equity in the property and the property is not necessary for an effective reorganization.[9] The debtor will often argue that it in fact has equity in the property or that the property is necessary for an effective reorganization. Moreover, the debtor may argue that it can provide adequate protection of the secured creditor's interest without resorting to the termination of the automatic stay. The creditor has the burden of proof on the issue of whether the debtor has eq-

---

6. *See* 11 U.S.C. § 362(b) (2006).
7. 11 U.S.C. § 362(d) (2006).
8. 11 U.S.C. § 362(d)(1) (2006).
9. *Id.*

uity in the property; however, the debtor bears the burden on the remaining issues.[10]

## 9.5 FILING REQUIREMENTS

Below are the filing requirements regarding stay-relief motions in bankruptcy courts.

- File motion for relief from stay, which commences a contested matter under Bankruptcy Rule 9014.
- Pay the filing fee, if required.
- File brief in support of the motion presenting discussion of relevant facts and issues.
- File affidavits describing the debt owed, secured status, cause, value of the collateral, etc.
- Request a hearing date from the court.
- File proposed order granting the motion with the court.

One must consult local rules and a judge's own peculiarities when considering relief from the stay.

## 9.6 WHY SEEK RELIEF FROM THE AUTOMATIC STAY

Various factors will affect a creditor's decision whether to seek relief from the stay; however, foremost in the majority of a creditor's thoughts is the debtor's ability to repay the indebtedness owed and to protect the collateral securing the creditor's loan. In order for a creditor to seek the release of its collateral from the debtor's estate, it is necessary to file a motion to terminate or modify the automatic stay. Such action may be brought at any time after the bankruptcy case is filed by a creditor claiming an interest in property or otherwise seeking relief to proceed against the debtor. The Bankruptcy Code requires that a court schedule a preliminary hearing on the motion for relief from the automatic stay within 30 days of filing the motion to consider whether the

---

10. *See* 11 U.S.C. § 362(g) (2006).

automatic stay should continue. Depending on the local rules, certain courts will hold a preliminary hearing to determine if the automatic stay should continue for up to 30 days, and then a final hearing will be held within another 30 days. Other jurisdictions, however, combine the preliminary and final hearings.

## 9.7 CRITERIA FOR OBTAINING RELIEF FROM THE AUTOMATIC STAY

As briefly stated above, the Bankruptcy Code sets forth four alternatives for requesting relief from the automatic stay: (1) "for cause, including lack of adequate protection of an interest in property"; (2)(a) "lack of equity in such property" *and* (b) "such property is not necessary to an effective reorganization"; (3) as an act against a single-asset real estate where the debtor has either failed to file a reasonable plan within 90 days from the order for relief or has failed to commence monthly payments to the secured creditor; or (4) the commencement of the case is determined to be part of a scheme to delay, hinder, or defraud creditors through a general assignment of interests in the specific real property at issue or through multiple bankruptcy filings.[11] The burden of proof is on the debtor for all elements except the issue of whether the debtor has equity in the property.[12]

Section 362(d)(1) specifies that cause may include lack of insurance to protect the collateral, bad faith in the filing of the bankruptcy case, or an inability to adequately protect the collateral securing the creditor's lien. Adequate protection is not defined in the Bankruptcy Code. However, methods of providing adequate protection are set forth in section 361. Adequate protection includes (1) a cash payment or periodic cash payments; (2) providing an additional replacement lien to the extent the use, sale, lease, or grant results in a decrease in the value of the property; or (3) granting other

---

11. 11 U.S.C. § 362(d) (2006) (emphasis added).
12. 11 U.S.C. § 362(g) (2006).

relief that will result in the realization of the "indubitable equivalent" of the creditor's interest in the property. As one can see, the concept of adequate protection is protean, its form limited by the imagination of counsel and the sensibilities of the court. Although adequate protection may take a multitude of forms, one theme remains constant: the purpose of adequate protection is to protect a creditor's interest in collateral from harm caused by the delays occasioned by the bankruptcy process itself; a creditor is not entitled to adequate protection from all harms. Moreover, adequate protection is not designed to protect a creditor's benefit of the bargain; rather, adequate protection protects impairment of the value of a creditor's lien from the delays inherent in the bankruptcy process.

Alternatively, pursuant to section 362(d)(2), a creditor may plead that a debtor does not have equity in the property, and the property is not necessary for an effective reorganization. To prove lack of equity, the creditor must show that the amount of indebtedness owed is greater than the value of the property. The creditor generally presents testimony regarding the amount of the indebtedness due and uses expert testimony with respect to the value of the collateral. Assuming the sufficiency of the expert testimony, the creditor has then met its burden with respect to proving lack of equity. The debtor may then rebut the creditor's evidence regarding lack of equity or prove that the property is necessary for an effective reorganization. Because stay disputes are generally heard by the court early in the bankruptcy case, courts tend to be lenient in receiving and considering the debtor's evidence on whether property is necessary for an effective reorganization. However, the debtor must still introduce some evidence to show the necessity of the property for an *effective reorganization*. Obviously, the debtor or trustee cannot show that the property is necessary to an effective reorganization in a chapter 7 case; thus, the only defense under subsection (d)(2) in a chapter 7 case is equity.

The focus of a section 362(d)(3) action in the context of single-asset real estate is to ensure prompt compliance with the Bankruptcy Code by the debtor to protect the secured creditor's interest in the property. This is done either by forcing a debtor to propose a plan with a reasonable prospect of success or by requiring the debtor to make monthly interest payments at the then-fair market rate.

Finally, the focus of a section 362(d)(4) action in the context of real property is to prevent a debtor from frustrating legitimate creditor foreclosure efforts by employing the petition filing as part of a scheme to delay, hinder, or defraud its creditors through a transfer of ownership interest in the property or through the use of multiple or successive bankruptcy filings. The intent of this subsection, added by BAPCPA, is to frustrate illegitimate efforts by a debtor to use a bankruptcy filing or multiple bankruptcy filings as a sword.

## 9.8 TERMINATION OF THE AUTOMATIC STAY

Section 362(c)(1) provides that the automatic stay ends for property that is no longer property of the estate. Property is no longer property of the estate when exempted under section 522, abandoned under section 554, or sold under section 363. Although the property may no longer be property of the estate, it may remain property of the debtor still protected by the automatic stay. Section 362(c)(2) further provides that the automatic stay terminates when the bankruptcy case is closed or dismissed, or the debtor receives a discharge under chapter 7, 11, or 13.

Pursuant to BAPCPA, sections 362(c)(3) and (c)(4) provide further limits to the automatic stay's protection in certain circumstances. These provisions are designed to prevent a debtor who employs successive bankruptcy filings to reap benefits from the stay and to minimize the unfair frustration of a creditor.

# CHAPTER 10

# THE BANKRUPTCY ESTATE

Along with the automatic stay, the definition and role of property of the bankruptcy estate are two of the most important issues in a bankruptcy case. The estate's property and distribution turn on the chapter under which the case is filed. The commencement of the case creates the estate, while the filing of the petition operates as a stay protecting the estate, the debtor, and the debtor's property.

## 10.1 SCOPE OF THE BANKRUPTCY ESTATE

Under Bankruptcy Code section 541(a), property of the estate includes all of the debtor's legal or equitable interest in property at the time of the filing of the petition wherever located and by whomever held. This is a question of federal law, but state law may also be consulted (although state law is not controlling).[1] After the section 541 rules have been applied, chapter-specific rules such as section 1115 for chapter 11 and section 1306 for chapter 13 should be applied to determine the full extent of the property of the estate. Under these two provisions, post-petition earnings of the debtor are included in the ambit of the bankruptcy estate, a result that is inconsistent with the treatment of post-petition earnings in a chapter 7 case as provided in section 541(a)(6).

---

1. Chicago Bd. of Trade v. Johnson, 264 U.S. 1 (1924).

Property subject to exemption under section 522 is included in the definition of property of the estate until it is, in fact, set aside as provided in section 522. Further, anti-forfeiture, recapture, and exclusion provisions under section 541(c) should also be applied. Moreover, all the interest of the debtor and the debtor's spouse in community property that is under the sole, equal, or joint management of the debtor is included in property of the estate. Furthermore, inheritances that come to the debtor within 180 days after the filing of the petition, an interest in property as a result of a divorce decree or property settlement agreement with the debtor's spouse, the proceeds of a life insurance policy or death benefit plan, and the proceeds, rents, and profits from property included in the estate are all included in the definition of property of the estate.[2] Additionally, in a chapter 11 or 13 case, post-petition earnings are property of the estate and are usually used to fund the plan. It is this property of the estate that is administered under the Bankruptcy Code and used to satisfy, among other things, prepetition allowed claims.

Occasionally, a difficult issue arises as to whether something (tangible or intangible) constitutes property of the estate. For example, in *In re Prudential Lines, Inc.,*[3] the Second Circuit addressed whether a debtor's net operating losses and carry-forwards (collectively, NOLs) constitute property of the estate. Under federal tax law, tax attributes (like the NOLs) are not property. However, the Second Circuit concluded that the NOLs were property of the estate protected by the automatic stay. A perusal of these difficult "at the margin" cases teaches that if the "thing" that the court is considering has value from the perspective of the unsecured creditors of the estate, then it will likely be determined property of the estate.

---

2. *See* 11 U.S.C. §§ 541(a)(1)-541(a)(7) (2006).
3. 928 F.2d 565, 572 (2d Cir. 1981).

## 10.2 LIMITS TO PROPERTY OF THE ESTATE

Under section 541, the estate only reaches the interests in the property possessed by the debtor as of the filing of the petition. Thus, if the debtor is a lessee or co-tenant in property, then the estate's interest in that property will not exceed the debtor's interest. However, section 541(c) ensures that any forfeiture provision under an agreement signed by the debtor that would be triggered by insolvency or a bankruptcy filing is not enforceable in bankruptcy.

# CHAPTER 11

# THE CHAPTER 11 CASE

A chapter 11 case is commenced in the same manner as a chapter 7 case. A trustee can be appointed in a chapter 11 case, but the appointment does not occur automatically and requires appropriate motions by creditors or other parties in interest.[1] As a general rule, the debtor in a chapter 11 case remains in possession and in control of its property and continues to operate its business in the ordinary course.[2] Generally, only transactions outside the ordinary course of business require approval of the bankruptcy court.[3]

## 11.1 THE DEBTOR IN POSSESSION

In a chapter 11 case, the debtor remains in possession of the estate under sections 1108 and 1101. Under section 1107, the debtor has most of the powers of a chapter 7 trustee. Specifically, the debtor may do the following: reject executory contracts and leases, use a secured party's collateral, borrow money, modify the debt and equity portion of its capital structure, bind dissenting members of a class, cram down a plan over the objection of most classes, and receive certain tax benefits through reorganization.

---

1. *See generally* 11 U.S.C. § 1104.
2. *See* 11 U.S.C. §§ 1107, 1108.
3. *See* 11 U.S.C. § 363(b)(1).

Although the debtor remains in possession and operates the business in the ordinary course without the necessity of court approval, there are situations where a debtor may be replaced or have its authority severely limited. Under section 1104, a trustee may be appointed for cause if it is in the best interests of the creditors. The appointment of a trustee terminates the period of exclusivity—that is, the time period in which only the debtor had the right to propose a plan and get it confirmed. However, a court may terminate the trustee's appointment and restore the debtor to possession and management of the property of the estate and business according to section 1105.

A debtor in possession may make ordinary course transactions without court approval. The court, however, must approve extraordinary transactions or unauthorized post-petition transfers. The determination of what is or is not in the ordinary course of business is not self-evident. Courts employ both the vertical and horizontal tests to make this determination. The vertical test looks to the history of the debtor and determines whether a creditor could claim unfair surprise when the debtor engages in the transaction at issue. The horizontal test considers comparable companies both in and out of bankruptcy and the types of transactions that a creditor would expect in the industry.

## 11.2 OTHER PLAYERS

The Official Committee of Unsecured Creditors plays a key role in a chapter 11 case. The United States trustee, a Department of Justice official, appoints the creditors' committee from the list of the seven largest unsecured creditors, although the trustee has the authority to depart from the top seven creditors to ensure that the committee represents a meaningful cross-section of the creditor class, including ensuring that a creditor with a relatively small claim (but large to that creditor) finds himself on the committee. The creditors' committee may retain professional assistance with the court's approval. Further, the court may order a change in the committee composition, additional creditor committees, and an equity security committee.

An examiner may be appointed in certain circumstances to investigate the debtor or current management, review potential causes of action, consider offers to purchase where there is a concern of management entrenchment, etc. In some circumstances, the appointment of an examiner may be mandatory. However, as opposed to a trustee, an examiner may not displace a debtor in possession and is limited to the scope of duties delineated in the order approving his or her retention.

## 11.3 FIRST-DAY MOTIONS

When a debtor files a chapter 11 case, generally the debtor also files a host of "first-day motions" seeking expedited relief from the bankruptcy court. These motions generally involve the request for approval for actions necessary to keep the debtor running during the bankruptcy case. Often these motions are entertained by the court well before any Official Committee of Unsecured Creditors has been formed by the U.S. trustee. Consequently, courts enter these motions generally without prejudice to revisit the motions upon formation of the committee.

### 11.3.1 Types of Motions

The motions may be clustered into three groups, including administrative motions, operational motions, and substantive motions. These motions generally include the following:

- Motion for Order Authorizing Joint Administration of Related (Affiliate) Bankruptcy Cases—Purpose is to promote judicial efficiency by procedurally consolidating related bankruptcy cases.

- Motion for Order Establishing Notice Procedures—Purpose is to manage the administrative burden posed in large bankruptcy cases in handling the sheer volume of parties involved.

- Motion for Order Extending Time to File Schedules and Statements—Purpose is to allow debtor more time to prepare reliable and accurate schedules and statements.

- Motion for Order Authorizing Employment of Professionals—Purpose is to hire lawyers, accountants, investment bankers, etc., in a case.

- Motion for Order Authorizing Employment of Ordinary Course Professionals—Used in some but not all jurisdictions, purpose is to provide an expedited, less onerous procedure for retaining certain classes of professionals, including tax preparers and auditors.

- Motion for Order Authorizing Interim Fee Procedures—Purpose is to provide procedures for interim payment of professional fees subject to review until the final fee application is approved.

- Motion for Order Approving Information Access Protocol Pursuant to Section 1102(b)(3)—Purpose is to comply with the information-sharing requirements imposed by the 2005 Amendments to the Bankruptcy Code to promote greater creditor access to financial information historically captured but not shared by the Official Committee of Unsecured Creditors.

- Motion for Order Authorizing Certain Documents to Be Filed Under Seal—Purpose is to protect certain proprietary or confidential information related to the debtor.

- Motion for an Order Approving the Use of Cash Management Systems—Purpose is to, among other things, permit use and access to bank accounts, intercompany accounts, etc.

- Motion for Order Approving Investment Guidelines Pursuant to Section 345—Purpose is to establish procedures and protection regarding cash deposits in a bankruptcy case.

- Motion for Order Authorizing Debtor to Pay Pre-petition Claims of Critical Vendors—Procedure is to ensure that debtor may maintain good relations with critical vendors while also protecting the general unsecured creditors from dissipation of the bankruptcy estate.

- Motion for an Order Authorizing Debtor to Honor Pre-petition Employee Benefits and Pre-petition Wage Claims—Purpose is to pay employees to keep them around for the reorganizational efforts of the debtor.

- Motion for an Order Authorizing Continuation of Customer Programs—Purpose is to honor commitments to customers, including gift cards and warranty programs, in order to continue operations.

- Motion for an Order Authorizing Payment of Custom Duties and Certain Pre-petition Claims of Shippers, Freight Handlers, and Warehousers—Purpose is to permit the continued flow of goods to the debtor.

- Motion for an Order Authorizing Payment of Contractors in Satisfaction of Liens—Purpose is to protect the providers of services that keep facilities in order to continue to attract customers.

- Motion for an Order Permitting the Debtor to Honor Workers' Compensation Programs and Pay Insurance—Purpose is to keep the business operational.

- Motion for Order Establishing Adequate Assurance of Payment for Utilities—Purpose is to trigger certain procedural protections embodied in the Bankruptcy Code and to ensure that utilities are not interrupted.

- Motion for an Order Authorizing Business Closure or Going Out of Business Sales—Purpose is to authorize and expedite the steps necessary to develop and execute such steps or sales.

- Motion for Order Authorizing Payment of Sales and Use Taxes—Purpose is to remit trust fund taxes (in some jurisdictions) and to continue operation of the business.

- Motion for an Order Authorizing Debtor to Return Goods Pursuant to Section 546(g)—Purpose is to provide procedures to return goods that are no longer necessary for an effective reorganization of the debtor.

- Motion for an Order Authorizing Post-petition Delivery of Goods Ordered Pre-petition—Purpose is to avoid disruption in the flow of goods.

- Motion for Order Establishing Reclamation Procedures—Purpose is establish procedures for either the return of goods or some form of adequate protection of such claim.

- Motion for Order Limiting Certain Transfers of the Debtor's Equity Securities or Trading in Claims—Purpose is to preserve certain options under section 382(l)(5) or (l)(6) of the Internal Revenue Code by preventing an ownership change through the transfer of equity securities or claims trading that prevents application of section 382(l)(5).

- Motion for an Order Authorizing Use of Cash Collateral—Purpose is to permit a debtor's use of cash or cash equivalents while at the same time protecting creditor rights in such cash or cash equivalents.

- Motion for an Order Authorizing the Debtor to Incur Secured Indebtedness—Purpose is to permit the incurrence of post-petition financing to maintain operations in a bankruptcy case, a form of bridge loan between the commencement of the case and the confirmation of the plan of reorganization in which exit financing would be obtained.

- Motion for an Order Authorizing the Rejection of Nonresidential Real Property Leases—Purpose is to ensure that non-performing leases that constitute a net liability are rejected to prevent dissipation of the bankruptcy estate.

- Motion for an Order Authorizing Key Employee Retention Programs (KERPs)—Purpose is to retain important employees to effectively reorganize the debtor.

### 11.3.2 Rule 6003

On December 1, 2007, the Federal Rules of Bankruptcy Procedure were amended and now weigh in on the practice of first-day motions, seeking to slow down the process by which so many critical decisions are made in many business bankruptcy cases. Before we turn to new Bankruptcy Rule 6003, a little history may be beneficial. It is not unusual for a flurry of activity to take place once a business has decided to commence a case under title 11 of the United States Code (the Bankruptcy Code). For some time now, a number of bankruptcy courts have been receptive to the use of first-day motions to ensure a relatively smooth transition for a business as it enters bankruptcy. These bankruptcy courts will entertain motions to retain professionals for the debtor, pay employees, provide adequate assurance to utility service providers, use cash collateral, obtain postpetition financing, maintain cash management systems, honor gift cards and warranty claims, and pay critical vendors. These first-day orders are defended on the grounds that granting them on limited notice and before formation of any official committees keeps the going-concern value of a company intact, benefits the estate, and does not compromise any ultimate objections by parties in interest who had little or no notice of these motions. Critics of these procedures turn to the emerging reality that these decisions made early in a case are difficult to revisit once the momentum of the case has developed, that often the burden of proof has drifted to the objectant, and that "putting the toothpaste back in the tube" may be impracticable. New Rule 6003 is an attempt to compromise the competing camps.

Rule 6003 provides:

> Except to the extent that relief is necessary to avoid immediate and irreparable harm, the court shall not,

within 20 days after the filing of the petition, grant relief regarding the following:

(a) an application under Rule 2014;

(b) a motion to use, sell, lease, or otherwise incur an obligation regarding property of the estate, including a motion to pay all or part of a claim that arose before the filing of the petition, but not a motion under Rule 4001; and

(c) a motion to assume or assign an executory contract or unexpired lease in accordance with § 365.[4]

Thus, new Rule 6003 sets forth new guidelines limiting relief in the early stages of a bankruptcy case. Rule 6003 limits the granting of interim and final relief by a bankruptcy court during the first 20 days after commencement of a case on certain delineated issues. Specifically, absent a showing of immediate and irreparable harm, a bankruptcy court cannot grant relief during the first 20 days of a case on applications for the employment of professional persons; motions for the use, sale, or lease of property of the estate; motions to pay claims (presumably including critical vendors, warranty claims, and gift cards); and motions to assume or assign executory contracts and unexpired leases. This rule is intended to protect parties in interest and to ensure that full consideration will be given to matters that are likely to have a fundamental impact on the bankruptcy case. The 20-day bar to the motions identified in the rule may be overcome by a showing that such relief is necessary "to avoid immediate and irreparable harm."[5] Mere allegations in the motions are not enough; rather, the movant must introduce evidence in the record that makes the case of immediate and irreparable harm—a heightened standard for relief.

A perusal of the Advisory Committee Notes on Rule 6003 flesh out the importance of this new rule. The purpose given

---

4. FED. R. BANKR. P. 6003.
5. FED. R. BANKR. P. 6003

for the rule is to "alleviate some of the time pressures present at the start of a case so that full and close consideration can be given to matters that may have a fundamental impact on the case." The committee noted that the "flurry of activity" in the beginning of a bankruptcy case often happens before the formation of a creditors' committee. The standard for relief is taken from Rule 4001(b)(2) and (c)(2), and the committee noted that "decisions under those provisions should provide guidance for the application of this provision."

A recent case addressed the application of Rule 6003 to a debtor's retention of counsel through a first-day application. In *In re First NLC Financial Services, L.L.C.*,[6] the bankruptcy court confronted a situation in which a chapter 11 debtor in possession requested the entry of an order at the first-day hearings to approve, on an interim basis, the application for employment of counsel. In response, the U.S. trustee objected, arguing that Rule 6003 does not provide for such interim relief. The court approved the retention application. In support, the bankruptcy court held that, notwithstanding the Rule 6003 20-day bar, the Advisory Committee directly suggested that in interpreting the new Rule 6003, courts refer to Rule 4001(b)(2) and (c)(2), which "provide for bifurcation of relief into interim and final components."[7] Furthermore, the court noted that a corporation, such as the debtor, may not appear in court pro se, but required legal representation to present first-day requests for relief. The court finally noted that *Collier on Bankruptcy*, which noted that no party would be prejudiced by the 20-day wait because a court could allow for full compensation from day one, overlooked the "unwieldy" procedure in which a court would have to enter several orders approving past compensation and then denying further employment in order to ensure compensa-

---

6. 382 B.R. 547 (Bankr. S.D. Fla. 2008),
7. 382 B.R. at 549.

tion for a professional who is ultimately not approved for employment.[8]

Although the court in *NLC* steered a pragmatic tack in addressing the application of new Rule 6003 to the retention of legal counsel for the debtor, one should be careful in reading too much into the opinion. Generally, interim relief for the retention of legal counsel does constitute immediate and irreparable harm, in that without counsel, a corporate debtor is legally dead in the water. This is not the same with other professionals, such as special or litigation counsel, who may be necessary for an effective reorganization but not necessary for the legal proceeding itself. Only time will tell whether courts will limit the rationale of *NLC* to its particular situation or whether the "camel's nose is in the tent."

## 11.4 FILING A PLAN OF REORGANIZATION

In a chapter 11 case, the debtor or its creditors formulate a plan or competing plans of reorganization that provide the means by which the claims of creditors, equity security holders (e.g., shareholders), and other parties in interest are satisfied from the assets or otherwise treated and how the future operations of the debtor's business will be conducted. Unless a trustee is appointed, only the debtor may file a plan of reorganization during the 120-day period following the filing of the petition, although that period can be, and generally is, extended.[9] If a debtor files a plan within this 120-day period, no other plan may be filed during the first 180 days following the filing of the bankruptcy petition.[10] If a trustee has been appointed or if the debtor fails to file the plan within 120 days and to have the plan confirmed by 180 days (unless these deadlines are extended by the bankruptcy court for cause),[11] a creditor or other party in interest may propose a plan of reorganization and eventually solicit votes in

---

8. *Id.* at 550.
9. 11 U.S.C. § 1121(b).
10. 11 U.S.C. § 1121(c).
11. *See* 11 U.S.C. § 1121(d).

favor of its plan. The 120-day period of exclusivity to propose a plan cannot be extended beyond 18 months from the order for relief. The 180-day period of exclusivity to propose and have a plan confirmed may not be extended beyond 20 months from the order for relief.

## 11.5 CONTENTS OF A PLAN AND DISCLOSURE STATEMENT

The plan deals with the claims of creditors and interests of equity security holders. The claims and interests are divided into classes based upon the priorities established by the Bankruptcy Code and the specific nature of the claims and interests.[12] Each secured creditor is generally placed in a class by itself. The classes of unsecured creditors are generally divided into priority and general unsecured claims, although other classes may be appropriate in certain cases, such as disputed, contingent, or unliquidated claims. The interests of equity security holders may be divided into classes based on the relative rights and priorities provided in the equity securities that the debtor has issued.

A disclosure statement must be prepared discussing the plan of reorganization before the debtor solicits any acceptances of the plan from parties in interest.[13] The court conducts a hearing to review and approve the form and content of the disclosure statement. The disclosure statement must provide information adequate to inform a hypothetical investor about the contents of the plan.[14] It must explain the treatment of each class of creditors and disclose the method for classification of claims. It must also contain an adequate liquidation analysis so that a claimant may compare its treatment under the plan to its recovery under a chapter 7 liquidation. The disclosure statement must also contain a discussion of the federal tax consequences of the plan. The disclosure statement is similar to a prospectus filed in connection with

---

12. *See* 11 U.S.C. § 1122.
13. *See generally* 11 U.S.C. § 1125.
14. 11 U.S.C. § 1125(a).

a public offering of stock under federal securities laws, in that it cannot be misleading.

## 11.6 CLASSIFICATION OF CLAIMS

Under a chapter 11 plan of reorganization, all creditors need not be treated alike. Rather, the Bankruptcy Code provides that creditors are divided into classes based upon the nature of their legal rights. The Bankruptcy Code also expressly provides that dissimilar claims are not to be placed within the same class of claims.[15] Although classification of claims can be a creative process (and an important one, too, if the debtor needs an affirmative vote of a non-insider-impaired creditor class to set up a cram-down of an objecting creditor class under section 1129(b)), there are certain basic tenets that are generally followed in classifying claims.

First, secured claims are generally placed in their own class. For example, the creditor who has a security interest in the equipment will be placed in one class, and the creditor who has a lien on real property will be placed in another class. Second, generally the taxing authorities are placed in a separate class. Third, generally the administrative priority expenses are placed in a separate class. Finally, all unsecured creditors are generally placed in one class. Classification is important, because all the members of a class receive the same treatment. Further, a majority of the class in number and two-thirds in amount of claims binds the minority of a class if a plan is confirmed.[16] Furthermore, in order to invoke the cram-down provisions under section 1129(b) of the Bankruptcy Code, the debtor must be able to point to an affirmative vote in favor of the plan cast by a non-insider creditor class. Consequently, the classification of claims has become a hot litigation topic. Debtors, in their attempt to seek confirmation of plans, have engaged in creative classifications in formulating a plan of reorganization. Creditors, on the other hand, vigorously object to what appears

---

15. *See* 11 U.S.C. § 1122(a), *see also* 11 U.S.C. § 1123(a) and 1322(b)(1).
16. *See* 11 U.S.C. § 1126(c).

to them to be the gerrymandering of classes of claims for the sole purpose of obtaining the consenting vote in order to invoke cram-down. At present, the issue of how far a debtor can go in creatively classifying claims under a chapter 11 plan of reorganization is unresolved.

## 11.7 FUNDING ALTERNATIVES FOR PLANS OF REORGANIZATION

Before the bankruptcy court will confirm a plan under chapter 11 of the Bankruptcy Code, the court must find that the plan is feasible. Essentially, feasibility is a reflection of the financial and economic realities of the proposed reorganization. Like railroad cars, for a chapter 11 plan to go anywhere it must have an engine; that engine is some type of funding mechanism. Below are discussed five of the more common funding alternatives that may be available to a debtor in attempting to propose, and ultimately confirm, chapter 11 reorganization. Bear in mind, however, that whether any of these funding alternatives is available will depend directly on the facts and circumstances of each case.

### 11.7.1 Sale of Assets

Often, a debtor's reorganization may be funded by selling certain of its assets. For example, a corporate debtor may have various divisions within the corporate structure that the debtor could "spin off" in efforts to raise funds for the reorganization. Furthermore, a parent corporation may decide to sell stock in certain of its subsidiaries in an effort to raise funds for reorganization. The sale of assets is one of the more traditional funding alternatives discussed.

### 11.7.2 Avoidance Powers

A debtor may argue that the recovery from certain avoidance powers, such as fraudulent transfer, post-petition transfer, and avoidable preference actions, will be sufficiently large (even discounting the probability that the debtor may not prevail) to fund a plan of reorganization. Nonetheless, a debtor that must rely on recoveries from avoidance powers actions to fund a plan is on very thin ice. Typically, courts will convert a case to a case under chapter 7 and allow the trustee to bring the actions for the benefit of all creditors.

## 11.7.3 Post-petition Financing

It may seem strange to the novice, but there are creditors who are interested in providing post-petition financing to a debtor in bankruptcy. There are many creditors, and the post-petition financing industry is becoming increasingly competitive. Creditors who provide post-petition financing may be entitled to administrative expense priorities discussed above, liens on unencumbered assets, and in some circumstances, superpriority liens that prime the liens of pre-petition secured creditors.[17] Along with the collateral package, post-petition creditors can shore up any pre-petition deficiencies through a mechanism known as cross-collateralization if certain requirements are met, may obtain origination fees in large amounts, and may extract a higher rate of interest from the debtor. Moreover, a lender could not envision a more cost-effective and more tightly monitored lending situation than that of a debtor in possession operating under the Bankruptcy Code. Typically, a lender will require certain promises or covenants in loan documents wherein the debtor will promise not to engage in transactions out of the ordinary course of business or grant further security interests in or liens on collateral. This is merely a promise, the breach of which would result in damages in any action brought by the creditor. However, in a chapter 11 case, although the debtor who operates as a debtor-in-possession has the right to continue to engage in business in its ordinary course, it must seek prior approval from a bankruptcy court after due notice and hearing before it can engage in transactions out of the ordinary course of business or grant *additional* security interests or liens.[18]

---

17. *See generally* 11 U.S.C. § 364.
18. *See* 11 U.S.C. § 363(b)(1).

### 11.7.4 Equity-for-Debt Swaps

Yet another funding alternative involves the cancellation of some or all of the debt held by a class or classes of creditors in exchange for an equity interest in the reorganized entity. One will often encounter this situation in the more consensual chapter 11 reorganization plan; however, the debtor may make such a proposal in other situations, and if it otherwise complies with section 1129, the court may confirm the plan of reorganization.

### 11.7.5 Equity Infusions

Probably the oldest form of funding discussed here is the equity infusion. The typical situation is where either one of the owners of the debtor agrees to infuse money in the reorganized debtor, or a third party binds himself or herself to do so. One of the major limitations of equity infusions, discussed in detail below, is the absolute priority rule.

### 11.7.6 Future Operations

Although rare by itself, a debtor may propose to fund a reorganization from future income generated by the reorganized enterprise. More commonly, this alternative is coupled with one of the above methods as a combined means of funding a reorganization.

## 11.8 ACCEPTANCE AND CONFIRMATION OF A REORGANIZATION PLAN

To gain approval of the plan, the debtor must receive the acceptance of the plan by each class of claims and interests. A class of claims accepts a plan if creditors holding two-thirds in amount and one-half in number of the allowed claims in the class vote in favor of the plan. A class of interests accepts a plan if holders of two-thirds in amount of the allowed interests of the class vote in favor of the plan. If a class of claims or interests is not "impaired"[19] by the plan, all members of the unimpaired class are deemed to have accepted the plan as a matter of law.

Even if all classes of claims vote in favor of the plan, the bankruptcy court may refuse to confirm the plan if it determines that the plan was not proposed in good faith.[20] Conversely, under certain "cram-down" provisions, a plan may be confirmed, even though most of the impaired classes reject the plan, if at least one class of impaired claims accepts the plan, the plan does not discriminate unfairly, and the plan is "fair and equitable" with respect to each impaired class of claims or interests that rejected the plan.[21]

The "fair and equitable" standard is based on the absolute priority rule. The absolute priority rule requires that no class of claims or interests that is junior to the claims or interests of a non-consenting impaired class may receive anything under the plan until all members of the non-consenting senior class have been fully compensated. The senior class is entitled to full (but not over-) compensation. The absolute priority rule also requires that any secured creditor be allowed to retain its lien on its collateral and receive payments in the amount of the value of its collateral or otherwise realize the indubitable equivalent of its secured claim.

Courts have generally recognized what has been called the new value exception to the absolute priority rule. To fit this exception, there must be a contribution to a reorganized debtor by old equity, that contribution must be in money or money's worth (future services or sweat equity is insufficient), the contribution must be necessary, and it must be substantially equivalent in value to the interest retained by the old equity.

---

19. A class is "impaired" if it receives under the plan less than the full amount of its allowed claim.
20. *See* 11 U.S.C. § 1129(a)(3).
21. *See* 11 U.S.C. § 1129(b).

## 11.9 PLAN CONFIRMATION

The Bankruptcy Code provides two means by which a chapter 11 plan may be confirmed. First, the debtor must meet all 11 requirements of section 1129(a) of the Bankruptcy Code, including subsection (a)(8), which provides that all impaired classes of claims or interests must accept the plan. Second, absent consent of all impaired classes, the debtor can achieve confirmation pursuant to the cram-down provisions of section 1129(b). Section 1129(b) provides that if the plan meets all of the applicable requirements of section 1129(a) except subsection (a)(8), the court, upon request by the debtor, shall confirm the plan if it does not discriminate unfairly and is fair and equitable with respect to each class of claims or interests that is impaired under, and has not accepted, the plan. Thus, a chapter 11 plan of reorganization can be confirmed over the objections of one or more impaired classes of creditors if at least one non-insider-impaired class of creditors votes in favor of the plan.

### 11.9.1 Confirmation under Section 1129(a)

The debtor has 180 days to propose and convince the court to confirm the plan without competing plans in play. Further, the period of exclusivity cannot be extended beyond 18 months (time to propose a plan) or 20 months (time to confirm a plan) from the order for relief. Section 1129(a) of the Bankruptcy Code provides that a court shall confirm a plan only if the following statutory requirements are met:

- The plan complies with the Bankruptcy Code. This requirement embraces such things as the reasonable classification requirement found in section 1122 and the plan content requirement found in section 1123. The plan proponent must comply with the Bankruptcy Code—for example, making the required disclosures under section 1125. The plan must be proposed in good faith and not by any means forbidden by law.

- Disclosure must be made of any payment made or promised by the proponent, the debtor, or the person issuing securities or acquiring property under the plan for services or for costs and expenses for, or in connection with, the case, or in connection with the plan. Moreover, any preconfirmation payment must be reasonable, and any post-confirmation payment must be approved by the court. The plan must disclose the identity and affiliations of any individual proposed to serve, after confirmation, as an officer, director, or voting trustee for the reorganized debtor. Furthermore, the plan must disclose the identity of any insider who will be employed or retained by the reorganized debtor and must disclose the nature of any compensation to be paid to the insider. Although the sixth requirement of confirmation is generally not applicable, it nevertheless requires that any regulatory commission having jurisdiction over the reorganized debtor must approve any rate change contained in the plan.

- Each holder of an impaired claim or interest must either accept the plan or, on the effective date of the plan, receive or retain an amount not less than the amount that such holder would so receive or retain if the debtor were liquidated under chapter 7. This is known as the "best interest of the creditors" test. Each class must accept the plan (or is unimpaired under the plan).

- The plan must comply with the absolute priority rule. In short, the absolute priority rule requires that no class of claims or interests junior to a particular class can receive any payment under the plan unless the senior class is paid in full. For example, the absolute priority rule prohibits payment to equity security holders until all creditors holding allowable claims have been paid in full.

- At least one class of claims that is impaired under the plan must accept the plan. The class cannot be an insider class.

- The plan must be feasible. In essence, this requirement ensures that a plan that is likely to be followed by liquidation or the need for further reorganization will not be confirmed. The feasibility focus is on future cash flow, amortized principal, and the net earnings needed to restructure. The new capital structure, including the relationship of debt to equity for the reorganized debtor, must also be sound.

- Certain fees must be paid at or before the effective date of the plan.

- Certain retiree benefits must continue to be paid after the plan's effective date.

- If all the requirements under section 1129(a) of the Bankruptcy Code are met, then the court shall confirm the plan of reorganization. However, if the requirement of consent under section 1129(a)(8) is lacking *but all other confirmation requirements are met*, the debtor may turn to section 1129(b) of the Bankruptcy Code.

### 11.9.2 *Tax Claims and Issues*

BAPCPA addressed bankruptcy tax issues in a robust fashion by including some 20 new provisions. For example, new section 507(a)(8) grants priority status to unsecured governmental claims for income or gross receipts taxes owed by the debtor (i) related to returns that became due (including extensions) during the three years before the debtor filed its bankruptcy petition; (ii) assessed within 240 days before the petition date; or (iii) that are still assessable. The 240-day rule is calculated exclusive of any time during which an offer in compromise with respect to that tax was pending or in effect during that 240-day period, plus 30 days. Further, this is also exclusive of any time during which a stay of proceedings against collections was in effect in a prior case under this title during that 240-day period, plus 90 days.

Furthermore, the rate of interest on tax claims is governed by section 511. If there is a requirement to pay the interest on a tax claim or on an administrative expense tax, or to enable a creditor to receive the present value of the allowed amount of a tax claim, the rate of interest is the rate determined under applicable non-bankruptcy law. However, in the case of taxes paid under a confirmed plan, the rate of interest is determined as of the calendar month in which the plan is confirmed. The non-bankruptcy tax rate is a terrible provision, because it is the only case where the creditor may receive more than the value of its claim. The federal rate makes the most sense, as it is closest to the market rate. The state rate, however, may be as much as 20 percent higher than the market rate.

Additionally, with respect to the periodic payments of taxes as governed in section 1129(a)(9), the claim holder receives regular installment payments in cash. These payments are of a total value, as of the effective date of the plan, equal to the allowed amount of such claim. This is to be taken over a period ending in less than five years after the date of the order for relief. The payment should not be in a manner less favorable than the most favored non-priority unsecured claim provided for by the plan. Further, with respect to a secured claim that would otherwise meet the description of an unsecured claim of a governmental unit, the claim holder receives cash payments in the same manner and over the same period.

Moreover, the standards for tax disclosures are covered in section 1125(a). Here, "adequate information" means information of a kind, and in sufficient detail, as far as is reasonably practicable in light of the nature and history of the debtor and the condition of the debtor's books and records, including a discussion of the potential federal tax consequences of the plan to the debtor, any successor to the debtor, and a hypothetical investor typical of the holders of claims or interests in the case, that would enable such hypothetical investor of the relevant class to make an informed judgment about the plan. However, adequate information need not include such information about any other possible or proposed plan and in determining whether a disclosure statement provides adequate information. Here, the court considers the complexity of the case, the benefit of additional information to creditors and other parties in interest, and the cost of providing additional information.

Finally, the Bankruptcy Code provides that there should be no discharge of fraudulent taxes in section 1141(d). Section 1141(d) defines the effect of confirmation of a chapter 11 plan and specifically discharges certain debts that arose before confirmation. There is an exception for tax liabilities from a chapter 11 discharge if the debtor corporation made a fraudulent return or willfully attempted in any manner to evade or defeat that tax or duty. Further, this provision also makes a discharge exception for any debt incurred under false pretenses or by making a false statement in writing. Corporations cannot discharge a debt based on fraud owed to a governmental unit arising out of false pretenses, false representations, or actual fraud, whether or not based on use of a financial statement in writing. The language of this provision makes it unclear whether these non-dischargeable debts to governmental units must arise from the debtor's own fraudulent dealings with the government or if this extends to claims or fines the government could impose on account of the debtor's defrauding of investors or creditors. Further, debt owed to an individual on a qui tam claim is also not dischargeable. With regard to individuals filing chapter 11 cases, the discharge may be delayed until full performance absent a chapter 11 hardship discharge.

### 11.9.3 Cram-down

Nothing conjures up the demons in the deep recesses of a creditor's mind quite like the concept of "cram-down." Cramdown is a euphemistic term for the process by which a debtor can obtain confirmation of its plan as long as the plan satisfies all the requirements of section 1129(a) except subsection (a)(8), which requires acceptance of the plan by all classes of claims and interest. Failing unanimous consent, cram-down is the only way to "cram" a plan "down the throat of the dissenting class." The debtor accomplishes cram-down by proving that all confirmation requirements except (a)(8) are met under section 1129(a) and by proving that the plan "does not discriminate unfairly, and is fair and equitable, with respect to each class of claims or interest that is impaired under, and has not accepted, the plan."

The concept of fair and equitable treatment turns on whether the class of claims at issue is a secured or unsecured class. Section 1129(b)(2)(A) defines fair and equitable treatment with respect to a class of secured claims. Section 1129(b)(2)(B) defines fair and equitable treatment with respect to a class of unsecured claims. Please read those provisions.

### 11.9.4 Competing Plans

Suppose competing plans have been filed and they all meet the requirements under section 1129(a) or (b). What is the court to do in that situation? Section 1129(c) expressly provides that the court may confirm only one plan. If more than one plan satisfies section 1129, the Bankruptcy Code requires the court to give due consideration to the preferences of creditors and equity security holders before confirming a plan.

## 11.10 EFFECT OF CONFIRMATION

Confirmation of a plan of reorganization under chapter 11 discharges the corporate debtor from all claims arising before the confirmation of the plan except those claims paid pursuant to the terms of the plan, subject to certain limitations.[22] Confirmation of the plan, however, does not relieve an individual debtor of any debt excepted from discharge under section 523. Furthermore, confirmation

---

22. *See* 11 U.S.C. § 1141(d).

of a plan of reorganization, except as otherwise provided in the plan, vests in the debtor all property of the estate free and clear of all claims and interests of creditors and other parties in interest.

Once a plan has been confirmed, it becomes a final order of the bankruptcy court and binds all creditors, all equity security holders, the debtor, and other parties in interest with notice of the bankruptcy case to the terms, conditions, and contents of the plan. Consequently, a creditor's pre-bankruptcy rights evaporate. Instead of resorting to pre-bankruptcy documents, a creditor who attempts to satisfy its claim against a reorganized debtor merely seeks to enforce the confirmation order. A confirmation order may be revoked by the court only in certain limited circumstances. Under section 1144, the confirmation order can only be revoked for fraud in its procurement, and only within 180 days after the entry of the order. These strict exceptions to the general effect of a confirmation order are necessary to promote and ensure finality in the proceedings. Consistent with that view, any entity that relied in good faith on the confirmation order is protected, even if it is later revoked under section 1144.

## 11.11 MODIFICATION OF THE PLAN

Because the plan of reorganization is an intensely negotiated document, it is not uncommon for modifications to be proposed by creditors, and for some of those modifications to be embraced by the debtor. Therefore, section 1127 of the Bankruptcy Code was enacted to regulate the modification of plans. A plan proponent may modify a plan at any time before confirmation. Of course, the requirements in sections 1122, 1123, 1125, and 1129 must be met by the modified plan.

The procedure for modification, however, is different if the reorganized debtor or a proponent of the plan seeks to modify the plan after confirmation but before substantial consummation. The plan may nevertheless be modified even after confirmation but before substantial consummation if, after notice and a hearing, the court concludes that circumstances warrant the modification. Again, any modified plan must comply with sections 1122, 1123, and 1129. To facilitate plan modifications, section 1127 further provides that "[a]ny holder of a claim or interest that has accepted or rejected a plan is deemed to have accepted or rejected . . . such plan as modified unless, within the time fixed by the court, such holder changes such holder's previous acceptance or rejection."

## 11.12 DISCHARGE UNDER CHAPTER 11

Under section 1141(d) of the Bankruptcy Code, the confirmation of the plan of reorganization discharges the debtor from any debt that arose before the confirmation of the plan. Unlike section 727(a), a partnership or corporation (as well as an individual) may receive a section 1141(d) discharge. The section 1141(d) discharge is broader than the section 727(a) discharge in that the latter discharges any debts that arose before the entry of the order for relief, while the former discharges any debts that arose before the confirmation of the plan.

Nevertheless, there are limits to the section 1141(d) discharge. First, debts excepted from discharge under section 523 are not discharged under section 1141(d) when the debtor is an individual. Second, if the plan provides for liquidation of all or substantially all of the property of the estate, the debtor does not continue in business, and the debtor would be denied a discharge under section 727(a), then confirmation of the plan does not discharge the debtor. These limitations are necessary so that an individual debtor may not employ a chapter 11 liquidation plan to evade the objections to discharge embodied in sections 523(a) and 727(a).

Section 1141 also excepts tax liabilities from chapter 11 discharge if the debtor corporation made a fraudulent return or willfully attempted in any manner to evade or defeat that tax or duty. Moreover, this section also excepts from discharge any debt incurred under false pretenses or by making a false statement.

# CHAPTER 12

# CASH COLLATERAL AND DEBTOR TRANSACTIONS

Implicit in the reorganization model is a viable business to reorganize. To remain viable, a business must continue in business. The Bankruptcy Code recognizes this basic fact.

## 12.1 CASH COLLATERAL

For a business to function, it needs cash. This axiom is true in or out of bankruptcy. Cash and cash equivalents are the lifeblood of a successful reorganization. Consequently, to continue operations in an attempt to successfully reorganize under the Bankruptcy Code, the debtor must be able to gain access to any cash and cash equivalents it may have on hand. On the other hand, a creditor may hold a validly perfected security interest in the cash and cash equivalents. Because in most instances once the cash is used the lien evaporates, a creditor can experience significant harm to its secured claim. The Bankruptcy Code recognizes this dilemma and attempts to accommodate the creditor's legitimate concern while providing a means by which the debtor can tap into its cash assets. This mechanism is found neatly in section 363(c)(2) of the Bankruptcy Code.

### 12.1.1 Definition of Cash Collateral

Before exploring the relationship of a debtor and a creditor who asserts an interest in cash collateral, cash collateral must be identified. Cash collateral is defined in section 363(a) as "cash, negotiable instruments, documents of title, securities, deposit accounts, or other cash equivalents whenever acquired in which the estate and an entity other than the estate have an interest and includes the proceeds, products, offspring, rents, or profits of property. . . ." Technical definitions aside, cash collateral means cash or some type of property that can be turned into cash very quickly.

### 12.1.2 The Debtor's Use of Cash Collateral

Cash collateral is evanescent; when used, it disappears forever. Recognizing that a creditor who has a secured claim is entitled to the protection of its claim at least for the value of the collateral, how then may the debtor ever use cash collateral? The answer lies in section 363(c)(2).

The rule is straightforward. The debtor is prohibited from using cash collateral except in two circumstances: first, the debtor can use cash collateral if it obtains the consent of the creditor claiming an interest in the cash collateral. If more than one creditor claims an interest in the cash collateral, consents from all creditors would be required. Second, absent consent, the debtor can move the court, after notice and a hearing, to authorize the debtor to use the cash collateral. The price, however, for the debtor to gain access to the cash collateral is the requirement of adequate protection. The court will not permit the debtor to use cash collateral unless the court is convinced that the creditor who claims an interest in the cash collateral is adequately protected.

Previous discussion centered on the role of adequate protection concerning relief from the automatic stay pursuant to section 362(d) of the Bankruptcy Code. Recall that failure to provide adequate protection may constitute one type of cause for relief from the automatic stay under section

362(d)(1). Adequate protection is a term that is defined under section 361. The definition is nonexhaustive and defines by example. Thus, adequate protection includes periodic cash payments, replacement liens, and additional liens, but does not include the granting of an administrative expense priority. It has been suggested that the concept of adequate protection is derived from the protection of property interests by the Fifth Amendment to the United States Constitution. Once the debtor convinces the court that it can adequately protect the creditor's interests, the debtor may use its cash collateral as long as such use is consistent with other provisions of the Bankruptcy Code.

## 12.2 TRANSACTIONS WITH THE DEBTOR

Under section 1108 of the Bankruptcy Code, the debtor in possession is authorized to operate its business unless the operation is curtailed by the court. Furthermore, section 363 of the Bankruptcy Code regulates the debtor's business activities. Both debtors and creditors should be aware of a debtor's ability to, and manner in which it may, conduct its business. If a debtor intends to engage in a transaction in the ordinary course of its business, it may do so under the Bankruptcy Code without prior court authorization. Furthermore, any creditor or third party who participates in an ordinary course transaction will be protected. However, a debtor cannot engage in a transaction outside of its ordinary course of business. Such transaction is an unauthorized post-petition transfer that may be attacked and unwound. Consequently, any creditor or third party that deals with the debtor in a transaction outside the ordinary course of business is not protected.

Thus, the paramount question in this area of bankruptcy law is, what is an ordinary course transaction? This determination depends on the facts and circumstances of each case, because the question is a factual one. In resolving the issue, courts will look at the historical operations of the particular debtor and the operations of similar persons in the industry. The court will also consider creditors' expectations concerning what is legitimately an ordinary course transfer by their debtor from the creditor's perspective.

As a general rule, when in doubt, before engaging in a transaction with a debtor you should obtain court approval of the transaction. An example may be helpful. Assume Baseball, Inc. has filed a chapter 11 bankruptcy petition. Baseball is in the business of manufacturing baseball bats, gloves, and balls. It operates three plants—one in Kentucky, one in Japan, and one in Haiti. Elrod Hendricks approaches Baseball and wants to purchase a shipment of bats, balls, and gloves for a sporting goods store outside Baltimore. This is the type of transaction that is Baseball's business. It sells bats, balls, and gloves to various businesses for resale. This is clearly an ordinary course transaction, and no prior court approval is necessary. Assume, however, that Jim French, an Elrod competitor, wants to buy every ball manufactured in Haiti. Also assume that Baseball has never entered into a contract of this type. Chances are that a court would conclude that the transaction between Baseball and Jim would be out of the ordinary course of Baseball's business; therefore, the transaction can be avoided under the Bankruptcy Code as an unauthorized post-petition transfer. Further assume that Jim decides that he would rather have the manufacturing plant in Haiti. Clearly, Baseball is not in the business of selling manufacturing plants, and any attempt to do so must be authorized by the court before the transaction.

# CHAPTER 13

# EXECUTORY CONTRACTS AND UNEXPIRED LEASES

In exploring the treatment of executory contracts and unexpired leases, one must become comfortable in identifying them. In this analysis, three general concepts must be discussed: (1) "assumption" of a contract or lease by the chapter 11 debtor in possession for its own continuing benefit, (2) "assignment" of the debtor's interest in a contract or lease to third parties, and (3) rejection of the debtor's interest.

## 13.1 WHAT IS AN EXECUTORY CONTRACT OR UNEXPIRED LEASE?

Bankruptcy Code section 365 permits a debtor in possession or a trustee to assume or reject executor contracts and unexpired leases. The Bankruptcy Code does not define the term "executor contract," leaving the determination to the courts. The appellate courts have accepted the operational definition to the effect that a contract is "executor" when there are performances due from each party to the contract as of the petition date, so that if one party were to commit a material breach of its obligations, the counterparty would be excused from having to perform its reciprocal obligations under applicable non-bankruptcy law. In other words, a contract under which both parties have unfulfilled future obligations other than the mere payment of money is an executor contract. Consequently, repayment of a promissory note is not an executor contract.

If one party has fully performed and the other party has not, the determination of whether a contract is executor becomes more difficult. Some courts hold that if one party has fully performed, then the contract cannot be executor, citing the test articulated above. Other courts, instead of employing the traditional test, assess whether the debtor's estate is benefited by characterizing the contract as executor. If yes, the court will hold that the contract is executor, thus allowing the trustee to assume or reject it.

The Bankruptcy Code also fails to identify the term "unexpired lease." What constitutes an unexpired lease is answered by consulting state law, particularly chapter 2A of the Uniform Commercial Code (UCC). Usually, however, unexpired leases will refer to real and personal property leases.

## 13.2 WHEN MUST THE TRUSTEE ASSUME OR REJECT?

If a trustee in a chapter 7 case does not expressly assume or reject an executory contract or unexpired lease within 60 days following the filing of the petition (or such additional time as the court, for cause, allows), the contract or lease is deemed rejected.[1] Further, in any non-residential lease situation, the assumption or rejection must be done within 120 days after the order for relief (with a 90-day extension for cause). In a chapter 11 case, as a general rule, the debtor or trustee (if a trustee has been appointed) may assume or reject an executory contract or unexpired lease at any time prior to confirmation of a plan.[2] There are several exceptions to this rule (discussed below). However, a party to the executory contract or unexpired lease can request the court to require the debtor or trustee to assume or reject the unexpired lease or executory contract within a specified time.

---

1. See 11 U.S.C. § 365(d)(1).
2. See 11 U.S.C. § 365(d)(2).

There is a "limbo" period between the filing of the petition and the time of assumption or rejection. If the debtor is not in default, the other party must continue to perform. Otherwise, the other party need not perform unless the contract is cured and assumed. If the matter deals with non-residential real property, performance must be executed.

## 13.3 ASSUME OR REJECT?

From the perspective of the debtor in possession, driving the decision whether to assume, to assign, or to reject any executory contract or unexpired lease is logically prior to the question whether the rejection of that contract or lease will assist in curtailing post-petition operating losses, whether the assumption of that contract or lease is integral or advantageous to the continuing business operations of the estate, or whether the assignment of that contract or lease will bring in any net proceeds. In other words, the perspective of the debtor in possession is completely opportunistic. It is more sensible to think about the debtor's legal interest in an executory contract or unexpired lease as an interest in property of the estate under section 541(a), and then to proceed to quantify the net benefit of assuming, assigning, or rejecting that interest.

## 13.4 CONSEQUENCES OF REJECTION

The general legal consequence of rejecting an executor contract or unexpired lease is to treat the act of rejection as an anticipatory repudiation of the contract, with the damages to be measured by applicable state or federal non-bankruptcy law. Note, however, that in the cases of employment agreements and non-residential real property leases, it is essential to consult section 502 of the Bankruptcy Code.

The important and unique point to remember about rejection damages is that even though the debtor in possession is authorized to reject the contract or lease by the bankruptcy court during the post-petition period, the effective date of rejection is defined under section 365 as occurring on the day before the petition date, thus giving rise to a general unsecured claim. In practical terms, the holder of a pre-petition allowed unsecured claim will receive its pro rata share of the distribution made to members of that class.

## 13.5 THE STANDARD FOR ASSUMPTION

Assumption binds the estate and the non-debtor party. Most contracts and leases may be assumed, except personal services and other financial accommodations under section 365(c). The effect is to make the contract an administrative expense of the estate as if the estate had originally entered into the contract. Post-assumption breach gives rise to an administrative expense under section 365(g)(2), but it is limited and capped.

A court must approve an assumption.[3] A clause that provides for termination of an executory contract or unexpired lease upon bankruptcy or insolvency events is not enforceable under the Bankruptcy Code to prevent the assumption of the executory contract or unexpired lease.[4] To assume an executory contract or unexpired lease, a debtor must cure any defaults, compensate the other party to the contract or lease for any pecuniary loss resulting from any defaults, and provide adequate assurance of the debtor's future performance.[5] Prior to assumption of an unexpired lease, the debtor or trustee must pay for any services or supplies furnished after commencement of the case under the lease and, if the lease is a lease of non-residential real property and the debtor is the lessee, perform all obligations of the debtor under the lease.

## 13.6 ASSIGNMENT

An unexpired lease or executory contract may be assumed and assigned by the trustee in accordance with the require-

---

3. *See* 11 U.S.C. §§ 365(a), 365(b)(2).
4. *See* 11 U.S.C. § 365(b).
5. 11 U.S.C. § 365(b).

ments described above and with adequate assurance of future performance by the assignee. In this situation, the debtor is effectively selling its rights under the contract or lease. The sale may be negotiated in advance with a prospective assignee, and the proposed sale is submitted on notice and hearing to the court for approval, subject to higher or better bids. The net proceeds to the bankruptcy estate of the assignment will be a value that falls between the cost to perform the balance of the contract or lease and the current and projected market cost for a substituted contract or lease. The great virtue of the Bankruptcy Code from the estate's perspective is that it allows the estate to bargain for and retain the negotiated or auctioned consideration for the assumption and assignment of the debtor's interest, with no part of this spread payable to the lessor by the estate.

Once the executory contract or unexpired lease is assigned, the non-debtor party to the contract no longer has a claim against the estate. Note, however, that certain contracts, such as an executory contract to make a loan or extend credit, may not be assumed under section 365.

## 13.7 THE SPECIAL CASES OF REAL PROPERTY

### 13.7.1 Unexpired Lease of Real Property Where the Debtor Is the Lessor

If a trustee (or debtor in a chapter 11 proceeding in which no trustee has been appointed) rejects an unexpired lease of real property of the debtor where the debtor is the lessor, the lessee under the lease may treat the lease as terminated by the debtor's rejection or, in the alternative, the lessee may remain in possession of the leasehold interest under the lease for the balance of the term of the lease and for any renewal or extension of the term that is enforceable by the lessee under applicable nonbankruptcy law.[6] If a lessee remains in possession under a lease rejected by

---

6. *See* 11 U.S.C. § 365(h)(1).

the trustee (or debtor in the applicable case) where the debtor is the lessor, the lessee may offset any damages caused by the nonperformance of any obligation of the debtor under the lease against the rent reserved under the lease for the balance of the term after the date of rejection of the lease plus any renewal or extension of the lease. The lessee does not have rights against the debtor's estate for damages arising after the date of the debtor's rejection of the lease, other than the setoff right described above. This power of the lessee to remain in possession under an unexpired lease of real property where the debtor is the lessor essentially makes any rejection by a trustee (or debtor) impractical if the purpose of the debtor's rejection is to terminate the leasehold estate of the lessee in order to regain possession of the leased premises.

### 13.7.2 Unexpired Lease of Non-residential Real Property Where the Debtor Is the Lessee

#### 13.7.2.1 Time Periods

One exception to the foregoing time periods by which the debtor (or the trustee) must either assume or reject exists with regard to an unexpired lease of non-residential real property in which the debtor is the lessee. If an unexpired lease of non-residential real property in which the debtor is the lessee is neither assumed nor rejected within 60 days of the commencement of a case under either chapter 7 or chapter 11 (or such additional time as the court, for cause, allows), then the unexpired lease is deemed rejected and the property subject to the lease must be surrendered to the lessor.[7]

BAPCPA took away the prior statutory standing of the commercial lessor to move for an order compelling the debtor in possession to exercise its option to assume or reject its lessee's interest under a commercial lease before the date of confirmation. The trade-off is that under BAPCPA, the debtor

---

7. 11 U.S.C. § 365(d)(4).

in possession is granted under subsection 365(d)(4)(A) an initial 120 days to decide (or an earlier date if that date is the date of confirmation of a plan) whether to accept or reject its lessee's interest under any of its commercial leases, and if the debtor in possession has not assumed the lease by that deadline, the lease is deemed rejected as a matter of law. The 120-day deadline may be extended for a further and final 60 days, thus totaling 210 days, for cause. This is a far cry from the earlier practice in the chapter 11 cases of extending the deadline in a first-day order until confirmation, with the burden placed upon the lessor to move for an earlier deadline.

### 13.7.2.2 Additional Restrictions for Commercial Leases in Shopping Centers

Further, there is an additional condition under subsections 365(b)(3)(A)–(D) to the assumption and assignment of a commercial lease in a shopping center beyond the curing of pre-petition defaults. The debtor in possession must also prove that as adequate assurance of future performance, (1) the proposed assignee will have, in brief, the same level of creditworthiness and operating history that the debtor had when it began the lease; (2) the percentage rents from the proposed assignee's business operations at the shopping center will not substantially decline; and (3) the proposed use (a) will not breach any provisions of a master lease agreement or the terms and conditions of the lessor's financing of the shopping center relating to radius, location, use, or exclusivity provisions, or (b) disrupt the existing tenant mix or balance in the shopping center.

## 13.8 SPECIAL CONTRACT TYPES

Certain types of executory contracts warrant further discussion. While each contract is different, there are certain classes of contracts that do present specific types of issues.

### 13.8.1 Franchisees

At the lower end of the middle market are the hundreds of chapter 11 cases filed annually by corporate debtors that operate as fast-food franchisees or as retail new car dealerships. The issue of whether the debtor in possession may assign its interest under its franchise agreement to another dealership is frequently litigated. In fact, many franchisee chapter 11 cases end in the first month with a motion to lift the stay based upon the franchisor's allegations that the franchise has been terminated before the petition date. Other car dealership cases end early due to the unwillingness of the floor-planning financier to consent to the use of cash collateral and a refusal to extended financing for the purchase of new vehicles.

Generally, a franchise agreement not terminated before the petition date is an executory contract, like any other that can be assumed and assigned regardless of the provisions. However, a provision intended to protect personal service contracts seems to alter that perception. Section 365(c) explicitly provides that:

> The [debtor in possession] may not assume or assign any executory contract . . . of the debtor, whether or not such contract . . . restricts assignment of rights or delegation of duties, if—
>
> (1)(A) Applicable law excuses a party, other than the debtor, to such contract . . . from, accepting performance from or rendering performance to an entity other than the debtor or the debtor in possession, whether or not such contract . . . prohibits or restricts assignment of rights or delegation of duties; and
>
> (B) Such party does not consent to such assignment or assumption [.]

At first glance, it may be difficult to understand what this provision has to do with a car dealership. However, many years ago the automobile manufacturers successfully lobbied state legislatures to enact statutes that upheld the manufacturers' refusal to allow the assignment by a dealership of its interest to a third party absent the discretionary consent of the manufacturer. Application of these state laws seem to run contrary, however, to subsection 365(f)(1), which states:

> Except as provided in subsections (b) and (c), notwithstanding a provision in an executory contract ... of the debtor, or in applicable law, that prohibits, restricts, or conditions the assignment of such contract ..., the trustee may assign such contract under subsection 2 of this subsection.

Subsections 365(f)(2)(A) and (B) require that the trustee or debtor in possession assume the contract and provide adequate assurance of future performance, and subsection 365(f)(3) reinforces and broadens subsection 365(f)(1) by overriding any provision under the contract or under applicable law that purports to terminate or modify the contract because of an assignment of the contract by the debtor.

The issue of statutory construction then becomes one of trying to divine what Congress intended when it conditioned subsection 365(f) upon subsections 365(b) and 365(c). No logical explanation seems to reconcile these provisions.[8] However, the result is that in most circuits, the debtor in possession or trustee cannot sell the estate's interest in a car dealership as an executory contract if the applicable state has enacted a statute precluding the assignability of car dealerships unless the manufacturer consents. Similarly, the case law in most circuits also applies this same approach to fast-food restaurant franchisees.

---

8. *See In re* Pioneer Ford Sales, Inc., 729 F.2d 27 (1st Cir. 1984); *In re* Magness, 972 F.2d 689 (6th Cir. 1992); *In re* CLFC, Inc., 89 F.3d 673 (9th Cir. 1996).

### 13.8.2 Assignments of Interests in Intellectual Property

This same issue of contradictory subsections 365(c) and (f) has also played out in connection with the assignment of non-exclusive patent licenses. The Ninth Circuit took the position that since the trustee is precluded from assigning an executory contract, here a non-exclusive license to use and sell a copyrighted video game, if that action is precluded under applicable non-bankruptcy law, then the debtor in possession cannot assume the executory contract either.[9] This means that the reorganized debtor cannot assume the very interest its "predecessor in interest" possessed, namely, the pre-petition debtor or the post-petition debtor in possession, even though the reorganized debtor has no intention of then assigning its interest to a third party. In cases where the right to use the patent license is of considerable value for the operation of the reorganized debtor, this construction has the effect of defeating any legitimate reorganization effort of failing companies with valuable non-exclusive license rights under federal patents or copyrights. However, this is not the case under First Circuit law.[10] There, the court determined that the identity of the licensee had not changed, just its ownership, and that change in ownership could not be defeated by the licensor's objection to the plan. Thus, the rights of the debtor to assume the licenses were protected.

It is important to point out that trademarks are treated differently from other intellectual property—trademarks are excluded from the definition of intellectual property under section 101(35)(A). Thus, the provisions of section 365(n), which incorporates the definition of intellectual property from section 101(A), do not reach the debtor's interests in trademarks.

---

9. *See In re* Catapult Entm't, Inc., 165 F.3d 747 (9th Cir. 1999).

10. *See In re* Inst. Pasteur v. Cambridge Biotech Corp., 104 F.3d 489 (1st Cir. 1997).

### 13.8.3 Equipment Leases

In general, the same rules for assumption, assignment, or rejection that apply to executory contracts also apply to unexpired leases of industrial or commercial equipment, which the Bankruptcy Code refers to as leases for personal property (other than personal property that is used by a consumer debtor for personal, family, or household purposes—that is, leased consumer goods). However, there is a host of additional burdens on equipment lessees imposed by BAPCPA.

#### 13.8.3.1 Preliminary Issues

Before proceeding further with this discussion, it is important to remember that the types of "personal property leases" or equipment leases that are covered by section 365 are "true" or actual "operating equipment leases," and not "financing or capitalized equipment leases." In this respect, the Bankruptcy Code implicitly carries over the distinctions between these two classes of equipment leases from Articles 2, 2A, and 9 of the Uniform Commercial Code as a matter of enacted state law. If an equipment lease is determined by the bankruptcy court to be a financing lease, then section 365 does not apply to the transaction, but sections 361 through 364 will apply; and then the issues change to those relevant to the rights and remedies of secured creditors. Sometimes these are referred to as recharacterization hearings when the parties dispute whether the underlying equipment transactions should be recharacterized from true equipment leases to financing leases or vice versa.

Note further that it is difficult to persuade a bankruptcy court that a lease agreement that covers a number of items described on a schedule is, in fact, separate agreements so that the debtor can assume the obligations for the items of equipment that it needs for continuing its business while rejecting the unnecessary items.

### 13.8.3.2 Under BAPCPA

BAPCPA imposed more pressure on equipment lessees to make up their minds about what they wished to do earlier in the administration of their chapter 11 cases. First, when a chapter 11 debtor in possession is a lessee under a true equipment lease, it is under a statutory duty under subsection 365(b)(5) to perform all of its obligations that become due 60 days after the petition date and thereafter until the equipment lease is assumed or rejected (unless for cause, the court provides some relief from this provision "based upon the equities" of the case—whatever that means). This obviously puts some pressure on the debtor in possession to make its business assessments fairly early in the administration of the case. Section 365(d)(2) continues in effect the general rule that the debtor in possession has until the date of confirmation to make its decisions to assume, reject, or assign its equipment leases, but BAPCPA also conferred standing upon the equipment lessor to file a motion compelling the debtor in possession to make its decision to assume or reject an equipment lease by an earlier date in an amended section 365(d)(2).

# CHAPTER 14

# Avoidance Powers

Avoidance powers substantially distinguish a bankruptcy case from state debt collection activity. Although some of the avoidance powers have state-law analogues, in bankruptcy, the avoidance powers are the most efficient and successful tool in reassessing the relative rights, powers, and duties between the debtor and its creditors and among creditors. In essence, the avoidance powers authorize a bankruptcy trustee (or a debtor in possession in a chapter 11 case where no trustee has been appointed) to unwind in a bankruptcy forum what the debtor and creditors have done before the commencement of the bankruptcy case.

A trustee (or a debtor in possession in a chapter 11 case in which no trustee has been appointed) is given extensive powers to avoid pre-petition transactions involving transfers of property by the debtor to the extent such transfers are avoidable by creditors under non-bankruptcy laws, are avoidable as preferences, or are avoidable as fraudulent transfers. A transfer subject to these avoidance powers may be voluntary as by a sale or exchange or involuntary (as by judgment, mechanics lien, or foreclosure), a simple payment through various forms, or an absolute transfer of title or the creation of a lien or security interest. The applicability of these avoidance powers to pre-petition transactions will bring additional assets into the debtor's estate. A debtor should be aware of the existence of the avoidance powers and the duty to examine pre-petition transactions to determine if any are subject to avoidance.

Although not without controversy, the purposes of the avoidance powers are generally well understood. These powers allow the trustee to enhance the property of the estate for the benefit of all creditors in circumstances where the pre-petition transfer resulted in the unjust diminution of the debtor's property on the verge of bankruptcy, or a transfer favored certain creditors at the expense of the general creditor body. The avoidance powers maximize the return to the unsecured creditors by bringing estate assets back into the estate for everyone to share in and dissuades creditors from opting out of the collective debt-collection action once bankruptcy is on the horizon.

The avoidance powers help the trustee in enhancing the Bankruptcy Code's goal of maximizing the distribution of property of the estate to creditors, a result that is one of the stated goals of bankruptcy, by avoiding and recovering for the benefit of the estate certain enumerated transfers that frustrate the goal. The avoidance powers are found in sections 543 through 553.

## 14.1 TRUSTEE'S STRONG-ARM POWERS UNDER SECTION 544(A)

One of the most powerful avoidance techniques can be found in section 544(a) of the Bankruptcy Code. Section 544(a), also known as the trustee's strong-arm power, endows the trustee with the status of a hypothetical judicial lien creditor with a lien on the debtor's personal property or a bona fide purchaser of the debtor's real property at the time of the filing of the bankruptcy petition. The trustee's status as a hypothetical judicial lien creditor or a bona fide purchaser is merely a derivative fictional status whose substantive effect must spring from some non-bankruptcy law, usually state law that defines the rights and priorities of judicial lien creditors or bona fide purchasers for value.

Under Article 9 of the Uniform Commercial Code (UCC), which has been enacted by every state, the powers of the trustee as a hypothetical judicial lien creditor are clear. Under UCC Section 9.301(1)(b), a judicial lien creditor who obtains a judicial lien before an Article 9 security interest in the debtor's personal property is perfected has priority over the secured party. Thus, a trustee in bankruptcy under section 544(a) almost always defeats a secured party who has not perfected its security interest as of the filing of the bankruptcy petition.[1] If, however, the secured party perfects its security interest five minutes before the petition in bankruptcy is filed, then the trustee cannot mount a successful attack solely under section 544(a).

Aside from bestowing upon the trustee the status of the hypothetical judicial lien creditor, section 544(a) also gives the trustee, as of the date of the bankruptcy petition, the status of a hypothetical bona fide purchaser of the debtor's real property. This additional strong-arm power enables the trustee to avoid transfers of real property that were unrecorded at the time the bankruptcy petition was filed. Thus, if Gomer sells his gas station to Floyd and Floyd fails to record the deed in the real property records, Floyd runs the risk that Gomer may file a petition in bankruptcy and his trustee may seek to avoid the transfer as a hypothetical bona fide purchaser under section 544(a)(3).

An example may be helpful. Assume that Andy owes money to Buford, the Chief, and Harold. Further assume that all three creditors are secured parties under Article 9 of the UCC. However, Buford, the Chief, and Harold have not perfected their security interest in accordance with state law. Smothered by an avalanche of debt, Andy decides to file a bankruptcy petition under chapter 7. Just before the bankruptcy petition is filed, Buford files a financing statement and perfects his security interest in accordance with state law. On the other hand, the Chief, without knowledge of Andy's

---

1. We use the modifier "almost" for these instances in which the Bankruptcy Code may permit the relation back of certain security interests.

bankruptcy filing, nevertheless files his financing statement in the appropriate place but only after the bankruptcy petition was filed. Unlike the Chief, Harold has actual knowledge of the bankruptcy filing, but nevertheless files a financing statement in an attempt to perfect his security interest in the collateral.

In these circumstances, the trustee will be successful under section 544 in attacking the Chief and Harold. As to the filing of the petition in bankruptcy, the trustee attains the status of a hypothetical judicial lien creditor. Under Article 9, a judicial lien creditor has priority over any secured party who was unperfected at the time the judgment lien creditor attains its status. Furthermore, both the Chief and Harold have violated section 362(a) of the Bankruptcy Code. A filing of the financing statement, with or without knowledge of the bankruptcy filing, is a violation of the automatic stay. Moreover, any act in violation of the automatic stay is void. Knowledge or intent to violate the automatic stay is irrelevant; the stay is self-enforcing and operates even if the party allegedly violating the stay had no knowledge of the bankruptcy filing. But because Harold did have actual knowledge of the bankruptcy filing and nevertheless attempted to perfect the security interest, the trustee may choose to seek sanctions under section 362(k)(1) of the Bankruptcy Code (provided that the debtor is an individual and not a business organization). These sanctions include actual damages, punitive damages, and possibly contempt of court for willful acts in violation of the automatic stay.

## 14.2 TRUSTEE'S POWERS UNDER SECTION 544(B)

Section 544(b) provides the trustee with yet another weapon in the avoidance powers arsenal. Under section 544(b), the trustee may avoid the debtor's transfers or obligations if any *actual unsecured creditor* with an *allowable claim* could do so under non-bankruptcy law. To invoke this power, the trustee must identify an actual unsecured creditor with an allowable claim that could avoid the transfer under state law. Unlike section 544(a), section 544(b) does not bestow upon the trustee the status of a hypothetical creditor who can attack the transfer. Section 544(b) requires that the trustee find an actual creditor with an allowable claim. Thus, the potency of the trustee's ability to attack a transfer under section 544(b) turns on the substantive effect of applicable state law.

Most often, section 544(b) will be successfully invoked to attack a transfer as fraudulent under applicable state fraudulent transfer laws. Although the Bankruptcy Code under section 548 contains its own fraudulent transfer provisions, the trustee can only avoid a fraudulent transfer that occurred on or within one year of the filing of the bankruptcy petition. Nonetheless, under the Uniform Fraudulent Transfer Act (UFTA), a creditor can attack fraudulent transfers as far back as four years. Consequently, if a trustee can locate an actual unsecured creditor with an allowable claim who can attack the transfer as fraudulent under the UFTA, the trustee can step into the actual unsecured creditor's shoes and reach back not two years, but four years in attacking a transfer.[2] Furthermore, if one actual unsecured creditor can be found, the trustee can void the transfer in its entirety and is not limited in the recovery to the amount of the claim of the creditor on whom the trustee relied.[3]

## 14.3 AVOIDABLE PREFERENCES UNDER SECTION 547(B)

An avoidable preference is (i) any transfer of an interest of the debtor in property (ii) to or for the benefit of a creditor (iii) for or on account of an antecedent debt owed by the debtor before the transfer was made; (iv) made while the debtor was insolvent; (v) made on or within 90 days before the date of the filing of the petition (or within one year if the creditor is an insider); and (vi) that enables the creditor to

---

2. The predecessor Uniform Fraudulent Conveyance Act (UFCA) remains in effect in only a few states, but probably in New York; the reach-back period is six years.

3. This is known as the doctrine of *Moore v. Bay*, 284 U.S. 4 (1931).

receive more than it would have received under a chapter 7 liquidation. The trustee, or the debtor in possession in a chapter 11 case, shoulders the burden of proof on all the elements of an avoidable preference action. However, there is a statutory presumption that the debtor is insolvent on or within 90 days of the filing of the petition in bankruptcy. Furthermore, if the creditor who received the alleged avoidable preference was an insider of the debtor, then the operative period is extended from 90 days to one year before the filing of the petition in bankruptcy.

## 14.3.1 Elements

The following is a more detailed analysis of the elements that must be satisfied before a transfer constitutes an avoidable preference under section 547(b) of the Bankruptcy Code.

### 14.3.1.1 A Transfer of the Debtor's Property

Transfer is broadly defined in section 101(54) to include every mode or disposition of an interest in property, voluntary or involuntary, and includes the creation of a lien on the debtor's property and foreclosure under the real property law. Once the triggering transfer has been identified, the fact that the transferred property was property of the debtor must be established. This is usually the case; however, if the debtor acts as a mere conduit of funds, or the funds that go from a third party through the debtor to the creditor are earmarked, then some courts have concluded that the transfer is not of the debtor's property. For example, an owner of the debtor corporation pays off a corporate debt for which the owner was not personally liable. In that situation, there is no transfer of an interest in the debtor's property. Furthermore, assume the owner directs the funds to the creditor through the debtor but that the funds were always earmarked for the creditor. In that case, some courts have held that the debtor has not transferred its property to the creditor. Under both scenarios, even assuming if all other elements of an avoidable preference are met, there is no avoidable preference under section 547(b) because the debtor has not transferred its property.

### 14.3.1.2 To or For the Benefit of a Creditor

The drafters of the Bankruptcy Code drafted the avoidable preference section in such a way as to ensnare not only transfers to a creditor, but also transfers for the benefit of a creditor. Assume the debtor owes a debt to A and A owes a debt to B. B, however, is not a creditor of the debtor. If the debtor paid A and then A paid B, assuming all other elements are met, the transfer is one between the debtor and its creditor A. However, if on directions from A the debtor pays B, assuming all other elements are met, the transfer is for the benefit of the debtor's creditor A. Either transfer satisfies the second element of an avoidable preference under section 547(b). These transfers are commonly called "indirect transfers."

### 14.3.1.3 For or on Account of an Antecedent Debt

Simply, this element requires that the creation of the debt occurred before the transfer was made. Usually, this element requires a straightforward comparison of the date the debt arose to the date of the transfer. Nonetheless, in some circumstances this simple comparison can be deceptive.

Bankruptcy Code section 547(e) employs an artificial test to establish when the transfer takes place. The general rule is the transfer takes place when the transfer becomes notorious by perfection rather than the actual date of the transfer. Section 547(e) is the drafters' attempt to protect against secret liens.

Section 547(e) provides that for real estate transfers, a transfer occurs when the transfer is effective against a bona fide purchaser of the real estate. With personal property transfers, the transfer occurs when it becomes perfected as against a judicial lien creditor [before the lien of the judicial lien creditor attaches to the same personal property]. Furthermore, a transfer perfected within 10 days after it is actually made is deemed to occur when it became effective between the parties as a matter of law under section 547(e)(2). Under BAPCPA, the 10-day period has been extended to 30 days. The new extended period applies to all preference actions commenced ancillary to any bankruptcy case filed on or after October 17, 2005.

An example should help explain this complex provision. Assume that two years before the debtor files a bankruptcy petition, it enters into a contract to borrow money from Johnny Bench. In return for the loan, the debtor grants a chapter 9 security interest in all of its inventory and equipment to Johnny. Johnny, busy with his many television appearances and car commercials, forgets to file the financing statement in the appropriate place. One month before the debtor files its bankruptcy petition, Johnny recognizes his mistake and files his financing statement. The filing of a financing statement is a transfer under Code section 101(54). The loan and the grant of the security interest occurred on the same date two years prior to the bankruptcy filing. That date is the date the debt was created. The actual transfer occurred on the same date the debt was created. Nevertheless, the "transfer" as defined by section 547(e) for avoidable preference purposes only occurs when the transfer is perfected as against a judgment lien creditor. The transfer does not become effective against a judgment lien creditor until the security interest is perfected. Recall that an unperfected security interest is junior to a judgment lien creditor. Thus, the transfer for avoidable preference purposes occurred one month before bankruptcy. Consequently, the transfer can be scrutinized to determine whether all the elements of an avoidable preference were met. This is the case even though the transfer actually occurred two years before the bankruptcy.

### 14.3.1.4 Made Within 90 Days Before Bankruptcy, or, if the Transferee Is an Insider, Within One Year of Bankruptcy

Again, the time of the transfer as determined by section 547(e) will be determinative as to whether the transfer occurred on or within 90 days of the filing of the bankruptcy petition. An insider is defined under section 101(31).

### 14.3.1.5 The Debtor Is Insolvent

Under section 101(32), insolvency is generally defined as the sum of the debtor's debts exceeding the debtor's property at a fair valuation—the balance sheet approach to insolvency. Under section 547(f), the debtor is presumed to be insolvent for the 90 days preceding the filing of the bankruptcy petition. The insolvency presumption is rebuttable.

### 14.3.1.6 Preferential Effect

The final element of an avoidable preference found at section 547(b)(5) requires that the transfer have the effect of giving the transferee more than it otherwise would receive in a straight chapter 7 liquidation proceeding. This preferential effect is the essence of an avoidable preference action.

The section 547(b)(5) element of an avoidable preference is almost always met if the creditor is an unsecured creditor. Conversely, if the debtor pays a fully secured creditor and the security interest is not avoidable under one of the avoiding powers, the transfer by the debtor is not a preference. A transfer to a fully secured creditor gives the fully secured creditor no more than it would have received under a chapter 7 liquidation.

However, this is not the case with an under-secured creditor. The law presumes that at least absent relinquishment of a portion of the collateral equal to the payment made by the debtor, any payment within the 90-day preference period is a reduction of an under-secured creditor's unsecured claim and therefore amounts to a preferential transfer for the benefit of the under-secured creditor.

BAPCPA changes to reclamation claims and the like will have an impact on the ability of the trustee to recover on preference actions. If the holder of a potential preference can show that it received no more than it would have been entitled to under a hypothetical chapter 7 case where the transfer had not been made, then there is no preferential effect. That may very well be the case in situations where trade creditors are being sued as recipients of alleged avoidable preferences when they were paid on goods received by the debtor within the 45-day and 20-day periods described below.

Prior to BAPCPA, Title 11 of the United States Code (the Bankruptcy Code) provided some level of protection to sellers of goods who delivered those goods to the debtor in the days preceding the filing of the debtor's petition by incorporating state law reclamation rights, as provided by the UCC, into the Bankruptcy Code in the form of section 546(c). However, the amendments made by BAPCPA via amended section 546(c)[4] and the inclusion of section 503(b)(9) dramatically change these rights.

---

4. 11 U.S.C.A. § 546(c)(1):

Except as provided in Subsection (d) of this Section and in Section 507(c), and subject to the prior rights of a holder of a security interest in such goods or the proceeds thereof, the rights and powers of a the trustee under Sections 544(a), 545, 547, and 549 of this title are subject to any statutory or common-law the right of a seller of goods that has sold goods to the debtor, in the ordinary course of such seller's business, to reclaim such goods if the debtor has received such goods while insolvent, within 45 days before the date of the commencement of a case under this title, but—(1) such a seller may not reclaim any such goods unless such seller demands in writing reclamation of such goods—
    (A) before 10 not later than 45 days after the date of receipt of such goods by the debtor; or
    (B) not later than 20 days after the date of commencement of the case, if such 10-day the 45-day period expires after the commencement of the case., before 20 days after receipt of such goods by the debtor; and
    (2) If a seller of goods fails to provide notice in the manner described in paragraph (1), the seller still may assert the rights contained in Section 503(b)(9).
    (2) the court may deny reclamation to a seller with such a right of reclamation that has made such a demand only if the court—
    (A) grants the claim of such a seller priority as a claim of a kind specified in Section 503(b) of this title; or
    (B) secures such claim by a lien.

An example may be in order. In *In re Georgetown Steel Company, LLC*,[5] the seller of goods was disputing the status of its reclamation claim regarding 12 supersacks of silicomanganese (SMI). There, the court determined that reclamation was a state law right, and thus, to prevail, the seller must prove up not only the timely written notice requirement contained in section 546(c), but also the elements of the state law right: (1) that the goods sold to the debtor on credit were of a type within the ordinary course of business of both parties; (2) that the debtor was insolvent pursuant to the Bankruptcy Code at the time of delivery of the goods; and (3) that the debtor was still in the possession of the goods or that the goods were not in the hands of a good-faith purchaser at the time the demand for reclamation was received.[6] In that case, the seller was unable to prove that the debtor had possession of the goods or that they were not in the hands of a good faith purchaser, thus the seller could not prevail.[7] The replacement of the words "any statutory or common law" with the word "the" in section 546(c)(1) appears to change the outcome of this case by rendering the possession requirement moot.

What if the seller in *Georgetown Steel* had prevailed? Old section 546(c)(2) gave the court the ability to deny reclamation (i.e., not require the debtor to return the goods) where the elements of reclamation were shown if the court granted the seller either a lien in property to secure its claim or a priority claim for the value of the goods. The elimination of old section 546(c)(2) in its entirety seems to divest the court of any option: If the seller shows that the goods were sold within 45 days of the commencement of the case to an insolvent debtor, and that a written demand was timely made, the seller appears to have an absolute right to reclaim the goods. How this will work with the definition of Property of the Estate as described by section 541 of the Bankruptcy

---

5. 318 B.R. 336 (Bankr. S.C. 2004).
6. *Id.* at 339.
7. *Id.* at 340.

Code and the Automatic Stay provided by section 362 is yet to be seen. The first instances of litigation may well come when the debtor seeks to sell the goods as part of a larger parcel of goods free and clear of liens and interests under section 363.

The reality is that, in most cases, asset-based financing provides a prior perfected lien on most goods so that the right of reclamation is rendered moot. Further, where a lien does not act to moot the reclamation rights, many vendors fail to provide the timely written notice.[8] So why all the concern about goods sold in the days immediately before the filing? One answer is that if the inventory of the debtor in possession is substantially reduced by reclamation, the estate will experience a substantial loss of operating income. Another answer is found in new section 546(c)(2), which refers to section 503(b)(9), which grants administrative expense status for:

> the value of any goods received by the debtor within 20 days before the date of commencement of a case under this title in which the goods have been sold to the debtor in the ordinary course of such debtor's business.[9]

This provision, in essence, appears to deem all vendors delivering goods within 20 days of the petition date "critical." Thus, as a result of this provision, it will become increasingly important that the debtor not order any goods for product lines or stores that will be shut down at, or immediately after, the filing of the petition, which will require additional planning on the part of the debtor and its advisors to avoid unnecessary administrative expenses.

---

8. Query, however, whether the increased time to provide that notice, and the absence of the requirement that the seller show that the goods are in the possession of either the debtor or an entity that is not a good-faith purchaser, taken with the absolute right to reclaim, will increase the instances of reclamation demands.

9. 11 U.S.C. § 503(b)(9).

## 14.3.2 Defenses

Section 547(c) of the Code provides a number of affirmative defenses that exclude certain transfers otherwise avoidable from the avoidable preference power. Of course, like any other affirmative defense, the section 547(c) affirmative defenses must be asserted and proved by the transferee.[10] Below is a discussion of the section 547(c) affirmative defenses.

### 14.3.2.1 Contemporaneous Exchange

Under section 547(c)(1), if the debtor and the transferee intended that the transfer be a contemporaneous exchange for new value given to the debtor and the exchange was in fact *substantially contemporaneous*, then the transfer is not an avoidable preference. Under section 547(c)(1), if a debtor and transferee *intend* the transfer to be a contemporaneous exchange for *new value* given to the debtor and the exchange is in fact *substantially contemporaneous*, then the transfer is not an avoidable preference. The test under section 547(c)(1) is both subjective and objective.

The first hurdle—the subjective component—is to determine whether the parties intended a contemporaneous exchange for new value. Without that intent, the fact that a transfer was contemporaneous or substantially contemporaneous does not save the transfer from avoidance under section 547(c)(1). Intent is a question of fact and, in this context, will generally be proved by circumstantial objective evidence, including the terms in any documents or memoranda between the parties, form of payment (for example, cash or check), prior relationships, custom in the industry, etc.[11] Additionally, the transfer must be in exchange for new value. New value includes "money or money's worth in goods, services, or new credit or release by a transferee of property previously transferred to such transferee in a transaction that

---

10. 11 U.S.C. § 547(g).

11. *See, e.g., In re* Arnett, 731 F.2d 358, 362 (6th Cir. 1984); *In re* Quade, 108 B.R. 681, 683 (Bankr. N.D. Iowa 1989).

is neither void nor voidable by the debtor or the trustee under any applicable law, including proceeds of such property, but does not include an obligation substituted for an existing obligation."[12] Obviously, money or money's worth is new value and generally poses no problem. Forbearance of a right or the substitution of an obligation is not new value and generally poses no problem.[13] Courts have concluded that the release of a lien does constitute new value.[14]

The second hurdle—the objective component—is to determine whether an intended contemporaneous transfer was in fact *substantially contemporaneous*. Whether a transfer is substantially contemporaneous is determined by the facts and circumstances of each case.[15] Courts generally hold that a 30-day delay generally passes muster, that 45 days begins to push the limit, and that 60 days or more usually does not constitute a substantially contemporaneous exchange.[16] But these guidelines may be misleading. The issue will generally turn on the particular facts and circumstances of each case, reasons for any delays, industry standards, and presence of events beyond the control of the parties.[17]

---

12. 11 U.S.C. § 547(a)(2).

13. Although substitution of an obligation does not constitute new value, authority does exist to support a finding of new value where terms of an existing loan have been modified in favor of the debtor, *see In re* F&S Cent. Mfg. Corp., 53 B.R. 842, 850 (Bankr. E.D.N.Y. 1985), or where the transferee pays a debt to a third party, thereby benefiting the debtor, *see In re* Bellanca Aircraft Corp., 850 F.2d 1275, 1279–1280 (8th Cir. 1988).

14. *See, e.g., In re* E.R. Fegert, Inc., 887 F.2d 955, 959 (9th Cir. 1989); *In re* Fuel Oil Supply & Terminaling, Inc., 837 F.2d 224, 231 (5th Cir. 1988); *In re* Phoenix Steel Corp., 76 B.R. 373, 376 (Bankr. D. Del. 1987).

15. *See In re* Arnett, 731 F.2d 358, 360 (6th Cir. 1984).

16. *See, e.g., In re* Bullion Reserve, 836 F.2d 1214, 1219 (9th Cir.), *cert. denied sub nom.* Bozeck v. Danning, 486 U.S. 1056 (1988); *In re* Foreman Indus., Inc., 59 B.R. 145, 152 (Bankr. S.D. Ohio 1986).

17. Recall that application of the earmarking doctrine may in fact be better understood as a special case of the § 547(c)(1) defense.

### 14.3.2.2 Payment Made in the Ordinary Course of Business

Prior to BAPCPA, the trustee could not avoid a transfer if it was in payment of a debt that was incurred by the debtor in the ordinary course of a business or financial affairs of both the debtor and the transferee, made in the ordinary course of business and in accordance with ordinary business terms.[18] These ordinary course transfers are treated similarly to cash transfers. This particular exception to the avoidable preference power is the one most often used by those creditors who provide valuable goods and services to the debtor on credit and is known commonly as the "Ordinary Course Defense" and is found at section 547(c)(2)

Historically, section 547(c)(2) had three prongs embodied in its three subsections. The first prong, whether the defendant was in the business of selling the goods sold during the preference period to the debtor, and whether the debtor was in the business of buying such goods, was very rarely at issue. This prong has been folded into the new section itself leaving only two subsections.[19] Further, where historically both of these two remaining subsections had to be met, now, for any preference action commenced ancillary to any bankruptcy case filed on or after October 17, 2005, only one of the subsections must be met.

The first of these subsections, section 547(c)(2)(A) (historically section 547(c)(2)(B)) as amended, also known as the

---

18. *See* 11 U.S.C. § 547(c)(2).
19. 11 U.S.C.A. § 547(c)(2) provides:

> (c) The trustee may not avoid under this Section a transfer— ...
> (2) to the extent that such transfer was—(A) in payment of a debt incurred by the debtor in the ordinary course of business or financial affairs of the debtor and the transferee,; and such transfer was—
> (BA) made in the ordinary course of business or financial affairs of the debtor and the transferee; and or
> (CB) made according to ordinary business terms; ....

"subjective test," requires that the transfers be "ordinary" as between the debtor and creditor, considering such factors as timing, amount, and manner.[20] Along with time between invoice and payment, other factors that may be analyzed include:

- the length of time the parties have been engaged in these types of transactions;

- whether the payments in question were larger than usual;

- whether the payments were made in the usual manner;

- whether the debtor or creditor took unusual actions to cause invoices to be paid; and

- whether the defendant took any actions within the preference period to put itself in a better position in the face of the debtor's deteriorating financial situation.[21]

The second prong, section 547(c)(2)(B) (historically section 547(c)(2)(C)) as amended, also known as the "objective test," requires that the transfers be made according to terms consistent with industry norms. An analysis of case law suggests that this prong does not require the determination of a single "industry metric," but rather that a range of terms used in the industry is a more reasonable and accurate depiction of ordinary course.[22] It is important to note that, as practitioners, we may be caught up in a battle of metrics—timing, manner and method of payment, days past due, etc.—and lose sight of what is most important in assessing the applicability of this defense—that is, in crafting

---

20. *In re* T.B. Home Sewing Enters., Inc., 173 B.R. 790, 795-96 (Bankr. N.D. Ga. 1993); *see also In re* First Jersey Sec., 180 F.3d 504, 512 (3d Cir. 1999).

21. *In re* T.B. Home Sewing Enters., Inc., 173 B.R. at 795-96; *see also* Global Tissue, LLC v. E.B. Eddy Forest Products, Ltd., 302 B.R. 808 (D. Del. 2003), *citing In re* Parkline Corp., 185 B.R. 164, 169 (Bankr. D.N.J. 1994).

22. Miller v. Florida Mining and Materials (*In re* A.W. Assoc., Inc.), 136 F.3d 1439, 1443 (11th Cir. 1998); *see also In re* First Jersey Sec., 180 F.3d at 513.

this defense, Congress sought to leave undisturbed normal business transactions between the debtor and its creditors as long as neither sought to opt out of the looming bankruptcy process.

The factors to be considered with regard to payments are as follows:

1) Character of payment

2) Method of payment

3) Type of check processing

4) Amount of check

5) Check invoice dates compared to payment dates

6) Term changes

7) Timing of payments

8) Proof-of-delivery issues

9) Lost invoices

10) Misplaced invoices

11) Returned or nonconforming goods

12) Custom goods

13) Credit and discount issues

14) Exposure

15) New preference period account

16) One invoice or payment situation

17) Stump period

18) Deviation from internal procedure

19) Horizontal comparison with regard to procedures

20) Extraordinary use of third parties

21) Meeting with customer

22) Classified as distressed credit

23) Appropriate model (no distress, distress, or entire market)

The following reveals the methodology for determining the ordinary course of business defense:

a) At some point, the expert, or someone working under the supervision of the expert (collectively, the expert), visits by phone or in person with the employees and/or professionals of the client to discuss the operations and procedures of the defendant and debtor. The expert analyzes the complaint and exhibits filed by the debtor in the preference action to determine the alleged preference payments, including the gross preference amount, net discounts, net charge-back, net credits, and other adjustments, to arrive at the net alleged preference amount.

b) Next, the expert assesses the available check posting and clearing (final payment) records to determine the date checks were posted to the defendant's records or cleared the debtor's bank. Further, the expert prepares and/or analyzes preference details, including check amounts and dates, invoice amounts and dates, any charge-backs, discounts, aging of invoices by due date, and other relevant data, including those factors identified above. Moreover, the expert analyzes the historical transactions between the debtor and the defendant to determine the payment experience with the debtor.

c) Now, the expert explicitly identifies the testing period—the time period of interest to and consideration by the expert. At this stage, the expert will also identify the relevant industry and then study relevant publications, trade journals, and other industry sources to become informed about collection practices and ordinary business terms. With this, the expert, through experience in the relevant industry and/or through an analysis of comparable companies and/or other accounts maintained by the parties, formulates an opinion of what constitutes ordinary business terms, considering the manner and amount of payment, the stated terms between the parties, the timing of payments, account status, and other common credit management practices and procedures. To the extent practicable, the expert might cross-validate the expert opinion based on a number of sources or methods, including research (preferably published), experience (including third-party experience), proprietary sources, and an assessment of the actual performance between the debtor and the defendant.

### 14.3.2.3 Enabling Loans

Under section 547(c)(3), the trustee cannot avoid a security interest if it secures new value given by the creditor that is given to enable the debtor to acquire a particular piece of property and is used by the debtor to acquire the property provided that the security interest must be perfected within 30 days from the time the debtor receives possession of the collateral. This affirmative defense recognizes a creditor's ability to protect its purchase money security interest status and mirrors protections common under Article 9 of the UCC for purchase money security interests.

### 14.3.2.4 Subsequent Advancement of Unsecured Credit

Under section 547(c)(4), a trustee cannot avoid the transfer if, after having received the transfer, the creditor extends unsecured credit. The courts are in conflict over whether the new value must remain unpaid at the date of the bankruptcy filing, with the better view being that all pre-petition new value be considered.

The policy rationale supporting the new value defense is that, by such actions, a creditor has essentially restored the status quo. Section 547(c)(4) is designed to insulate that restoration. Section 547(c)(4) immunizes repeated repayments of debt followed by extensions of credit, viewing the series of transactions as a whole. Section 547(c)(4), however, places two limits on the use of the defense. First, any subsequent advance of new value must be unsecured or secured by an interest that could be avoided in bankruptcy. Second, any subsequent advance must itself be an avoidable transfer, subject to avoidance under the Bankruptcy Code.

### 14.3.2.5 Floating Liens

Under section 547(c)(5), a trustee cannot attack a validly secured pre-petition creditor with an after-acquired inventory[23] or accounts receivable[24] clause except to the extent that the secured creditor improves its position during the applicable preference period. The affirmative defense, by its terms, does not apply to after-acquired equipment. Prior to the enactment of the Bankruptcy Code, debate existed over whether the attachment of a lien to after-acquired property occurred at the time the debtor acquired rights in the property or at some earlier date. Section 547(e)(3) ended the debate and provides that a transfer is not made until a debtor has acquired rights in the property transferred. Nonetheless, section 547(e)(5) permits avoidance of a security interest only to the extent that a transfer places the creditor in a better position as of the bankruptcy petition date than it had been on the latter of (1) the first date on which new value had been given under the security agreement or (2) 90 days prior to the bankruptcy petition date (one year if the creditor is an insider). Any improvement in position goes unprotected under section 547(c)(5). In other words, any decrease in the deficiency during the preference period may be recaptured by the trustee. Thus, accommodation of le-

---

23. "Inventory" is defined as:

> personal property leased or furnished, held for sale or lease, or to be furnished under a contract for service, raw materials, work in process, or materials used or consumed in a business, including farm products such as crops or livestock, held for sale or lease....

11 U.S.C. §547(a)(1).

24. "Receivable" "means right to payment, whether or not such right has been earned by performance." 11 U.S.C. § 547(a)(3).

gitimate inventory and receivables financing is the purpose of section 547(c)(5).

### 14.3.2.6 Statutory Liens

Under section 547(c)(6), the fixing of a statutory lien that is not avoidable under section 545 is insulated from attack under section 547(b). In particular, the fixing of a federal tax lien is generally not subject to preference scrutiny.[25] Statutory liens are governed by section 545.

### 14.3.2.7 Payment of Debt for Domestic Support Obligations

Section 547(c)(7) removes from the scope of the avoidable preference power any transfers to the extent that they are a bona fide payment of a debt for a domestic support obligation. Prior to BAPCPA, the language included *all transfers* for support, maintenance, or alimony to spouses, former spouses, and children, and did not limit itself to a payment as a form of transfer. Moreover, BAPCPA injected the requirement that the payments be bona fide, not a controversial addition, and that such payments be of a debt under a *domestic support obligation*. The term "domestic support obligation" is defined in section 101(14A) in an expansive manner. This provision is one in a line of provisions designed to alleviate the harsh effects of bankruptcy following a divorce.

### 14.3.2.8 Small Consumer Debt Payments

Under section 547(c)(8), the trustee in a case of an individual debtor whose debts are primarily consumer debts cannot avoid the preferences to any creditor that aggregates less than $600. This is a rule of administrative convenience and efficiency.

---

25. For a detailed treatment of federal tax liens and avoidance powers, *see* C. RICHARD MCQUEEN & JACK F. WILLIAMS, TAX ASPECTS OF BANKRUPTCY LAW AND PRACTICE § 16.21 (3d ed. 2006).

### 14.3.2.9 Small Business Debt Payments

Under section 547(c)(9), the trustee in a case filed by a debtor whose debts are not primarily consumer debts cannot avoid a preference to any creditor that aggregates less than $5,000. This rule also appears to be a rule of administrative convenience and efficiency.

### 14.3.2.10 BAPCPA Changes

There seems to be some debate among bankruptcy professionals about the legitimacy of many of the preference actions currently being pursued. Some liken to blackmail the practice of simply reviewing the debtor's check register and sending a demand letter and/or a complaint to any entity receiving a check within 90 days of the petition date with no consideration to possible defenses. The "ordinary course and new value are affirmative defenses that they have to prove and I'm not going to worry about until then" attitude has given rise to a great deal of irritation on the part of vendors, the people who represent them, and the courts. Several of the amendments in BAPCPA appear to be Congress's attempt at rectifying at least part of the problem.

First, the change frequently mentioned herein—the grant of administrative expense status for the value of goods delivered within 20 days of the petition date—appears to eliminate payments on account of these deliveries from any potential preference action. Unless the debtor is administratively insolvent, any payment on account of these goods would have to be paid in cash to confirm a plan, so the creditor could not have received more than under the confirmed plan (excluding the time value of money, of course). Thus, the debtor will not be able to make a prima facie case against these vendors on account of payments on these goods.

However, questions about these goods remain. For instance, can the delivery of goods the value of which is protected by an administrative expense constitute new value for the purposes of section 547(c)(4), or will the administrative expense priority be treated as a payment? And what exactly does "value" mean? If "value" is determined to be the wholesale cost and the debtor paid retail, then some room may still remain for a preference action regarding these goods.

Historically, there was no limit on the size of preference the trustee could pursue in cases where the debtor's debts were not primarily consumer in nature.[26] The only limitation was a jurisdictional restriction pursuant to 28 U.S.C. section 1409(b), which previously required that actions to recover a money judgment of, or property worth, less than $1,000, or a consumer debt worth less than $5,000, be brought only in the district where the defendant resides. Thus, as a practical result, while some trustees may have sent demand letters regarding smaller preferences, they generally did not file complaints unless the potential defendant was local. Pursuant to the act, these jurisdictional thresholds have been increased. While the $1,000 limit on money judgments and property remains the same, BAPCPA increased the amount of a consumer debt to $15,000 and added a provision for the collection of any other debt against a non-insider to $10,000.[27] Thus any preference action worth less than $10,000 must be brought in the district in which the defendant resides, which is generally not where the case is proceeding.

Additionally, a new affirmative defense has been added—Section 547(c)(9), which some refer to as the "why are you

---

26. In cases where the debts are primarily consumer in nature, 11 U.S.C.A. §547(c)(8) continues to set the threshold amount at $600.

27. 11 U.S.C.A. § 1409(b) provides:

> Except as provided in Subsection (d) of this Section, a trustee in a case under title 11 may commence a proceeding arising in or related to such case to recover a money judgment of or property worth less than $1,000 or a consumer debt of less than ~~$5,000~~ $15,000, or a debt (excluding a consumer debt) against a noninsider of less than $10,000, only in the district court for the district in which the defendant resides.

Note that subsection (d) refers to transactions occurring post-petition.

bothering me" defense—which prohibits the trustee from recovering transfers that total less than $5,000 if the debtor is a business debtor. Interestingly, this is added as an affirmative defense rather than an element of the trustee's case in chief, which means that the defendant will still have to hire an attorney to file an answer if such an action is brought. However, if a trustee does bring a preference action where the total amount demanded is less than $5,000, the trustee and the trustee's attorney can reasonably expect a motion under Federal Rule of Bankruptcy Procedure 9011 to be attached to the answer.

Prior to BAPCPA, when applying the ordinary course defense, where the relationship between the parties was longstanding, conformance with the ordinary practices of the parties gained in significance, as opposed to those of the industry, in reaching a determination regarding the ordinary course of business, as long as the terms between the parties did not deviate from those utilized by the relevant industry to an extent that they were clearly not "usual."[28] However, after BAPCPA, if either provision is met, the challenged transfer is considered within the ordinary course of business defense and, thus, not recoverable by the trustee.

In the Bankruptcy Reform Act of 1Buford4 (the 1Buford4 Act), Congress amended section 550 in an attempt to overrule *Levit v. Ingersoll Rand Financial Corp. (In re DePrizio)*.[29] However, despite the 1Buford4 Act, the *DePrizio* question lingered on. Therefore, in BAPCPA, Congress has once again addressed the question. In *DePrizio*, the law of unintended consequences reached up and smacked the lender in the nose. When making the loan that was the subject of the alleged preference, the lender had asked for and received personal guarantees by an insider. Thus, every payment on the loan reduced the insider's contingent liability, benefiting the insider. The trustee argued that because the transfers

---

28. Miller v. Florida Mining and Materials (*In re* A.W. Assoc., Inc.), 136 F.3d at 1443.
29. 874 F.2d 1186, 1187 (7th Cir. 1989).

benefited the insider, the reach-back period should be one year rather than 90 days. Thus, by attempting to secure a loan with a personal guarantee by an insider, which created contingent liabilities for that insider, the lender became a de facto insider for the purposes of preference actions.

In the 1Buford4 Act, Congress amended section 550 by adding subsection (c) to prohibit recovering a transfer such as the one in *DePrizio* from the non-insider transferee. However, this did not really solve the problem for some transfers, as highlighted by *Roost v. Associates Home Equity Servs., Inc. (In re Williams)*.[30] In *Roost*, a lender had perfected a security interest in a mobile home and the land upon which it sat greater than 90 days, but less than one year, before the petition date. There, the trustee argued that since both the debtor and his wife executed the security agreement, the debtor's wife, as an insider, benefited from the security interest. The trustee then sought to avoid the security interest, arguing that it benefited an insider. When the lender sought protection under section 550(c), the trustee argued that it was not trying to recover anything, but simply trying to avoid the security interest. The court, citing rules of construction and precedent recognizing the separation of avoidance and recovery, found the security interest avoidable.

To close the loophole highlighted by *Roost*, BAPCPA added subsection (i), which provides:

> If the trustee avoids under Subsection (b) a transfer made between 90 days and 1 year before the date of the filing of the petition, by the debtor to an entity that is not an insider for the benefit of a creditor that is an insider, such transfer shall be considered to be avoided under this section only with respect to the creditor that is an insider.[31]

---

30. 234 B.R. 801 (Bankr. D. Or. 1999).
31. 11 U.S.C.A. § 547(i).

## 14.4 STATUTORY LIEN AVOIDANCE UNDER SECTION 545

Section 545 permits the trustee to invalidate those statutory liens that lack the characteristics of a true property interest and are merely disguised priority provisions enacted by states in an attempt to circumvent the priority provisions embodied in the Bankruptcy Code. As a general principle, the following types of statutory liens are avoidable under section 545:

- Statutory liens that become perfected at the time of certain kinds of deterioration in the debtor's financial condition.

- Statutory liens that are not perfected at bankruptcy as against a hypothetical bona fide purchaser from the debtor.

- Statutory liens that are in favor of the debtor's landlord.

Additionally, in liquidation cases under section 724(a), the trustee may avoid any lien, statutory or otherwise, that secures a governmental or private penalty. Furthermore, in liquidation cases under section 724(b), statutory tax liens on either real or personal property that are otherwise valid are subordinated to bankruptcy administration expenses, particularly chapter 7 expenses and certain unsecured employee and consumer priority claims, although BAPCPA limits this partial subordination in many common situations.

## 14.5 FRAUDULENT TRANSFERS UNDER SECTION 548(A)

A trustee, or debtor in possession under a chapter 11 case, may avoid any fraudulent transfer under section 548(a) of the Code. The Bankruptcy Code recognizes two types of fraudulent transfer: (1) actual fraudulent transfer and (2) constructively fraudulent transfer. An actual fraudulent transfer is a transfer made by the debtor with the actual intent to hinder, delay, or defraud its creditors. With this type of transfer, the court's focus is exclusively on the actual intent of the debtor. In a constructive fraudulent transfer, the debtor's intent is irrelevant. Rather, the focus is on whether the debtor received less than a reasonably equivalent value in exchange for the transfer and whether the debtor was in a precarious financial condition as defined by section 548 of the Bankruptcy Code.

Sections 548(a) and 544(b) (incorporating state fraudulent transfer law) of the Bankruptcy Code recognize the power of the trustee to challenge transfers or obligations incurred as fraudulent transfers. Section 548(a)(1)(B) provides:[32]

> The trustee may avoid any transfer (including any transfer to or for the benefit of an insider under an employment contract) of an interest of the debtor in property, or any obligation (including any obligation incurred to or for the benefit of an insider under an employment contract) incurred by the debtor, that was made or incurred on or within ~~one year~~ 2 years before the date of the filing of the petition, if the debtor voluntarily or involuntarily—
>
> > (A) made such transfer or incurred such obligation with actual intent to hinder, delay, or defraud any entity to which the debtor was or became, on or after the date that such transfer was made or such obligation was incurred, indebted; or
> >
> > > (B)(i) received less than a reasonably equivalent value in exchange for such transfer or obligation; and
> > >
> > > (ii)(I) was insolvent on the date that such transfer was made or such obligation was incurred, or became insolvent as a result of such transfer or obligation;

---

32. This outline does not address transfers made or obligations incurred with the actual intent to hinder, delay, or defraud creditors.

(II) was engaged in business or a transaction, or was about to engage in business or a transaction, for which any property remaining with the debtor was an unreasonably small capital; ~~or~~

(III) intended to incur, or believed that the debtor would incur, debts that would be beyond the debtor's ability to pay as such debts matured; or

(IV) made such transfer to or for the benefit of an insider, or incurred such obligation to or for the benefit of an insider, under an employment contract and not in the ordinary course of business.[33]

Section 544(b)(1) authorizes a trustee to avoid any transfer by the debtor that an unsecured creditor with an allowable claim could avoid under state fraudulent transfer law. Under section 544(b)(1), a trustee's cause of action rises and falls under state law; therefore, the elements of state law fraudulent transfers must be referenced. Although the UFTA is similar in many respects to section 548, some states (e.g., New York) still operate under the predecessor Uniform Fraudulent Conveyance Act (UFCA), and some states (e.g., Texas) have adopted non-uniform amendments to the UFTA.

Section 548 grants to the trustee the power to avoid a fraudulent transfer accomplished with either actual or constructive fraudulent intent. The fraudulent transfer is an infringement of the creditor's right to realize upon the available assets of its debtor. The law imposes a substantive prohibition: the debtor may not dispose of its property with the intent, actual or implied by law, of placing the property beyond the reach of its creditors. Although most commenta-

---

33. The "strike-out" language has been removed from the section but will continue to govern fraudulent transfer actions brought ancillary to all bankruptcy cases filed before Oct. 17, 2005. The bold and italicized language will govern all fraudulent transfer actions brought ancillary to all bankruptcy cases filed on or after Oct. 17, 2005.

tors agree that one of the fundamental thrusts of fraudulent transfer law is to protect the unjust diminution of the debtor's estate, the authorities disagree about where the proper limits of fraudulent transfer law should be drawn.[34]

### 14.5.1 Constructively Fraudulent Transfers

To make out a successful section 548(a)(1)(B) claim, the trustee must prove (1) a transfer to the defendant of (2) an interest in property of the debtor[35] (3) during two years pre-

---

34. *See, e.g.,* Douglas G. Baird & Thomas H. Jackson, *Fraudulent Conveyance Law and Its Proper Domain,* 38 VAND. L. REV. 829 (1985); David Gray Carlson, *Is Fraudulent Conveyance Law Efficient?,* 9 CARDOZO L. REV. 643 (1987); Frank R. Kennedy, *The Uniform Fraudulent Transfer Act,* 18 U.C.C. L.J. 195 (1986); Jonathan C. Lipson, *First Principles and Fair Consideration: The Developing Clash between the First Amendment and the Constructive Fraudulent Conveyance Laws,* 52 U. MIAMI. L. REV. 247 (1997); Marie T. Reilly, *The Latent Efficiency of Fraudulent Transfer Law,* 57 LA. L. REV. 1213 (1997); Emily Sherwin, *Creditors' Rights Against Participants in a Leveraged Buyout,* 72 MINN. L. REV. 449 (1988); Kathyrn Smyser, *Going Private and Going Under: Leveraged Buyouts and the Fraudulent Conveyance Problem,* 63 IND. L.J. 781 (1988); Paul M. Shupack, *Confusion and Policy and Language in the Uniform Fraudulent Transfer* Act, 9 CARDOZO L. REV. 811 (1987); Mary Jo Newborn Wiggins, *A Statute of Disbelief?: Clashing Ethical Imperatives in Fraudulent Transfer Law,* 48 S.C. L. REV. 771 (1997); Jack F. Williams, *Revisiting the Proper Limits of Fraudulent Transfer Law,* 8 BANKR. DEV. J. 55 (1991); Jack F. Williams, *The Fallacies of Contemporary Fraudulent Transfer Models as Applied to Intercorporate Guaranties: Fraudulent Transfer Law as a Fuzzy System,* 15 CARDOZO L. REV. 1403 (1994); Barry L. Zaretsky, *Fraudulent Transfer Law as the Arbiter of Unreasonable Risk,* 46 S.C. L. REV. 1165 (1995); Todd J. Zywicki, *Rewrite the Bankruptcy Laws, Not the Scriptures: Protecting a Bankruptcy Debtor's Right to Tithe,* 1998 WIS. L. REV. 1223.

35. The Bankruptcy Code does not define the phrase "interest of the debtor in property." Although the question of what constitutes an interest of the debtor in property is a question of federal law, the courts will consult state law in determining whether this element is met. 1A Bankr. Serv. L. Ed. §§ 5D:12, at 19 & n.1 (cases cited therein). The property requirement enjoys a broad scope and is generally construed in light of the purposes of fraudulent transfer law. Generally, the transfer must have depleted the debtor's estate. *Id.* § 5D:12, at 19–20 & n.2 (cases cited therein).

ceding the filing of the petition in bankruptcy[36] (4) without reasonably equivalent value[37] in exchange for such transfer (5) while the debtor was insolvent or left in some other statutorily defined precarious financial condition.[38]

Transfer is broadly defined in section 101(54) of the Bankruptcy Code to include "every mode, direct or indirect, absolute or conditional, voluntary or involuntary, of disposing of or parting with property or with an interest in property, including retention of title as a secu-

---

36. It is the filing of the petition in bankruptcy and not any subsequent petition that is used as the timing reference under § 548. *See* Bluford v. First Fidelity Mtg. Co. (*In re* Bluford), 40 Bankr. 640, 644 (Bankr. W.D. Mo. 1984). The appropriate reach-back period is often one of the most hotly contested issues in a fraudulent transfer action. Section 548(a) constitutes a grant of power to the trustee to avoid certain transfers deemed to have been made within one year of the filing (two years for bankruptcy cases filed on or after Oct. 17, 2005) of the bankruptcy petition. The reach-back period is not a statute of limitations. The reach-back requirement cannot be waived; it is not an affirmative defense. It serves as a means by which the trustee's power is limited in time so that § 548 does not serve as a form of unlimited insurance for creditors against the debtor's striking a bad deal. Consequently, transfers "deemed" to have taken place outside the one-year period (or for cases filed on or after Oct. 17, 2005, two years) are not subject to attack under § 548. However, one must be careful not to be misled by the realities of the transactions. Section 548(d)(1) states a policy and is not a recantation of the actual events. Thus, the law on when a transaction is deemed to have occurred (as opposed to when it actually happened) must be consulted. Finally, all transfers within the applicable time period must be examined by the court.

37. The analogous phrase was "fair consideration" under the Bankruptcy Act of 1898; it incorporated a requirement of good faith that no longer exists under § 548(a)(1)(B) or §§ 4 and 5 of the UFTA. *See* Carr v. Demusis (*In re* Carr), 34 Bankr. 653, 656 (D. Conn. 1983); *see also* UFCA § 3, 7A U.L.A. *supra* note 53, at 448–49 (employing a "fair consideration" standard).

38. Murphy v. General Elec. Credit Corp. (*In re* Rodriguez), 77 B.R. 939, 940 (Bankr. S.D. Fla. 1987), *aff'd*, 895 F.2d 725 (11th Cir. 1990); *In re* Ristich, 57 B.R. 568, 574 (Bankr. N.D. Ill. 1986). The corresponding UFTA sections are §§ 4, 5, 7A U.L.A. *supra*, at 652–53, 657. Although obvious, it is occasionally overlooked that post-petition (as opposed to pre-petition) transfers are not voidable under § 548. Nemeti v. Seaway Nat'l Bank (*In re* Nemeti), 65 B.R. 391, 394 (Bankr. N.D.N.Y. 1986).

rity interest and foreclosure of the debtor's equity of redemption."[39] A transfer is a protean and embracive term,[40] including a gift,[41] a foreclosure sale,[42] final pay-

---

39. 11 U.S.C. § 101(54).
40. *See* Venice Western Motel, Ltd. v. Venice Motor Inn, Ltd. (*In re* Venice Western Motel, Ltd.), 67 B.R. 777, 780 (Bankr. M.D. Fla. 1986).
41. Schafer v. Hammond, 456 F.2d 15, 17 (10th Cir. 1972).
42. BFP v. Resolution Trust Corp., 511 U.S. 531 (1994); Durrett v. Washington Nat'l Ins. Co., 621 F.2d 201, 204 (5th Cir. 1980) (seminal case holding that a foreclosure sale is a transfer); *accord,* First Fed. Sav. & Loan Ass'n v. Hulm (*In re* Hulm), 738 F.2d 323, 325 (8th Cir.), *cert. denied,* 469 U.S. 990 (1984); *but cf.* Madrid v. Lawyers Title Ins. Corp. (*In re* Madrid), 725 F.2d 1197, 1198 (9th Cir.), *cert. denied,* 469 U.S. 833 (1984); *In re* Winshall Settlor's Trust, 758 F.2d 1136, 1138–39 (6th Cir. 1985). Does the *Durrett* analysis apply to the personal property context? For example, if a debtor grants a security interest in all of its assets, there is little trouble finding a transfer once the interest is perfected. But if the debtor defaults, is the creditor's repossession and subsequent sale of the assets a new transfer? One bankruptcy court held that a pledge of securities as collateral and the subsequent involuntary sale of those securities upon the debtor's default each constituted separate transfers. Calairo v. Pittsburgh Nat'l Bank (*In re* Ewing), 33 B.R. 288, 291–92 (Bankr. W.D. Pa. 1983), *rev'd,* 36 B.R. 476 (W.D. Pa.), *aff'd,* 746 F.2d 1465 (3d Cir. 1984), *cert. denied,* 469 U.S. 1214 (1985). The court reasoned that the UCC sale must be a transfer, at least where the debtor's interest in the collateral exceeded the bank's secured debt. *Id. Calairo* was subsequently reversed by the district court. 36 B.R. 476 (W.D. Pa. 1984). The district court held that the only transfer was the original pledge of the collateral and not the subsequent sale, failing to discuss the new 1984 amendments to the Bankruptcy Code. *Id.* at 478. The district court was later affirmed by the Third Circuit in a summary disposition. 746 F.2d 1465, 1465 (3d Cir. 1984). It seems that the *Durrett* analysis and the *Calairo* analysis cannot live side-by-side. A little background may be helpful. In *Durrett,* the Fifth Circuit addressed a foreclosure sale, pursuant to a power of sale in a deed of trust, under Texas law. In Texas, the debtor's right of redemption of the real property ceases when the property is sold at the courthouse steps. Furthermore, only the debtor and any guarantors or co-owners have a right to notice of the foreclosure sale. In other words, junior lienholders, even those who have perfected their liens in the county's real property records, are not entitled to notice of the foreclosure sale that will, under Texas law, extinguish their perfected lien. Thus, only where notifying a junior lienholder of the proposed foreclosure sale would be beneficial to the senior lienholder—where, for example, the senior believes the junior will purchase its debt and take it out of its credit relationship with the debtor—will the junior receive notice. Nonetheless, the usual practice is not to provide notice to junior lienholders. This result almost always amazes

ment on a check,[43] a filing of a lis pendens for alimony,[44] an execution on a judgment lien,[45] a renewal of a loan and payments thereunder,[46] a pledge of securities and subsequent involuntary sale,[47] a termination of a lease,[48] a settlement agreement,[49] a consignment of goods,[50] a bonus,[51] a plant-

---

those practitioners from other jurisdictions who forcefully argue that such a foreclosure scheme violates the Due Process Clause of the Fourteenth Amendment. To them, one could quote at length the Texas cases finding no state action in private foreclosure sales. If still unconvinced, one could just observe that "[i]n Texas, however, people do things their own way." Steven Nickles, *The Objectification of Debtor-Creditor Relations*, 74 MINN. L. REV. 371, 378 (1990). Although not sound legal analysis, the answer does have the attribute of foreclosing debate on the state action doctrine. It was in this context that the Fifth Circuit addressed the issues in *Durrett*. I cannot help but believe that the system itself poisoned the court's analysis of the transfer and the reasonably equivalent value requirements. Furthermore, we cannot help but believe that the *Durrett* analysis, if good law, should apply to the Article 9 foreclosure sale as well. After all, the Article 9 foreclosure sale extinguishes the debtor's right of redemption in the same manner as real property foreclosure under Texas law, an act that appears to be a transfer by the debtor under § 101(54). Certainly, there are more provisions in Article 9 to ensure a commercially reasonable disposition, *see* U.C.C. § 9-504, but these provisions go to the question of value and not whether the triggering transfer exists.

43. Barnhill v. Johnson, 503, U.S. 393, 112 S. Ct. 1386 (1992).

44. *In re* Ottaviano, 63 B.R. 338, 341 (Bankr. D. Conn. 1986).

45. Frank v. Berlin (*In re* Frank), 39 B.R. 166, 167–69 (Bankr. E.D.N.Y. 1984).

46. B.Z. Corp. v. Continental Bank, N.A. (*In re* B.Z. Corp.), 34 B.R. 546, 548 (Bankr. E.D. Pa. 1983).

47. Kelley v. Horner (*In re* Kelley), 7 B.R. 384, 388–89 (Bankr. D.S.D. 1980).

48. Eder v. Queen City Grain, Inc. (*In re* Queen City Grain, Inc.), 51 B.R. 722, 725–26 (Bankr. S.D. Ohio 1985); *see also* Darby v. Atkinson (*In re* Ferris), 415 F. Supp. 33, 39 (W.D. Okla. 1976) (lease cancellation because of default is transfer subject to fraudulent transfer analysis); *but see* UFTA § 8(e)(1), 7A U.L.A. *supra* note 37, at 662 (leases terminated pursuant to their terms excluded from fraudulent transfer liability).

49. *In re* Edward Harvey Co., 68 B.R. 851, 858 (Bankr. D. Mass. 1987).

50. Campbell v. Macartie (*In re* Factory Tire Distribs., Inc.), 64 B.R. 335, 338 (Bankr. W.D. Pa. 1986).

51. *Id.* at 339.

ing of crops,[52] a bank's forbearance in collection of indebtedness in exchange for a security interest in livestock,[53] a garnishment of the debtor's bank account,[54] an attachment of a judgment lien,[55] a leveraged buyout,[56] an upstream, downstream, or cross-stream guaranty,[57] a ratification of a security interest,[58] a draw on a credit line,[59] a collusive judgment,[60] an encumbrance,[61] a release by a beneficiary of an interest in a trust estate,[62] a change in a beneficiary of a life insurance policy,[63] a divorce or separation agreement,[64] a rescission of a profitable contract,[65] a payment of a dividend,[66] and a payment of usurious interest.[67] This list

---

52. Lemley-Cabbiness Farms v. FDIC (*In re* Lemley Estate Business Trust), 65 B.R. 185, 189 (Bankr. N.D. Tex. 1986).

53. *In re* Bob Schwermer & Assocs., Inc., 27 B.R. 304, 310 (Bankr. N.D. Ill. 1983).

54. Ellenberg v. DeKalb County, Ga. (*In re* Maytag Sales and Serv., Inc.), 23 B.R. 384, 388 (Bankr. N.D. Ga. 1982) (case under § 547(b)).

55. Suppa v. Capalbo (*In re* Suppa), 8 B.R. 720, 722 (Bankr. D.R.I. 1981) (case under § 547(b)).

56. Kupetz v. Continental Ill. Nat'l Bank & Trust Co., 77 B.R. 754, 759–60 (C.D. Cal. 1987), *aff'd sub nom.* Kupetz v. Wolf, 845 F.2d 842 (9th Cir. 1988); *see* United States v. Tabor Court Realty Corp., 803 F.2d 1288 (3d Cir. 1986), *cert. denied*, 483 U.S. 1005 (1987); *see generally* David Gray Carlson, *Leveraged Buyouts in Bankruptcy*, 20 GA. L. REV. 73 (1985).

57. Lawrence Paperboard Corp. v. Arlington Trust Co. (*In re* Lawrence Paperboard Corp.), 76 B.R. 866, 874–76 (Bankr. D. Mass. 1987); *see generally* Daniel R. Coquillette, *Guaranty of and Security for the Debt of a Parent Corporation by a Subsidiary Corporation*, 30 CASE W. RES. 433 (1980); Robert J. Rosenberg, *Intercorporate Guaranties and the Law of Fraudulent Conveyances: Lender Beware,* 125 U. PA. L. REV. 235 (1976).

58. Mitchell v. Travis (*In re* Jackson Sound Studios, Inc.), 473 F.2d 503, 506 (5th Cir. 1973).

59. Rubin v. Mfrs. Hanover Trust Co., 661 F.2d 979, 989–91 (2d Cir. 1981).

60. Petrides v. Park Hill Restaurant, Inc., 265 A.D. 509, 511, 39 N.Y.S.2d 645, 647 (1943).

61. Service Mtg. Corp. v. Welson, 293 Mass. 410, 412, 200 N.E. 278, 279 (1936).

62. Schaefer v. Fisher, 137 Misc. 420, 426, 242 N.Y.S. 308, 314 (1930).

63. *Id.*

64. FDIC v. Malin, 802 F.2d 12, 18 (2d Cir. 1986).

65. Wilson v. Holub, 202 Iowa 549, 552, 210 N.W. 593, 595 (1926).

does not attempt to exhaust all of the possibilities of the term "transfer."[68]

The time when a transfer is deemed made for purposes of fraudulent transfer actions depends on section 548(d)(1) and applicable state law. Section 548(d)(1) states:

> For the purposes of this section, a transfer is made when such transfer is so perfected that a bona fide purchaser from the debtor against whom applicable law permits such transfer to be perfected cannot acquire an interest in the property transferred that is superior to the interest in such property of the transferee, but if such transfer is not so perfected before the commencement of the case, such transfer is made immediately before the date of the filing of the petition.

Thus, a fraudulent transfer is deemed to have occurred under section 548(d)(1) when the transfer becomes valid against a subsequent bona fide purchaser pursuant to applicable state law.[69] If the transfer is not perfected against a bona fide purchaser before the filing of the petition, the trans-

---

66. Mancuso v. Champion (*In re* Dondi Fin. Corp.), 119 Bankr. 106, 109 (Bankr. N.D. Tex. 1990).

67. Larrimer v. Feeney, 411 Pa. 604, 607, 192 A.2d 351, 353 (1963).

68. Because what constitutes a transfer is a question of federal law, state law on the issue is not controlling. *See* McKenzie v. Irving Trust Co., 323 U.S. 365, 369–70 (1945); First Fed. Sav. & Loan Ass'n v. Hulm (*In re* Hulm), 738 F.2d 323, 326 (8th Cir.), *cert. denied*, 469 U.S. 990 (1984); Lovett v. Shuster, 633 F.2d 98, 104 (8th Cir. 1980). For purposes of § 548, "transfer" should be construed to include an obligation incurred. *See* 11 U.S.C. §§ 101(54), 548(a); *see also* 1A Bankr. Serv. L. Ed. § 5D:6, at 13–14 (1990) ("a 'transfer' should be construed as including the incurring of an obligation").

69. *See* Sandoz v. Bennett (*In re* Emerald Oil Co.), 807 F.2d 1234, 1237 (5th Cir. 1987); Madrid v. Lawyers Title Ins. Corp. (*In re* Madrid), 725 F.2d 1197, 1200 (9th Cir.), *cert. denied*, 469 U.S. 833 (1984); *Lovett*, 633 F.2d at 104; Furedy v. Appleman (*In re* Vodco Volume Dev. Co.), 567 F.2d 967, 970 (10th Cir. 1977), *cert. denied*, 439 U.S. 806 (1978); Main v. Brim (*In re* Main), 75 B.R. 322, 326 (Bankr. D. Ariz. 1987); Frank v. Berlin (*In re* Frank), 39 B.R. 166, 171 (Bankr. E.D.N.Y. 1984); Schatzman v. Campo (*In re* Oesterle), 2 B.R. 122, 124 (Bankr. S.D. Fla. 1979).

fer is deemed to have occurred immediately before the date of the filing.[70] The purpose of section 548(d)(1) is twofold: first, the time of perfection serves as an objective point in computing the reach-back period of the trustee; and, second, it discourages secret, i.e., unperfected, liens.[71]

As mentioned, "transfer" is broadly defined in section 101(54) to include every mode or disposition of an interest in property, voluntary or involuntary. Once the triggering transfer has been identified, you must determine whether the transfer is one of an interest in the debtor's property. This is usually the case; however, it is important to realize that the estate can only recover that interest the debtor possessed.

### 14.5.1.1 Lack of Reasonably Equivalent Value

Under section 548(a)(1)(B)(i), receiving less than a reasonably equivalent value for a transfer made or obligation incurred is one of the necessary elements of a constructive fraudulent transfer. The assessment of reasonably equivalent value is objective and is generally a question of fact.[72] Courts have employed a case-by-case approach in assessing reasonably equivalent value while observing the unfairness of applying mechanical tests.[73] Reasonably equivalent

---

70. *See Oesterle*, 2 B.R. at 124 (actual "transfer" made well before one year of the filing of the petition but recorded two days after the filing; held, transfer deemed to have occurred immediately before filing).

71. *In re* Madrid, 725 F.2d at 1200; Nemeti v. Seaway Nat'l Bank (*In re* Nemeti), 65 B.R. 391, 395 (Bankr. N.D.N.Y. 1986); *see* 4 COLLIER ON BANKRUPTCY ¶ 548.08, at 548-87 to -88.

72. *See* Klein v. Tabatchnick, 610 F.2d 1043, 1047 (2d Cir. 1979); Jacoway v. Anderson Cajun's Wharf (*In re* Ozark Restaurant Equip. Co.), 74 B.R. 139, 143 (Bankr. W.D. Ark.), *remanded*, 77 B.R. 686 (W.D. Ark.), *on remand*, 83 B.R. 591 (Bankr. W.D. Ark. 1987), *aff'd in part and rev'd in part*, 850 B.R. 342 (8th Cir. 1988); *but see* BFP v. Resolution Trust Corp., 511 U.S. 531, 114 S. Ct. 1757 (1994) (bid price held to constitute reasonably equivalent value in noncollusive nonjudicial foreclosure sale); Durrett v. Washington Nat'l Ins. Co., 621 F.2d 201, 203 (5th Cir. 1980) (question of law in mortgage foreclosure context).

value is not susceptible to simple formulation. Ideally, it should signify the reasonable estimate of what can be realized from the debtor's assets by converting them into cash under possibly guarded (but not forced-sale) conditions. It is wrong-headed to think of reasonably equivalent value as a "number," or more correctly, a point estimate of value.[74] Rather, data on prices and market fluctuations suggest that a careful analysis of value must begin with an interval estimate of values that captures a more accurate and reliable picture of property, market, and value. Thus, value that falls short of a reasonably equivalent value is value that falls outside the range of values one would expect reasonable parties to reach based on the information available to each at the time of the transfer. The value that is the fruit of ordinary business dealings, that is consistent with the ordinary business practices of others, and that is in the range of values one could reasonably anticipate strongly suggests a reasonably equivalent value. The value that is the product of secret dealings, extraordinary business practices, or falls outside the range of values one could reasonably anticipate strongly suggests a failure of a reasonably equivalent value. Any greater precision comes at the sake of clarity.

"Value" is defined as "property, or satisfaction or securing of a present or antecedent debt of the debtor, but does not include an unperformed promise to furnish support to the debtor or to a relative of the debtor."[75] Under the Code, the proper valuation of an asset for purposes of assessing rea-

---

73. *See, e.g.*, Adwar v. Capgro Leasing Corp. (*In re* Adwar), 55 B.R. 111, 115 (Bankr. E.D.N.Y. 1985); *see also* Rubin v. Mfrs. Hanover Trust Co., 661 F.2d 979, 994 (2d Cir. 1981) (rejecting any requirement of "mathematical precision" in determining reasonably equivalent value); *but see Durrett*, 621 F.2d at 203 (observing that a foreclosure bid price of less than 70% of fair market value would not constitute reasonably equivalent value), *rejected in* BFP v. Resolution Trust Corp., 511 U.S. 531, 114 S. Ct. 1757 (1994).

74. *See* David S. Salsburg & Jack F. Williams, *A Statistical Approach to Claims Estimation in Bankruptcy*, 32 WAKE FOREST L. REV. 1119 (1997).

75. 11 U.S.C. § 548(d)(2)(A).

sonably equivalent value appears to be that "amount which can be realized from the assets within a reasonable time" and not upon immediate liquidation.[76] In addition, where the assets have a greater value as an ongoing business, that value is usually determinative.[77] Although it is clear that payment on an antecedent debt constitutes value, the payment is not dispositive of the issue of reasonably equivalent value.[78] Rather, the debt must be legitimate and bona fide; moreover, the debt must be compared to the value transferred by the debtor to see if reasonably equivalent value is lacking.[79] Unlike the UFTA or the Bankruptcy Code, the Texas UFTA[80] does provide a noninclusive definition of reasonably equivalent value. Under Texas UFTA section 24.004(d), reasonably equivalent value includes, without limitation, a "transfer or obligation that is within the range of values for which the transferor would have willfully sold

---

76. *See, e.g.,* Utility Stationery Stores, Inc. v. Am. Portfolio (*In re* Utility Stationery Stores, Inc.), 12 B.R. 170, 176 (Bankr. N.D. Ill. 1981) (§ 547(b) action).

77. Danning v. Progressive Pharma. Sys., Inc. (*In re* Western Adams Hosp. Corp.), 609 F.2d 929, 930 (9th Cir. 1979) (per curiam).

78. Demusis v. Carr (*In re* Carr), 40 B.R. 1007, 1008 (D. Conn. 1984). For a discussion of different categories of value, *see* 1A Bankr. Serv. L. Ed. §§ 5D:34 to :44, at 36–41.

79. *See* Plymouth United Sav. Bank v. Lee, 278 Mich. 545, 548, 270 N.W. 781, 782 (1936). How about the situation where a debtor who has borrowed $1 million grants a security interest to its creditor in all of its assets worth $5 million: is the perfection of the security interest a fraudulent transfer? We believe common sense would lead one to conclude no. Regardless of the breadth of the security interest, a creditor is only entitled to satisfaction of the debt. In other words, although $5 million in assets are encumbered, it is only to the extent of the $1 million indebtedness. The UFTA follows this commonsense approach. *See* UFTA, Prefatory Note, 7A U.L.A. 639, 641 (1984). This, however, may not be the case under the UFCA. Bad faith coupled with property securing a present advance or antecedent debt in an amount disproportionately small compared with the value of the property may lead a court to find a lack of fair consideration. UFCA § 3(b), 7A U.L.A. 427, 449 (1984).

80. Tex. Bus. & Com. Code Ann. § 24.004(d) (Vernon).

the assets in an [arm's-] length transaction."[81] This definition is consistent with the decision in *Anderson Industries, Inc. v. Anderson (In re Anderson Industries, Inc.)*,[82] which analyzed reasonably equivalent value in light of the fact that the bargained for exchange was reached through arm's-length negotiations where, presumably, the purchaser was the best informed party as to the value of the asset.[83]

Reasonably equivalent value as commonly understood suggests a comparison of the value transferred by the debtor with the value actually received by the debtor.[84] The bargaining position of the parties, their relationship, the adequacy of the price, the prevailing market conditions, and the marketability of the property transferred are all relevant considerations.[85] Beyond this simple formulation, unfortunately, the case law on reasonably equivalent value is hopelessly confused. Aside from several general rules regarding reasonably equivalent value discussed above, each court seems to address the issue in a subjunctive manner. For example, one court, resigned to the fact that no true market comparison could be made to determine reasonably equivalent value because no such market existed, nevertheless created a hypothetical market to gauge the price paid by the transferee.[86] All in all, the cases on reasonably equivalent value have been deficient in providing a sensible and pre-

---

81. *Id.*; *see* Kjeldahl v. United States (*In re* Kjeldahl), 52 B.R. 926, 934 (Bankr. D. Minn. 1985) (reasonably equivalent value is the amount that reasonable minds would agree is a close or fair exchange given all the circumstances surrounding the transfer).

82. 55 B.R. 922 (Bankr. W.D. Mich. 1985).

83. *Id.* at 927–28.

84. *See* 1A Bankr. Serv. L. Ed. § 5D:45, at 42 (1990).

85. *See also* Jacoway v. Anderson (*In re* Ozark Restaurant Equip. Co.), 850 F.2d 342 (8th Cir. 1988) (analysis of reasonably equivalent value in fraudulent transfer context requires consideration of "the entire situation," including market conditions).

86. *See* Cooper v. Ashley Commc'ns, Inc. (*In re* Morris Commc'ns NC, Inc.), 75 B.R. 619, 622–25 (Bankr. W.D.N.C. 1987), *rev'd*, 914 F.2d 458 (4th Cir. 1990).

dictable manner to judge whether a debtor has transferred an asset for less than a reasonably equivalent value.

Based on a careful distillation of the cases, it does appear that a model of reasonably equivalent value may be constructed. The approach suggests that if the process actually employed by the parties to reach a value is reasonable, then the fruit of that process is itself reasonable. Thus, the purchase price of an asset transferred wherein the price was reached by arm's-length negotiations will generally approximate reasonably equivalent value.

For example, the Supreme Court addressed the issue of what constituted reasonable equivalent value in the context of a real property foreclosure in *BFP v. Resolution Trust Corporation*.[87] In that case, the Supreme Court put to rest the issue of how to gauge reasonably equivalent value in the context of a real property foreclosure, where it held that the bid price at a non-collusive real property foreclosure sale, conducted in accordance with state law, was per se reasonably equivalent value. Some commentators have chalked the *BFP* case up to the sanctity of certainty of title in real property. Although an important point, a better view is that a reasonable sale process (that is, a sale process that the legislature has deemed reasonable by its enactment) results in a reasonable sale price. Thus, at a greater level of abstraction, the Supreme Court case in *BFP* contains a treasure trove of valuable lessons on the general questions of what constitutes a reasonably equivalent value.

Another example of the process approach suggested above may be found in the context of intercorporate guaranties. Guaranties may also constitute fraudulent obligations in certain circumstances. This is especially the case in the context of intercorporate guaranties. If you were to study the guaranty cases, you would find that three rules may be deduced. First, an upstream guaranty from a subsidiary guar-

---

87. 511 U.S. 531 (1994).

anteeing the debt of a parent is presumptively for less than a reasonably equivalent value unless the guaranties result from an arm's-length negotiation where the common enterprise was a going concern at the time of the incurrence of the guaranty obligations. Courts reach this result under either the identity of interests rubric or the indirect benefits approach. However, the benefits must be demonstrable and supported by the evidence. Likewise, a cross-stream guaranty where one subsidiary guarantees the debt of another subsidiary may presumptively fail the reasonably equivalent value test, according to many opinions, unless demonstrable benefit can be adduced. Finally, a downstream guaranty, where a parent guarantees the subsidiary's debt, is presumptively valid.

Thus, fraudulent obligations, such as some guaranties, may be proscribed under section 548.[88] It is, however, incorrect to cast aspersions on all guaranties. An emerging trend is developing that embraces a robust, process-sensitive approach[89] to assessing reasonably equivalent value in the context of guaranties, particularly where affiliates are involved, from an enterprise or common group lens. For example, in *In re Image Worldwide*,[90] the Seventh Circuit observed that any indirect benefits to a guarantor may be considered in evaluating whether a reasonably equivalent value was received in exchange for the guaranty obligation.[91] While dated authorities exist to the contrary, recent authority generally rejects the notion that an intercorporate guaranty constitutes a fraudulent obligation per se.

---

88. *See* Jack F. Williams, *The Fallacies of Contemporary Fraudulent Transfer Models as Applied to Intercorporate Guaranties: Fraudulent Transfer Law as a Fuzzy System*, 15 CARDOZO L. REV. 1403 (1994).
89. For a detailed treatment of robust or fuzzy logic in the nature of fraudulent transfers, *see id.*
90. 139 F.2d 574 (7th Cir. 1998).
91. *Id.* at 582.

### 14.5.1.2 Statutorily Defined Financial Distress

Under fraudulent transfer law, a lack of reasonable equivalent value is necessary but not sufficient before a court condemns a transfer made or obligation incurred as constructively fraudulent. In addition to lack of a reasonably equivalent value, the transfer made or obligation incurred must occur when the debtor is (1) insolvent or rendered insolvent, (2) left with unreasonably small capital, or (3) left with an inability to pay its debts as they became due.

### 14.5.1.3 Insolvent or Rendered Insolvent

Although a thorough discussion of the solvency question is beyond the scope of this text,[92] several additional observations should be made. First, insolvency is a legal term of art. Accounting or finance principles inform the inquiry; they do not constrain it. Thus, the definition of asset or liability, for example, is not a Generally Accepted Accounting Principles (GAAP) question; it is a legal one. Second, in this context, the question is one of bankruptcy law. Finally, the test for insolvency for fraudulent transfers is the same test used to determine insolvency for preference action with one notable exception. In a fraudulent transfer analysis, you must assess insolvency immediately before and after the transfer is made; section 548(a)(1)(A) ensnares transfers made by the debtor while insolvent *or that render a debtor insolvent.* However, under section 547(b)(3), a preference is avoidable when a debtor makes the transfer while insolvent.

Insolvency is not a well-understood or universal term of art. To the contrary, it is a content-driven term. If you ask that insolvency be defined, you must first specify the purpose for which you seek the definition. To be sure, classic

---

92. For a thorough discussion of solvency, including proof issues, *see* Frank R. Kennedy, Vern Countryman, & Jack F. Williams, Kennedy, Countryman, & Williams on Partnerships, Limited Liability Entities, and S Corporations in Bankruptcy, ch. 6 (2000).

definitions abound, often captured in reference to a balance sheet: Solvency is that condition whereby a company's liabilities exceed its assets. Of course, financial statements employ book values, and, in all likelihood, do not reflect assets at fair market value or all liabilities. Thus, insolvency law forced consideration of a company's assets and liabilities at some version of fair value. Adjusted balance sheet formulas also quickly slipped the moors of GAAP, requiring a consideration of additional assets (such as causes of action) and additional liabilities (such as contingent liabilities). GAAP became the handmaiden of insolvency tests and not its jailor.

The Bankruptcy Code applies the adjusted balance sheet approach to determine solvency. Under this approach, a debtor is insolvent when the sum of its debts is greater than its property at a fair valuation. In employing the Bankruptcy Code's adjusted balance sheet test of insolvency, a fair valuation—not the book value or cost of an asset—is used.[93] Equitable rights, such as the rights of subrogation and of contribution, are assets that must be quantified.[94] Further, goodwill, other intangible property, and, to the extent not reflected in goodwill or some other asset already accounted for, discounted cash flow constitute assets that should be quantified and considered in assessing insolvency in a going-concern analysis only.

The "fair valuation" standard under the Bankruptcy Code is not self-evident. A fair valuation does not mean the amount the property would bring in the worst circumstances or in the best. For example, a forced sale price is not necessarily fair value, though it may be used as evidence on the question of fair value, particularly where the debtor is on its financial deathbed as of the transfer date. Likewise, fair market value is not necessarily fair value, though it may be

---

93. *Euro-Swiss Int'l Corp.*, 33 B.R. at 885–86.
94. Join-In Int'l (U.S.A.) Ltd. v. N.Y. Wholesale Distribs. Corp. (*In re* Join-In Int'l (U.S.A.) Ltd.), 56 B.R. 555, 560 (Bankr. S.D.N.Y. 1986); *see* 1A Bankr. Serv. L. Ed. § 5D:76, at 60 (1990).

used as evidence on the question of fair value, particularly where the debtor is a going concern as of the transfer date.

In the quest of employing reasonable approaches to the determination of a fair valuation, some courts have embraced going-concern values for inventory and not for equipment,[95] while others have disregarded illiquid assets in the insolvency calculus altogether.[96] Still other courts have employed a temporal standard in assessing which valuation to use, that is, a presumption that going-concern value is applicable unless at the time of transfer the business is in such a precarious financial condition that the liquidation value of the assets is more appropriate.[97] It appears that the present consensus among cases suggests that where at the time of the transfer under scrutiny, if the debtor's business is a going concern and not on its financial deathbed, then a going concern valuation is appropriate. However, where at the time of the transfer or action under scrutiny, if a debtor's business is in such a financial state as to lead one to conclude that it was more likely than not that the debtor would liquidate in the reasonably foreseeable future, then a fair valuation should more closely approximate orderly liquidation value to liquidation value.[98] Therefore, one must assess the business status of the debtor at the time of the transfers made or obligations incurred.

### 14.5.1.4 Left with Unreasonably Small Capital

In addition to the adjusted balance sheet test for insolvency, the Bankruptcy Code fraudulent transfer provision can also condemn a transfer made for less than a reasonably equivalent value if the debtor was left with unreasonably small capital. While adequate market capitalization may be a rel-

---

95. *See, e.g.*, *Ohio Corrugating Co.*, 91 B.R. at 437–38.
96. *See, e.g.*, Wieboldt Stores, Inc. v. Schottenstein, 94 B.R. 488, 505 (N.D. Ill. 1988).
97. *See, e.g.*, Vadnais Lumber Supply, Inc. v. Byrne (*In re* Vadnais Lumber Supply, Inc.), 100 B.R. 127, 131 (Bankr. D. Mass. 1989).
98. *See* KENNEDY, COUNTRYMAN & WILLIAMS, *supra* note 90.

evant indicator in assessing whether the debtor was left with unreasonably small capital, the primary focus by the use of the term "capital" is on current assets, total assets, working capital, and both current and long-term liabilities.

Garrick Hollander does an excellent job in introducing the concept of unreasonably small capital as required under fraudulent transfer law.[99] His analysis of the components of capital is illuminating and worth careful consideration. He observes:

> Total capital consists of: (i) fixed capital (capital invested in fixed assets); and (ii) working capital (capital invested in current assets). Fixed assets cannot be employed without the existence of current assets. Cash is necessary to meet the day to day obligations. Receivables are necessary in any business because many customers cannot afford to pay cash and thus depend on the ability to buy goods and services on credit. The company's inventory is essential for production and sales. Marketable securities are a good source of liquidity, yet provide a company with a greater return on its investment than would the investment in cash. Hence, "the main function of working capital is to keep the wheels of business moving."[100]

Hollander then presses for a more precise meaning of working capital. He states:

> Working capital consists of two types: (i) gross (total of all current assets); and (ii) net (excess of current assets over current liabilities). The concept of gross working capital (a going concern concept) is important to the management of a company because

---

99. Garrick A. Hollander, *Defining "Unreasonably Small Capital" in Fraudulent Transfer Cases: Ration Analysis May Provide an Answer*, 49 Bus. Law. 1185, 1200 (1994).

100. *Id.* (quoting N.K. Agrawal, *Working Capital—Concepts, Planning and Financing*, Chartered Accountant, Apr. 1987, at 865–68).

> the profitability of fixed assets depends upon use of all the current assets. The concept of net working capital is important to management because it helps them ascertain the financial soundness of the company, "and is of special interest to sundry creditors and suppliers of short-term loans and advances. It creates confidence among the creditors about the security of their credits."[101]

Hollander correctly notes that gross working capital itself can be further classified into two types: permanent and variable.

> Permanent working capital represents that portion of total current assets that must remain at all times to maintain the minimum level of operations. Generally, permanent working capital is financed from long-term sources, preferably from owners/shareholders capital. Variable working capital, however, fluctuates in volume according to a company's expansion or contraction in its production or trading. The variable portion of working capital may be financed from short-term sources such as bank financing.[102]

Working capital investment is both industry- and company-specific. Factors that ought to be considered include:

- type of business;
- business cycle;
- production cycle;
- credit policy;
- supply/demand conditions;
- market conditions;
- growth potential;

---
101. *Id.*
102. *Id.*

- dividend policy;
- inflation; and
- financing of working capital either through internal or external sources.[103]

In addition to these factors, an assessment of unreasonably small capital would include both a horizontal and vertical analysis of the company's balance sheets and income statements as described above. For example, a trend analysis of the balance sheets would show over time a more robust picture of current assets, total assets, working capital (current assets net current liabilities), and leverage (both current and long-term liabilities). Ratios based on the financial statements calculated over time could include total current liabilities to total assets, current assets to current liabilities (working capital). A trend analysis of the income statements would show over time sales, operating income, interest expense, net income before taxes, and earnings before interest, taxes, depreciation, and amortization (EBITDA). Furthermore, a trend analysis of the financial statements should pick up any increase in debt maturities because of transactions, any unforeseeable or unplanned intervening events that arose after the transfer date, and borrowing availability.

In addition to the analysis described above, an expert would routinely undertake a financial ratio analysis to determine whether the debtor was left with unreasonably small capital. Thus, the expert would calculate the key financial ratios of the debtor in an effort to assess its financial position based on its financial statements as reported and as constructed for the testing period. In undertaking this analysis, an expert would employ both a trend analysis (comparison of the debtor's ratios across time) and an analysis of comparable companies in the industry.

---

103. *Id.*

### 14.5.1.5 Left with an Inability to Pay Debts as They Become Due

A third alternative test for financial distress is where the debtor is left with an inability to pay debts as they become due. Thus, an expert would also investigate and analyze whether a debtor intended to incur debts beyond the debtor's ability to pay those debts as they come due. Employing this test, the expert would assess the existing liquidity ratios and working capital levels discussed above. An expert would also consider the debtor's borrowing availability under any financing arrangement, which would strongly bolster the view that the debtor was able to pay current obligations as they came due. Additional factors would include history of payables performance, violation of financial covenants, actual business operations, the fact that the debtor continued operations and generated profits for some significant time after the transfer (if applicable), that public bondholders invested in the debtor (if a public company), that equity continued to invest in the debtor, and that sophisticated creditors continued to do business with the debtor, including extending credit for goods provided and services performed.

## 14.6 CHANGES TO FRAUDULENT TRANSFER LAW

There are several amendments to fraudulent transfer law found under section 548. Three are addressed in these materials. Please note that these changes generally apply to all fraudulent transfer actions commenced ancillary to any bankruptcy case filed on or after October 17, 2005.

### 14.6.1 *Two-Year Reach-Back Period*

As mentioned previously, BAPCPA amended section 548 to expand the reach-back period for scrutinizing transfers made and obligations incurred as either actually or constructively fraudulent. The amendment increased the period from one year to two years under general section 548(a)(1) attack. The intent was to expand the powers of the trustee, especially in the areas of fraudulent transfer attacks on transactions to insiders, although the language does not limit itself to those special situations. Whether this expansion is significant is subject to debate in light of the much longer periods already embodied in section 544(b) as that section incorporates state fraudulent transfer law. Of course, one can surmise that where a situation presents itself outside the one-year period but within two years from the petition date, and the trustee cannot find an actual creditor with an allowed unsecured claim who could have avoided the transfer, then the expanded reach-back period would be welcome relief.

### 14.6.2 *Insider Employment Contracts*

BAPCPA also sought to ensure the trustee and the courts that the power to scrutinize insider employment contracts existed and that the standards to avoid such contracts, in the appropriate circumstances, should be loosened. First, BAPCPA amends the general flush language of section 548 to include as a modifier of both "transfer" and "obligation" any transfer or obligation to or for the benefit of an insider under an employment contract. "Insider" is broadly defined at section 101(31) to include, in the situation where the debtor is a corporation, a director, officer, or person in control of the debtor, or an affiliate of the debtor, among others. The term "employment contract," while not directly defined under the Bankruptcy Code, will continue to maintain the meaning that it has under applicable non-bankruptcy law. Whether this amendment is necessary is also subject to debate; it appeared that the existing definitions of "transfer" and "obligation" were sufficiently broad to include both the creation of the employment contract and any payments or transfers thereunder.

Second, BAPCPA amends the conditions of financial distress that may result in the avoidance of any transfer made or obligation incurred. Specifically, once a court finds a lack of a reasonably equivalent value[104] in exchange for any obligation incurred or transfer made pursuant to an employment contract with an insider, the trustee need only show that such transfer made or obligation incurred was not in the ordinary course of business. Much is left to imagination under this new replacement for financial distress. For example, is it the transfer made or obligation incurred that must be outside the ordinary course, or is it the employment contract in the first instance? A reading consistent not only with the language of section 548(a)(1)(B)(ii)(IV) but also with other provisions in the Bankruptcy Code that mandate scrutiny on a transaction-by-transaction basis is suggested.[105] Additionally, when assessing ordinary course, whose ordinary course are we considering? Is it the ordinary course of the debtor? The insider? The industry? Healthy members of the industry only? The proper focus should be to borrow from the authorities under section 363 and employ both a horizontal and vertical assessment of ordinary course. However, the proper focus should also be on whether the creditors may maintain a legitimate claim of unfair surprise based on all the circumstances known or reasonably known to them at the time of the transfer made or obligation incurred under the insider employment contract. Of course, even if the insider employment contract falls within the ordinary course, it may nonetheless fail section 548 under the general dictates of financial distress coupled with a lack of a reasonably equivalent value, nothing in that section suggesting otherwise.

### 14.6.3 Condemnation of Certain Asset-Protection Strategies

BAPCPA adds a new subsection (e) to section 548, designed to condemn certain asset-protection strategies commonly

---

104. One must note that value as defined in § 548(d)(2)(A) does not include an unperformed promise to furnish support to the debtor.

105. *See, e.g.,* 11 U.S.C. § 547(c)(2) (ordinary course of business defense on transfer-by-transfer basis); 11 U.S.C. § 363 (transfers made in and out of ordinary course).

employed under applicable non-bankruptcy law. Specifically, section 548(e)(1) provides:

> In addition to any transfer that the trustee may otherwise avoid, the trustee may avoid any transfer of an interest of the debtor in property that was made on or within 10 years before the date of the filing of the petition, if—
>
> (A) such transfer was made to a self-settled trust or similar device;
>
> (B) such transfer was by the debtor;
>
> (C) the debtor is a beneficiary of such trust or similar device; and
>
> (D) the debtor made such transfer with actual intent to hinder, delay, or defraud any entity to which the debtor was or became, on or after the date that such transfer was made, indebted.[106]

Again, although some may argue that the main thrust of new section 548(e) is already covered by existing fraudulent transfer law, one cannot argue with the proposition that the trustee's powers to scrutinize the self-settled trust scenario have expanded greatly. Two key changes include the following: First, the new subsection extends the reach-back period to ten years. Second, the new subsection broadens the definition of self-settled trust by including the ambiguous language "similar device." The ramifications of the addition of "similar device" to section 548(e)(1)(A) are presently not well understood. To what extent will the "similar device" language be used to scrutinize favorite asset-protection planning devices such as IRAs, retirement funds, or even the limited liability entity? The ambiguity and importance of the language means that bankruptcy courts will be left to interpret the meaning of "similar device." Thus, for example, if one were to identify the primary attributes of

---

106. 11 U.S.C. § 548(e)(1).

the self-settled trust, it would be found that the self-settled trust is simply the alter ego of the debtor and that the self-settled trust protects assets from the claims of creditors because it acts as a restraint on the alienation of property. Thus, would a bankruptcy court embrace a definition of "similar device" to include any alter ego form that restrains alienation? Only time will tell.

## 14.7 POST-PETITION TRANSFERS UNDER SECTION 549(B)

With a couple of enumerated exceptions at sections 549(b)-549(c), a trustee may avoid a transfer of property of the estate that occurs after the commencement of the case and is not authorized by the Bankruptcy Code or by the bankruptcy court. Recall the discussions about unauthorized transactions with the debtor, such as the transaction outside the ordinary course of the debtor's business. Absent court approval of the outside-the-ordinary-course-of-business transaction, the trustee under section 549(a) may avoid the transaction and recover any transfer of estate property.

## 14.8 SETOFF UNDER SECTION 553

Pursuant to section 553, any right of setoff that existed under state law is preserved in a bankruptcy. Thus, there is no right to setoff created by bankruptcy law; section 553 merely recognizes a state-created right to setoff, but only in certain circumstances.

### *14.8.1 Right to Setoff*

Setoff is a time-honored creditor's remedy whereby mutual debts may be "netted out." The genesis of the doctrine of setoff can be traced to Roman law and, although not a part of early English common law, has been a part of American common law since the middle seventeenth century. As the U.S. Supreme Court cogently observed, the doctrine of setoff is grounded on the absurdity of making A pay B when B owes A.

Because the Bankruptcy Code does not create any independent right of setoff, one must review state law to assess whether a right to setoff exists at all. Traditionally, the right to setoff exists when the following four conditions are met:

- The fund to be set off is the property of the debtor.
- The fund is deposited without restrictions.
- The existing indebtedness is due and owing.
- There is a mutuality of obligation between the debtor and the creditor, and between the debt and the fund on deposit.

Setoff is thus a method to net debts, usually arising out of unrelated transactions. Although state law is not uniform as to how one effects a right to setoff, generally, the courts have concluded that a creditor must take three steps to effectuate its setoff right. First, the creditor must decide to exercise the right to setoff. Second, the creditor must take some action that accomplishes the setoff. Third, the creditor must make some record that evidences that the right to setoff has been exercised. Under the majority rule, the mere declaration of intent to setoff is ineffective to accomplish setoff. There are, however, several jurisdictions where no overt act is necessary.

A typical example of the right to setoff often arises in the traditional bank/customer relationship. For example, a customer maintains a deposit account at a bank. This relationship is traditionally viewed as a creditor/debtor relationship. The customer then executes a promissory note, promising to pay the bank a sum of money in return for a car loan. Upon the execution of the note, an additional customer/bank relationship exists. In this relationship the customer is the debtor, the bank is the creditor. If the customer defaults on the promissory note, the bank's right to setoff arises. The customer is the bank's creditor in relation to the deposit account, but is also a debtor in relation to the promissory note. The bank is a creditor as to the promissory note, but is a debtor as to the deposit account. Mutuality of obligation exists. The conditions necessary for the right to setoff are all present.

Only mutual debts may be set off under section 553(a). A debt is considered mutual when it is between the same parties in the same right or capacity. The debts need not, and usually do not, arise out of the same transaction. Section 553 requires that both the funds and the debt arise prior to the filing of the bankruptcy petition.

### 14.8.2 Limitations on a Creditor's Right to Setoff

Although the Bankruptcy Code does not create any right to setoff, it does delineate the procedure by which a creditor can exercise its non-bankruptcy setoff right. There are several limitations on a creditor's ability to effectuate a setoff.

- If the creditor's claim is disallowed other than under section 502(b)(3), any setoff can be avoided.

- If a creditor effects the setoff within 90 days of bankruptcy, while the debtor is insolvent, and if it can be proved that the deposit was made for the purposes of obtaining a right to setoff, the setoff is voidable by the trustee under section 553(a)(3).

- If a creditor effects a setoff within 90 days of bankruptcy, while the debtor is insolvent, and if it can be proved that the creditor's claim was transferred to it by an entity other than the debtor, the setoff is voidable by the trustee under section 553(a)(2).

The Bankruptcy Code modifies prior law dramatically in granting the trustee power to avoid a setoff exercised within 90 days of bankruptcy, not only where deposits have been built up with an intent to exercise setoff or a claim has been transferred to set up a setoff right, but also where there has been an improvement in position by the creditor within the 90-day period. Under section 553(b), the trustee may void a setoff to the extent that an insufficiency existing at the date of setoff is less than an insufficiency existing on the latter of (i) the first day of the 90-day period or (ii) the first day within that period on which an insufficiency existed. The insufficiency relates to the extent to which the amount owed by a debtor exceeds the amount owed to that debtor.

Significantly, the power to recover under section 553(b) is absolute; the power does not hinge on the insolvency of the debtor. Furthermore, of great significance is the fact that the improvement in position test under section 553(b) only applies to the pre-petition setoff. Thus, mere improvement of a creditor's position is not voidable by the trustee when the creditor does not set off prior to bankruptcy. The creditor who rolls the dice and refrains from pre-petition setoff can ride the tide of any increase in the debtor's funds.

The dual standard between the treatment by the Bankruptcy Code of pre-petition and post-petition setoff reflects a policy to discourage pre-petition setoff, thus maintaining a source of working capital for the debtor's reorganization.

### 14.8.2.1 Calculation of Possible Recovery

To calculate the amount the trustee is entitled to recover from the creditor, one must make the following basic calculations:

- calculate the insufficiency, if any, at the time of the setoff;
- calculate the insufficiency, if any, as of the 90th day preceding the bankruptcy filing; and
- if the insufficiency at the time of the setoff is greater than the insufficiency at the time of the bankruptcy filing, calculate the insufficiency for every successive day from the bankruptcy filing date until you reach 90 days back.

The trustee may then recover from the creditor the amount equal to the difference between (i) the setoff date insufficiency and (ii) the "first date insufficiency" (or the insufficiency amount on the first date in the 90-day window when such amount is less than the setoff date insufficiency). This amount is the improvement in position. If the amount subject to setoff is always greater than the debt (i.e., the lender is always oversecured), or the amount of the setoff date insufficiency is always greater than the "first date" insufficiency amount (i.e., no improvement), then there is no insufficiency and no funds can be recovered by the trustee.

### 14.8.2.2 Additional Analysis and Illustrations

The following three examples illustrate, in a step-by-step fashion, the workings of the recovery provisions of the statute.

(Example 1)

*Step 1.* Ninetieth day preceding the filing of the petition in bankruptcy, or the first date within the 90-day period on which there was an insufficiency:

Amount debtor owed—$1 million

Amount subject to setoff—$500,000

Insufficiency—$500,000

*Step 2.* At time of setoff:

Amount debtor owed—$1 million

Amount subject to setoff—$700,000

Insufficiency—$300,000

*Step 3.* Amount subject to recovery by trustee:

Trustee could recover $200,000. The basis for this conclusion is that the insufficiency on the 90th day preceding the date of filing, or on the first date within the 90-day period in which there was an insufficiency, exceeded the insufficiency at the time of setoff by $200,000.

(Example 2)

***Step 1.*** Ninetieth day preceding the filing of the petition in bankruptcy:

Amount debtor owed—$1 million

Amount subject to setoff—$1 million

Insufficiency—None

***Step 2.*** First day within the 90 days preceding the filing on which there was an insufficiency:

At all times during the 90-day period, the amounts on deposit equaled or exceeded the amount owed to creditor.

***Step 3.*** Amount setoff:

Creditor setoff the amount on deposit against the entire amount owed to creditor.

***Step 4.*** Amount subject to recovery by trustee:

Since there was no insufficiency at any time during the 90 days preceding filing of the petition, creditor did not improve its position during that time; consequently, no part of the amount setoff was subject to recovery under section 553.

(Example 3)

***Step 1.*** Ninetieth day preceding the filing:

Amount debtor owed—$1 million

Amount subject to setoff—$1 million

Insufficiency—None

***Step 2.*** The first date within the 90-day period in which there was an insufficiency:

The debtor borrowed an additional $200,000, creating a total debt of $1.2 million. At the same time, the debtor withdrew $100,000, leaving a total amount of $900,000 subject to setoff.

Insufficiency—$300,000

*Step 3.* At time of setoff:

The debtor had paid down its debt to $400,000. The amount on deposit equaled or exceeded $400,000. The creditor setoff the amount on deposit against the debt owed.

Insufficiency—None

*Step 4.* Amount subject to recovery by the debtor:

The debtor could recover $300,000. The basis for this conclusion is that the first insufficiency within the 90 days prior to the filing exceeded the insufficiency at the time of setoff by $300,000. In the type of factual setting illustrated by Example 3, it is conceivable that the entire setoff amount could be recovered by the trustee. This would be the result if in Step 2 of Example 3, the trustee had withdrawn $200,000. The result would have been an insufficiency of $400,000, which would then be the amount of the improvement in position in Step 3; consequently, the entire $400,000 setoff could be recovered.

## 14.9 AVOIDANCE POWER LIABILITY UNDER SECTION 550

The liability of a transferee of an avoided transfer is governed by section 550(a). After avoiding a transfer, the trustee may recover the actual property transferred or, if the court orders, the value of the property transferred. The stated policy of preferring return of the property rather than its value is to avoid unnecessary contests over valuation. Any avoidable transfer is automatically preserved for the benefit of the estate under section 551, thus promoting equality of distribution among creditors and honoring priorities established in the Bankruptcy Code.

Not only is the initial transferee or the entity for whose benefit the transfer is made liable under section 550(a), but also any subsequent transferee. Nevertheless, any subsequent transferee from the initial transferee may absolve its liability if it can show it has given value in good faith. Although unable to absolve itself from total liability, any initial transferee is entitled to a credit for any "improvements" made to the property in good faith. Finally, although the trustee may have several legitimate target defendants, the trustee will receive but one satisfaction.

# CHAPTER 15

# CLAIMS AND DISTRIBUTION

The historic core of bankruptcy law is the claims process. Holders of claims[1] participate in the bankruptcy case and ultimately receive a distribution from property of the estate. Moreover, it is the claim that is discharged in bankruptcy, and claims that are subject to the stay. Thus, a broad definition of *claim* enlarges the universe of parties in interest in a bankruptcy case and expands the debtor's right to discharge. The claims process can be highly technical. Although a commonality exists throughout the Bankruptcy Code, each substantive chapter harbors its own peculiarities regarding the claims process. In general, proofs of claim set out the nature and grounds of the claim and circumstances surrounding it. Proofs of claim also identify the amount, extent, and status of the claim.

In some situations, when a claim arises is not self-evident. There are three tests to determine when a claim arises. First, the state law test examines whether the holder of the claim has an action under state law. Second, the pre-petition relationship test seeks to establish whether there is some pre-petition privity, contact, impact, or hidden harm affecting the holder. Lastly, the conduct test looks to the time of the debtor's wrongful conduct to establish when the claim arose.

In some situations, a court may need to estimate claims for purposes of voting and plan feasibility. For these purposes,

---

1. *See* 11 U.S.C. § 101(5) (2006) (defining *claim*).

an estimation of claims is outlined in section 502(c). The methods for estimation include face value, zero value, market theory, forced settlement, discounted value, and summary trial. Ultimately, bankruptcy courts make the determinations, and their findings are regularly upheld on appeal. However, reconsiderations for cause are permitted under section 502(j).

## 15.1 CHAPTER 7 CASE

In a chapter 7 case, all creditors who believe they have a claim against the estate must file a proof of claim before the bar date or their claim will be forever barred and can no longer be satisfied from the property of the estate or enforced against the debtor. The proof of claim must usually be filed within 90 days from the first scheduled date of the first meeting of creditors. The government, including the IRS, has 180 days from the order for relief to file its claim.[2] The proof of claim sets out the nature and grounds for the claim, the circumstances surrounding the claim, and the amount, status, and extent of the claim. If the trustee or any party in interest fails to dispute the proof of claim, the claim is deemed allowed and approved.[3] The distribution of estate assets to satisfy claims in a chapter 7 case is made in strict accordance with section 726. Here, the estate agrees to distribute unencumbered estate property to the allowed priority and unsecured claims. The secured creditor generally receives its collateral or the value of the collateral.[4]

## 15.2 CHAPTER 11 CASE

Although a creditor generally need not file a proof of claim in a chapter 11 case unless the creditor's claim is listed in the debtor's schedules as unliquidated, contingent, or disputed, or the creditor's claim is not listed in the debtor's

---

2. *See* 11 U.S.C. § 502(b)(9) (2006).
3. 11 U.S.C. § 502(a) (2006).
4. *See* 11 U.S.C. § 725 (2006).

schedules, it is usually a good practice to do so.[5] That way, if the case is later converted from a chapter 11 case to a chapter 7 case, the creditor is protected. Moreover, the filing of a proof of claim provides notice to the trustee or debtor-in-possession of the status, extent, and circumstances of the claim in question.

The distribution of estate assets and the treatment of claims in a chapter 11 case are accomplished pursuant to a plan of reorganization usually filed by the debtor. The plan of reorganization will set out the various assets of the estate, the classes of creditors, the amounts and distribution creditors are to receive, and the treatment of the claims. Before soliciting votes on approval of the plan, the debtor must file and have the court approve a disclosure statement. The disclosure statement serves as a prospectus, explaining the plan of reorganization and the treatment of classes of claims. After the disclosure statement is approved, the debtor then solicits votes on the plan, hopefully convincing a majority of the creditors *and* the holders of two-thirds of the amount of claims in each designated impaired class that it is in their best interests to approve the plan. If the plan is approved by the creditors and the bankruptcy court, then the plan is the mechanism by which the various creditors are paid. If the plan is not approved, then creditors may file competing plans in an attempt to obtain a majority approval, or the debtor or creditors may convert the case to a liquidation case under chapter 7.[6]

## 15.3 CHAPTER 13 CASE

Generally, a creditor must file a proof of claim in a chapter 13 case within 90 days from the date of the first scheduled meeting of creditors—the bar date. The proof of claim provides notice to the chapter 13 standing trustee and the debtor of the status, amount, extent, and circumstances of the claim in question.

---

5. *See* 11 U.S.C. § 1111(a) (2006).
6. 11 U.S.C. § 1112 (2006).

The distribution of estate assets and the treatment of claims in a chapter 13 case are accomplished pursuant to a plan filed by the debtor. A chapter 13 plan must provide for full payment of all priority claims (although, unlike in chapter 11, the payments may be extended over the period of the plan), must not discriminate unfairly among claims of the same legal type, and must not modify claims that are secured only by the debtor's principal residence, except that a default on such a claim can be cured and any debt that has been accelerated can be reinstated. Furthermore, a chapter 13 plan cannot extend over three years, or up to five years with the court's permission.

Other than the restrictions above, a chapter 13 plan can alter or affect secured or unsecured claims. A chapter 13 plan can provide for extended payments, a composition, or pro rata monthly payments to creditors until the funding for the plan dissipates. Unlike chapter 11 plans of reorganization, creditors do not have a vote on a chapter 13 plan. After notice and a hearing, if the plan meets the requirements of section 1325, the court can confirm the plan even though a creditor objects.

## 15.4 CLAIMS AND DISTRIBUTION

The Bankruptcy Code establishes certain rules and priorities with respect to the allowance, treatment, and satisfaction of claims. Filing a proof of claim makes the prima facie case for an allowance. Further, the proof of claim is deemed allowed unless there is a timely objection. The grounds for disallowance are set out in section 502(b)(1)–(9), which includes unenforceable claims against the debtor, claims on unmatured interests, and claims that are not timely filed.

One of the major modifications of the Bankruptcy Code is the focus on and characterization of claims. State law generally focuses on the status of creditors as secured or unsecured. The Bankruptcy Code, however, focuses on the status of claims. Thus a creditor is said to have a fully secured claim, an undersecured claim, an oversecured claim, or an unsecured claim. For example, a creditor who is owed $100,000 and possesses a lien in collateral worth $75,000 possesses a secured claim for $75,000 (the value of the underlying collateral) and an unsecured claim for $25,000 (the deficiency).[7] Such a creditor is also known as an undersecured creditor. Further, there is no distinction between consensual and nonconsensual creditors.

## 15.5 SUPPLIERS OF GOODS LEADING UP TO THE BANKRUPTCY

### 15.5.1 Reclamation Rights

The Bankruptcy Code incorporates the state law and Uniform Commercial Code right of a seller of goods to reclaim those goods through the inclusion of section 546(c), which provides:

(1) Except as provided in subsection (d) of this section and in section 507(c), and subject to the prior rights of a holder of a security interest in such goods or the proceeds thereof, the rights and powers of the trustee under sections 544(a), 545, 547, and 549 are subject to the right of a seller of goods that has sold goods to the debtor, in the ordinary course of such seller's business, to reclaim such goods if the debtor has received such goods while insolvent, within 45 days before the date of the commencement of a case under this title, but such seller may not reclaim such goods unless such seller demands in writing reclamation of such goods—

(A) not later than 45 days after the date of receipt of such goods by the debtor; or

(B) not later than 20 days after the date of commencement of the case, if the 45-day period expires after the commencement of the case.

---

7. *See generally* 11 U.S.C. § 506(a) (2006).

(2) If a seller of goods fails to provide notice in the manner described in paragraph (1), the seller still may assert the rights contained in section 503(b)(9).[8]

Timing is a key issue when making a reclamation demand. However, reclamation under section 546(c) of the Bankruptcy Code is rarely an issue, as most debtors have asset-based financing, which provides a prior perfected lien on most goods so that the right of reclamation is rendered moot.[9] Thus, while many creditors still go through the motions of reclamation, it rarely produces results.

### 15.5.2 503(b)(9) Administrative Expenses

On the other hand, the inclusion of a new section 503(b)(9) gives vendors supplying goods in the 20 days before the petition is filed significantly more power. This section states:

(b) After notice and a hearing, there shall be allowed administrative expenses, other than claims allowed under section 502(f) of this title, including— . . .

(9) the value of any goods received by the debtor within 20 days before the date of commencement of a case under this title in which the goods have been sold to the debtor in the ordinary course of such debtor's business.[10]

The series of decisions in *In re Plastech Engineered Products, Inc., et al.* provides a wealth of information on how at least one court views this provision. The first decision, *Plastech I*,[11] begins by summarizing the previous decisions on this provision, stating that in both *In re Global Home*

---

8. 11 U.S.C. § 546(c).
9. Some thought that the changes to this provision made by BAPCPA somehow created a federal right of reclamation different from the UCC and state law, but at least one court has found otherwise. *See In re* Dana Corp., 367 B.R. 409 (Bankr. S.D.N.Y. 2007).
10. 11 U.S.C. § 503(b)(9).
11. 394 B.R. 147 (Bankr. E.D. Mich. 2006), decided on Sept. 16, 2008.

*Products, LLC*[12] and *In re Bookbinder's Restaurant, Inc.*,[13] the courts determined that the allowance of a claim under 503(b)(9) does not give an unqualified right to immediate payment. Further, other than as of the effective date of the chapter 11 plan, payment of administrative expenses is left to the discretion of the court. In determining when the payment should be made, the court in *Global Home* determined that it should consider three factors:

1. The prejudice to the debtor of making the payment;

2. The hardship on the administrative expense holder of not making the payment; and

3. The potential detriment to other parties in the case (i.e., how the cash drain would impact the ongoing operations of the debtor).[14]

There, the court denied the motion seeking immediate payment. It would seem that filing a motion seeking such a payment may be a way to cause the court to (a) direct the payment, (b) direct the debtor to determine if the case is administratively solvent, and/or (c) convert the case to chapter 7.

The court in *Plastech I* then addressed the question at hand, which was the interplay of section 501, which governs the filing of claims; section 502, which governs the allowance of claims; and section 503, administrative expenses. Specifically, the question was whether section 502(d) of the Bankruptcy Code, which provides for the disallowance of a claim filed under section 501 due to the failure to repay an allegedly preferential transfer under section 547, should apply to section 503(b)(9) administrative expenses. Noting that no other court had ruled on the matter, the court reviewed decisions on the question of whether section 502(d) applies to section 503(b) in general and noted a split in the

---

12. 2006 WL 3791955 (Bankr. D. Del. Dec. 21, 2006)
13. 2006 WL 3858020 (Bankr. E.D. Pa. Dec. 28, 2006)
14. *Global Home*, 2006 WL 3791955 at *4.

circuits. The court found that section 502(d) did not apply to section 503(b)(9) for a variety of reasons. Among the most important were:

1. The court agreed with the line of cases finding that section 502(d) was not applicable to section 503, but applied only to claims filed under section 501 and allowed under section 502;

2. Requests for administrative expenses, including 503(b)(9), are not filed under section 501 but rather under section 503(a); and

3. Determining that 502(d) did apply to section 503(b)(9) violates statutory rules of construction.[15]

The second decision in the *In re Plastech Engineered Products, Inc., et al.* (*Plastech II*) case involving section 503(b)(9) is an unpublished decision dated October 7, 2008.[16] This decision determined the question of whether the actual goods in question had to be received by the debtor or simply the value of the goods. The court stated: "In the Court's view, the word *received* modifies the word *goods* and not the *value* that must be received by the debtor to trigger § 503(b)(9)."[17] Thus, the goods in question must actually be received by the debtor to give rise to the claim under section 503(b)(9). This line of reasoning is cited heavily in *In re Goodys' Family Clothing, Inc.*[18]

The third decision in this case is dated December 10, 2008 (*Plastech III*).[19] This decision provided several important points. First, the UCC definition of goods applies to section 503(b)(9) so that there is no claim for services provided.[20] The court cited favorably to *In re Samaritan Alliance*,[21] which

---

15. *Plastech I*, 394 B.R. at 161–64.
16. 2008 WL 5223014.
17. *Id.* at *2.
18. 2009 WL 294384 (Bankr. D. Del. 2009).
19. 397 B.R. 828 (Bankr. E.D. Mich. 2008).
20. *Id.* at 835–36.
21. 2008 WL 2520107 (Bankr. E.D. Ky. June 20, 2008).

provided that electricity is more in the form of a service and does not give rise to a 503(b)(9) expense, and *In re Deer*,[22] which also consulted the UCC to determine the definition of goods when determining if advertising was a good or a service.[23]

Second, *Plastech III* states that the predominant purpose test used in some instances to determine if a contract was for goods or services is not applicable to section 503(b)(9). Where an entity provides both goods and services, it is entitled to section 503(b)(9) treatment for the goods provided, but not the services in a bifurcated manner, unlike the "winner take all" result of the predominant purpose test.[24]

Finally, *Plastech* III states that the goods need not be reclaimable (i.e., identifiable, still in the hands of the debtor, in their original state, and not subject to a superior lien) to give rise to section 503(b)(9) treatment. The court states: ". . . there is nothing in § 503(b)(9) that requires a claimant to also be entitled to a reclamation right under § 546. Section 546 does not limit or control in any way the rights that a claimant has under § 503(b)(9)."[25]

The decision of *In re Brown & Cole Stores, LLC*[26] filed on August 17, 2007, addressed a different set of questions: specifically, whether the creditor needed to be unsecured to be entitled to section 503(b)(9) treatment and whether the 503(b)(9) expense's pre-petition nature possessed the requisite mutuality for setoff purposes with regard to alleged pre-petition breach of contract claim against the holder of the section 503(b)(9) expense. There, the court determined that the provision of goods on a wholly secured basis can give rise to a section 503(b)(9) expense. In answer to the debtor's contention that this was unfair to other creditors,

---

22. No. 06-02460, slip op. at 2 (Bankr. S.D. Miss. June 14, 2007).
23. *See also In re* Goodys' Family Clothing, Inc., 2009 WL 294384 (Bankr. D. Del. Feb. 6, 2009).
24. *Plastech III*, 397 B.R. at 837.
25. 397 B.R. at 838.
26. 375 B.R. 873 (9th Cir. B.A.P. 2007).

the court stated: ". . . if AGI's twenty-day sales claim is fully secured, then payment of it by B&C will free the value of the security for that claim for the benefit of other creditors. If AGI's claim proves to be undersecured or unsecured, then to deny administrative priority would be to ignore the statute, something we cannot do."[27] The court then noted that there was mutuality under the test set forth in *Biggs v. Stovin* (*In re Luz Int'l, Ltd.*),[28] which states:

1. The debtor owes the creditor a pre-petition debt;
2. the creditor owes the debtor a pre-petition debt;
3. the debts are mutual.[29]

Since both the potential breach of contract claim and the sale giving rise to the 503(b)(9) expense were pre-petition, setoff was available.[30] The court went on to note, however, that the issue was premature because the debtor simply alleged a breach of contract claim and had not filed a contested matter or an adversary proceeding to determine those rights. Until the right to payment from the creditor was established, there was nothing to set off against.[31]

## 15.6 SECURED CLAIMS

Secured claimants are generally entitled to the collateral or to the value of the collateral securing their claims. Generally, the trustee will surrender the collateral under section 725, abandon the collateral under section 554, sell the collateral and turn over the proceeds under section 363, or allow the creditor to terminate the stay under section 362(d) and repossess and foreclose on the collateral.

A secured claim is allowed for the full amount of the claim, including post-petition interest on the claim and possible

---

27. 375 B.R. at 878.
28. 219 B.R. 837 (9th Cir. B.A.P. 1998).
29. 219 B.R. at 843–44.
30. 375 B.R. at 879–80.
31. 375 B.R. at 880–81.

attorneys' fees to the extent, but not in excess, of the value of the collateral securing the claim, but only if the creditor is oversecured.[32] Thus, if a creditor is undersecured, it will not be entitled to attorneys' fees or post-petition interest as part of its allowable secured claim.

Property acquired by the debtor's estate after commencement of a case is not subject to any security interest granted under a security agreement executed prior to commencement of the case except to the extent of proceeds, products, offspring, rents, or profits of property if such proceeds, products, offspring, rents, or profits are covered by the security agreement and financing statement. Thus, the Bankruptcy Code extinguishes the effect of after-acquired property clauses contained in the bulk of security agreements.

## 15.7 UNSECURED CLAIMS

Unsecured claims arising prior to the filing of the petition are allowed only to the extent of the amount of the claim as of the date of filing. Except with respect to fully or oversecured *secured* claims, no post-petition interest is allowed on any claim unless a surplus remains after all creditors' claims are paid in full.[33]

Claims filed by insiders and attorneys for services rendered to the debtor are disallowed to the extent that these claims exceed the reasonable value of services rendered by the parties. An insider of a corporate debtor includes a director, officer, person in control, partnership in which the debtor is a general partner, general partner of the debtor, a relative of a general partner, director, officer or person in control of the debtor, or an affiliate.[34]

---

32. *See* 11 U.S.C. § 506(b) (2006).
33. *See* 11 U.S.C. §§ 502(b), 726 (2006).
34. *See* 11 U.S.C. § 101(31) (2006).

## 15.8 CLAIMS FOR UNEXPIRED NON-RESIDENTIAL REAL PROPERTY LEASES

Certain types of claims are capped under the Bankruptcy Code. The policy reason seems to be that in certain types of cases these damages claims would encompass all available assets. The most prominent of these caps is on non-residential real property where the landlord is allowed to recover any unpaid rent due under the lease as of the date of commencement of the case—like any other unsecured claims—but where damages due to the breach of the lease are capped as follows:

The *greater* of:

(1) One year's rent; and

(2) The *lesser* of:

    (a) 15 percent of the remaining lease period's rent; and

    (b) Three years' rent.[35]

The easiest way to unpack this provision is with an example. For the purposes of the example, assume the lease provisions are as follows

- Lease term (LT) = 30 years on a calendar basis beginning on 1/1/2003
- Petition Date (PD) = 6/1/2008
- Rejection Date (RD) = 7/15/2008
- The Monthly Lease Amount starts at $10,000 and escalates at 2.5 percent per year, with the following representing the monthly lease amounts:

---

35. *See* 11 U.S.C. § 502(b)(6) (2006).

| Year | Monthly Rent | Year | Monthly Rent | Year | Monthly Rent |
|---|---|---|---|---|---|
| 2003 | $ 10,000.00 | 2013 | $ 12,800.85 | 2023 | $ 16,386.16 |
| 2004 | $ 10,250.00 | 2014 | $ 13,120.87 | 2024 | $ 16,795.82 |
| 2005 | $ 10,506.25 | 2015 | $ 13,448.89 | 2025 | $ 17,215.71 |
| 2006 | $ 10,768.91 | 2016 | $ 13,785.11 | 2026 | $ 17,646.11 |
| 2007 | $ 11,038.13 | 2017 | $ 14,129.74 | 2027 | $ 18,087.26 |
| 2008 | $ 11,314.08 | 2018 | $ 14,482.98 | 2028 | $ 18,539.44 |
| 2009 | $ 11,596.93 | 2019 | $ 14,845.06 | 2029 | $ 19,002.93 |
| 2010 | $ 11,886.86 | 2020 | $ 15,216.18 | 2030 | $ 19,478.00 |
| 2011 | $ 12,184.03 | 2021 | $ 15,596.59 | 2031 | $ 19,964.95 |
| 2012 | $ 12,488.63 | 2022 | $ 15,986.50 | 2032 | $ 20,464.07 |

### 15.8.1 Known Factors

The case law is clear about the following:

- The *measuring date* is the earlier of:

  i. the date of the filing of the petition; and

  ii. the date on which such lessor repossessed, or the lessee surrendered, the leased property.

  Thus, for our example, the *measuring date = 6/1/2008*

- The *one-year period* equals the 12 months after the measuring date. Thus, from our example, this equals"

  | 6* | $ 11,314.08 | $67,884.49 |
  |---|---|---|
  | 6* | $ 11,596.93 | $69,581.61 |
  | | | **$137,466.10** |

- The *three-year period* equals the 36 months after the measuring date. Thus, from our example, this equals:

  | 6* | $ 11,314.08 | $67,884.49 |
  |---|---|---|
  | 12* | $ 11,596.93 | $139,163.21 |
  | 12* | $ 11,886.86 | $142,642.29 |
  | 6* | $ 12,184.03 | $73,104.17 |
  | | | **$422,794.17** |

## 15.8.2. Questioned Factor

The courts are split on what the 15 percent means. Some say it is 15 percent of the remaining period in a time-based calculation (.15*24.5*12 = 44.1 months) applied to the immediately following months, while others say it is 15 percent of the money due. In our case this means:

15% of the Remaining Time[36] = 44 Months:

| | | |
|---|---|---|
| 6 | $ 11,314.08 | $67,884.49 |
| 12 | $ 11,596.93 | $139,163.21 |
| 12 | $ 11,886.86 | $142,642.29 |
| 12 | $ 12,184.03 | $146,208.35 |
| 2 | $ 12,488.63 | $24,977.26 |
| | | **$520,875.60** |

15% of the Remaining Money[37] =

| | | | | | |
|---|---|---|---|---|---|
| | | 2012 | $ 153,610.15 | 2022 | $ 196,633.97 |
| | | 2013 | $ 157,450.40 | 2023 | $ 201,549.82 |
| | | 2014 | $161,386.66 | 2024 | $ 206,588.57 |
| | | 2015 | $165,421.33 | 2025 | $ 211,753.28 |
| | | 2016 | $169,556.86 | 2026 | $ 217,047.11 |
| 2008 | $67,884.49 | 2017 | $173,795.78 | 2027 | $ 222,473.29 |
| 2009 | $139,163.21 | 2018 | $178,140.67 | 2028 | $ 228,035.12 |
| 2010 | $142,642.29 | 2019 | $182,594.19 | 2029 | $ 233,736.00 |
| 2011 | $146,208.35 | 2020 | $187,159.05 | 2030 | $ 239,579.40 |
| 2012 | $149,863.56 | 2021 | $191,838.02 | 2031 | $ 245,568.89 |
| | $645,761.90 | | $ 1,720,953.10 | | $2,202,965.47 |
| | | | | | $4,569,680.46 |
| | | | | *.15 | **$685,452.07** |

---

36. *In re* Connectix Corp., 372 B.R. 488, 491–94 (Bankr. N.D. Cal. 2007); *In re* Allegheny Int'l, Inc., 136 B.R. 396, 402–03 (Bankr. W.D. Pa. 1991), *aff'd*, 145 B.R. 823, 827–28 (W.D. Pa. 1992); *In re* Ace Elec. Acquisition, *LLC*, 342 B.R. 831, 833 (Bankr. M.D. Fla. 005); *In re* Peters, 2004 WL 1291125, at *6, n.20 (Bankr. E.D. Pa. 2004); *In re* Iron-Oak Supply Corp., 169 B.R. 414, 419–20 (Bankr. E.D. Cal. 1994); *In re* Bob's Sea Ray Boats, Inc., 143 B.R. 229, 231 (Bankr. D.N.D. 1992).

37. *In re* New Valley Corp., 2000 WL 1251858, at *11–12 (D.N.J. 2000); *In re* Andover Togs, Inc., 231 B.R. 521, 545–46 (Bankr. S.D.N.Y. 1999); *In re*

### 15.8.3. Applying 502(b)(6)(A)

The section works out to be as follows:

The greater of one year's rent and (the lesser of 15 percent of the remaining and three years). Thus,

> The greater of:
> $137,466.10 and

> The lesser of:
> ($685,452.07 or $520,875.60) and
> $422,794.17

> Therefore, in our case, it is the three years — $422,794.17

## 15.9. PRIORITIES UNDER THE BANKRUPTCY CODE

Distributions in a chapter 7 case are made in accordance with priorities established by the Bankruptcy Code.[38] Unsecured claims are placed in various categories under the following priorities:

1) Domestic support obligations owed as of the petition date subject to certain trustee fees.

2) Administrative expenses of the case as defined in sections 507(a) and 503(b). These include post-petition tax claims of the estate for which the debtor may not be liable.

3) Claims arising out of authorized post-petition transactions in involuntary cases as defined in section 502(f).

4) Certain employee claims for wages and attendant payroll taxes accrued within 180 days of the bankruptcy filing (or cessation of business) and up to $10,950 per claimant.

---

Today's Woman of Fla., Inc., 195 B.R. 506, 507–08 (Bankr. M.D. Fla. 1996); *In re* Gantos, Inc., 176 B.R. 793, 795–96 (Bankr.W.D. Mich. 1995); *In re* Financial News Network, Inc., 149 B.R. 348, 351 (Bankr. S.D.N.Y. 1993); *In re* Communicall Central, Inc., 106 B.R. 540, 544 (Bankr. N.D. Ill. 1989).

38. *See* 11 U.S.C. § 507(a) (2006).

5) Certain contributions to employee benefit plans arising out of services rendered within 180 days before the filing of the petition and to the extent of the number of covered employees multiplied by $10,950, less the aggregate amount paid to employees in level 4 and by the estate to other benefit plans.

6) Certain farmer and fishermen claims up to $5,400 per individual claimant.

7) Certain deposits in connection with consumer transactions up to $2,425 per claimant.

8) Certain federal, state, and local tax claims, including income or gross receipts for a taxable year ending on or before the petition filing date incurred within three years[39] of the filing of the petition or assessed within 240 days of the filing, taking into account the still-assessable rule.[40]

9) Certain FDIC claims.

10) Wrongful death or personal injury claims as a result of the debtor driving under the influence of alcohol or some other substance.

The claims described in clauses 1 through 10 are defined as priority claims under section 507(a). Priority claims are unsecured claims afforded priority status over other *unsecured claims*; as a general rule, priority claims do not disrupt *secured claims*. The priority scheme delineated in section 726 and set forth above provides that unsecured claims are paid in the priority established above, and no claim in a lower

---

39. 11 U.S.C. § 507(a)(8) priority tax rules are designed to give taxing authorities three years to collect taxes before such taxes become non-priority and dischargeable or 240 days after assessment in long-running tax shelter cases.

40. This subsection applies to certain property taxes incurred before but payable within one year of filing, trust fund taxes, employer employment taxes incurred within three years, certain excise taxes where the transaction is within three years, customs duties, and certain penalties for actual pecuniary loss associated with the aforementioned claims.

class of priority will be paid prior to payment in full of all allowed claims in a higher class of priority. This concept is known as the absolute priority rule.

A further point is necessary when dealing with priority taxes that hinge on certain time periods. The question is whether a prior bankruptcy case has tolled the time periods. The hanging paragraph after 507(a)(8)(G) describes tolling. Time periods in this subsection are tolled if a taxing authority is prohibited under applicable non-bankruptcy law from collecting a tax as a result of a request of a debtor for a hearing and an appeal of any collection action taken or proposed against the debtor. Further, there must be an automatic stay in effect. Lastly, the collection must be precluded by one or more confirmed plans. However, this is a tolling add-on of 90 days if the priority time period is suspended.

Late-filed priority claims may participate in distribution if filed earlier than either 10 days after the mailing to creditors of the summary of the trustee's final report or the date that the trustee commences the final distribution.

## 15.10 DISTRIBUTION TO CREDITORS IN A CHAPTER 11 CASE

In a chapter 11 case, distribution to creditors is governed by the plan of reorganization. The plan must designate and specify the treatment of the classes of claims. Each member of a class must be treated the same as other members of the class. Holders of priority claims (clauses *a* through *h* in the priorities listed above) generally must be paid in full, in cash, under the plan at its consummation. One exception is with priority tax claims, which may be paid in full over a six year period.

Each holder of a claim must either accept the plan or receive as much under the plan as the holder would have received in a liquidation under chapter 7.[41] This requirement

---

41. *See* 11 U.S.C. § 1129(a)(7) (2006).

is known as the "best interests of the creditors" test. Along with the absolute priority rule, the best interests of the creditors test establishes the parameters of all chapter 11 plans. A creditor, however, can be forced under the "cram-down" provisions of chapter 11 to accept a plan notwithstanding its rejection by the creditor's class only if at least one non-insider-impaired class votes in favor of the plan, the plan complies with the absolute priority rule, and the plan is in the best interests of the creditors.[42]

## 15.11 DISTRIBUTION TO CREDITORS IN A CHAPTER 13 CASE

In a chapter 13 case, distribution to creditors is governed by the plan. The chapter 13 plan may designate classes of claims and specify the treatment of the classes.[43] The plan may not discriminate unfairly among claims of the same legal type.[44] The plan must provide for full payment of all priority claims, though the payments may be extended over the period of the plan. Recall that a chapter 13 plan cannot be extended over more than three years, or up to five years with the court's permission. Otherwise, the chapter 13 plan may alter or affect any kind of secured or unsecured debt, provided the plan cannot modify a claim that is secured only by the debtor's principal residence, except that a default on such a claim can be cured, and any debt that has been accelerated can be reinstated.[45] Additionally, a plan can affect secured claims if the lien is left untouched and the stream of payments provided for the secured claim has a present value at confirmation that is at least equal to the value of the secured claim. Nonetheless, if a creditor is fully secured, it must be compensated in full under chapter 13. If a creditor is only partially secured, it is entitled to full compensation to the extent of the value of the collateral. The creditor's unsecured claim, which is repre-

---

42. *See* 11 U.S.C. § 1129(b) (2006).
43. *See* 11 U.S.C. § 1322(a) (2006).
44. *Id.*
45. 11 U.S.C. § 1322(b) (2006).

sented by the deficiency, may be treated like any other unsecured claim.

Unlike chapter 11 reorganization plans, creditors do not vote on a chapter 13 plan. Rather, the court must determine whether the chapter 13 plan satisfies the confirmation requirements under section 1325. If so, the court can confirm the plan even over the objections of creditors. Section 1325 contains a single financial protection for all unsecured creditors: The court cannot confirm a plan if an unsecured creditor would receive more from a distribution under chapter 7 liquidation than he would under the chapter 13 plan. However, the plan must be proposed in good faith.

## 15.12 SUBORDINATION OF CLAIMS

Under the Bankruptcy Code, a claim can be subordinated based on contractual, statutory, or equitable subordination agreements.[46] Generally, the creditor whose claim is to be subordinated on equitable grounds must have committed fraud or other inequitable conduct that has resulted in an unfair advantage to the creditor at the expense of some other claimant. Since equitable subordination is remedial in nature, a claim will be subordinated only to the extent necessary to rectify the harm done. Furthermore, any equitable subordination must be consistent with the provisions of the Bankruptcy Code.

What is the effect of equitable subordination? A claim that is subordinated on equitable grounds does not share in distribution of property of the estate with other claims in its class; rather, the subordinated claim will participate in the estate distribution only after those claims it has been subordinated to are paid in full. An IRS claim or federal tax lien may be subordinated under section 510(c) where the IRS has engaged in misconduct.

---

46. *See* 11 U.S.C. § 510(a)–(c) (2006).

## 15.13 ESTABLISHING AND PROTECTING CLAIMS

All creditors who intend to share in the assets or participate in the administration of the estate should file a proof of claim within the allowable time. The proof of claim should be served on the debtor and the trustee, if one is appointed, and should be filed with the bankruptcy court. A proof of claim evidences a creditor's claim or interest.

A claim is defined under section 101(5) as:

(A) Right to payment, whether or not such right is reduced to judgment, liquidated, unliquidated, fixed, contingent, matured, unmatured, disputed, undisputed, legal, equitable, secured, or unsecured; or

(B) Right to an equitable remedy for breach of performance if such breach gives rise to a right to payment, whether or not such right to an equitable remedy is reduced to judgment, fixed, contingent, matured, unmatured, disputed, undisputed, secured, or unsecured.[47]

There are significant differences and traps for the unwary between the claim rules for a chapter 11 bankruptcy case and for cases in chapters 7 and 13. In chapters 7 and 13 cases, a proof of claim must be filed within 90 days from the first date set for the first meeting of creditors under section 341.[48] The Bankruptcy Rules contain limited exceptions to the deadline.

In a chapter 11 case, the rules are more lenient. The filing of a proof of claim is required only when the debtor schedules a creditor's claim as disputed, contingent or unliquidated; fails to schedule the claim at all; or schedules the wrong amount.[49] However, when a chapter 11 case is converted to chapter 7, a proof of claim should be filed. The bankruptcy courts have generally held that the "deemed

---

47. 11 U.S.C. § 101(5).
48. Bankr. R. 3002(c).
49. 11 U.S.C. § 1111(a) (2006); *see also* Bankr. R. 3003.

filed" provisions of section 1111(a) are applicable only for the chapter 11 case. Thus, upon a conversion to a chapter 7 (or chapter 13) case, the "deemed filed" creditor is out of luck unless it timely files a proof of claim. Further, the debtor may amend its original schedules to alter its treatment or the acknowledged amount of a claim. However, if the debtor lists a claim as "disputed" for the first time in an amended schedule, a creditor is entitled by due process to receive sufficient notice and additional time to subsequently file a proof of claim.[50]

The proof of claim itself is a relatively simple document, but it must be accurately filled out, signed by the party holding the claim, and substantiated by documents (e.g., the note, deed of trust, and security agreements). There are substantial criminal penalties for filing a fraudulent or false claim.

In most cases, it is extremely important to timely file a proof of claim in order to protect a creditor's claim in a bankruptcy case. A properly filed claim is prima facie evidence of the validity and the amount of the claim.[51] The proof of claim will then be relied upon by the chapter 7 trustee, or the debtor-in-possession in a chapter 11 case, as evidence of the amount owed to the creditor and the security held for the claim. Assets of the estate will later be distributed based on the allowed claims filed against the bankruptcy estate. The debtor or the trustee may later object on the basis of the amount, status, or validity of the proof of claim; however, by filing a proof of claim prior to the bar date, the creditor can shift the burden of proof on issues of allowability to the objecting party.

## 15.14 WHY NOT FILE A PROOF OF CLAIM?

As a general rule of thumb, regardless of the chapter under which the case is filed or whether the claim is properly scheduled, one should file a proof of claim. However, as with

---

50. *See* Bankr. R. 1009.
51. 11 U.S.C. § 501 (2006); *see also* Bankr. R. 3001(f).

everything under the law, there are exceptions. When filing a proof of claim, one files an appearance in the bankruptcy case and, thus, submits to the jurisdiction of the bankruptcy court and waives a jury trial for matters related to that claim or core to the bankruptcy case and the debtor's liquidation/ reorganization.[52] This includes most avoidance actions under Title 11. This does not mean that one submits to this jurisdiction and waives a jury trial for all purposes,[53] but it may be an issue that should be considered when filing a proof of claim. Thus, if the debtor scheduled the claim properly and there may be jurisdictional issues, one may not want to file a proof of claim. Note, however, that failing to file a proof of claim in any other circumstances generally means that the claim is lost forever.

---

52. Granfinanciera S.A. v. Nordberg, 492 U.S. 33, 58, 109 S. Ct. 2782 (1989); Lagenkamp v. Culp, 498 U.S. 42, 44, 111 S. Ct. 330 (1990).

53. See 28 U.S.C. 157(b), which excludes personal injury and wrongful death claims from the bankruptcy court's jurisdiction.

# CHAPTER 16

# THE DISCHARGE

To an individual debtor, the single most important feature of modern bankruptcy law is the discharge.[1] Along with exemptions and the carve-out of future income from property of the estate under section 541(a)(6) for chapter 7 cases, the discharge fuels the fresh start of the debtor—a policy of singular importance in individual bankruptcies. There is no need for a discharge for corporations under chapter 7, as the entity ceases to exist. However, both individual debtors and corporations can obtain a discharge under chapter 11 of the Bankruptcy Code (individuals also receive a discharge under chapter 13 of the Bankruptcy Code as well), although the chapter 11 discharge for an individual conforms more to the new chapter 13 discharge as to timing.[2]

## 16.1 DISCHARGE IN GENERAL

In filing for relief under the Bankruptcy Code, an individual's most important objective is a discharge from his debts. The discharge is the heart of the fresh start policy promoted by the Bankruptcy Code. The discharge is granted virtually automatically unless an objecting party can establish that the debtor has engaged in certain prohibited conduct, usu-

---

1. *See* 11 U.S.C. § 727 (2006).
2. *See* 11 U.S.C. §§ 1141(d), 1328(a)–(b) (2006).

ally some type of fraud or bankruptcy crime.[3] The objecting party has the burden of establishing a ground for the denial of a discharge.

## 16.2 EFFECT OF DISCHARGE

A discharge in a bankruptcy case voids any judgment to the extent that it is a determination of the personal liability of the debtor with respect to a pre-petition debt.[4] The discharge also operates as an injunction against the commencement or continuation of an action, the employment of process, or any act, including telephone calls, letters, and personal contacts, to collect, recover, or offset any discharged debt.[5] In effect, the discharge is a total prohibition on debt-collection efforts. Further, under section 524, any attempt to reaffirm a particular debt is void unless the particular provisions of the Bankruptcy Code delineating the requirements of reaffirmation are specifically followed.[6]

## 16.3 NON-DISCRIMINATION PROVISION

To ensure the effectiveness of the discharge, section 525 prohibits a governmental unit from denying, suspending, or refusing to renew a license or permit or deny employment solely because the person involved was discharged under the Bankruptcy Code, was insolvent before the bankruptcy case, or has not paid a dischargeable debt. Additionally, under section 525(b), no private employer may terminate the employment of, or discriminate with respect to employment against, an individual who is or has been a debtor under the Bankruptcy Code, or an individual associated with a debtor under the Bankruptcy Code, solely because the debtor is or has been a debtor under the Bankruptcy Code, was insolvent before the commencement of case un-

---

3. *See* 11 U.S.C. § 727(a) (2006).
4. *See* 11 U.S.C. § 524(a) (2006).
5. *Id.*
6. *See generally* 11 U.S.C. § 524(c) (2006).

der the Bankruptcy Code, or has not paid a debt that is dischargeable under the Bankruptcy Code.

## 16.4 SECTION 1141 DISCHARGE

Under section 1141(d), confirmation of the plan of reorganization discharges the debtor from any debt that arose before the confirmation of the plan. Unlike section 727(a), a partnership or corporation (as well as an individual) may receive a section 1141(d) discharge. Section 1141(d) discharge is broader than the section 727(a) discharge in that the latter discharges any debts that arose before the entry of the order for relief, while the former discharges any debts that arose before the confirmation of the plan.

Nevertheless, there are limits to the section 1141(d) discharge. First, debts excepted from discharge under section 523 are not discharged under section 1141(d) when the debtor is an individual. Second, if the plan provides for liquidation of all or substantially all of the property of the estate, the debtor does not continue in business, and the debtor would be denied a discharge under section 727(a), then confirmation of the plan does not discharge the debtor. These limitations are necessary so that an individual debtor may not employ a chapter 11 liquidation plan to evade the objections to discharge embodied in sections 523(a) and 727(a).

Section 1141 also excepts tax liabilities from chapter 11 discharge if the debtor corporation made a fraudulent return or willfully attempted in any manner to evade or defeat that tax or duty. Moreover, this section also excepts from discharge any debt incurred under false pretenses or by making a false statement.

## 16.5 TAX CLAIMS

A closer look at section 507(a)(8) reveals that priority tax claims are allowed on unsecured claims of governmental units to the extent that such claims are for a tax on or measured by income or gross receipts for a taxable year ending on or before the date of the filing of the petition for which a return is last due (including extensions) after three years before the date of the filing of the petition, assessed within 240 days before the date of the filing of the petition. This is exclusive of any time during which an offer in compromise with respect to that tax was pending or in effect during that 240-day period, plus 30 days. Further, this is also exclusive of any time during which a stay of proceedings against collections was in effect in a prior case under this title during that 240-day period, plus 90 days.

Non-priority/non-dischargeable taxes include:

- Taxes connected with fraudulent returns

- Taxes connected with late returns or a failure to file

- Taxes connected with a willful attempt to evade or defeat a tax

- Governmental fines and penalties to the extent that they are not compensation for actual pecuniary loss. (This category of non-dischargeable debt does not include tax penalties relating to dischargeable taxes or to any transaction or event that occurred more than three years before the filing of the bankruptcy petition.)

The Bankruptcy Code provides that there should be no discharge of fraudulent taxes in section 1141(d). Section 1141(d) defines the effect of confirmation of a chapter 11 plan and specifically discharges certain debts that arose before confirmation. There is an exception for tax liabilities from a chapter 11 discharge if the debtor corporation made a fraudulent return or willfully attempted in any manner to evade or defeat that tax or duty. Further, this provision also makes a discharge exception for any debt incurred under false pretenses or by making a false statement in writing. Corporations cannot discharge a debt based on fraud owed to a governmental unit arising out of false pretenses, false representations, or actual fraud, whether or not based on use of a financial statement in writing. The language of this provision is unclear as to whether these non-dischargeable debts to governmental units must arise from the debtor's own fraudulent dealings with the government or if they extend to claims or fines the government could impose on account of the debtor's defrauding of investors or creditors. Further, debt owed to an individual on a qui tam claim is also not dischargeable. With regard to individuals filing chapter 11 cases, the discharge may be delayed until full performance of the plan absent a chapter 11 hardship discharge.

# CHAPTER 17

# SUBSTANTIVE CONSOLIDATION

Substantive consolidation is not found expressly in the Bankruptcy Code. Instead, it is an equitable remedy that most courts have determined to be consistent with the Bankruptcy Code and policy. If a court orders that two or more bankruptcy estates are to be substantively consolidated, then the multiple estates merge together and are treated as one for the purposes identified in the substantive consolidation order. Substantive consolidation should be contrasted with administrative consolidation or joint administration. Administrative consolidation results in separate bankruptcy estates being consolidated for administrative purposes but retaining their separate substantive character; substantive consolidation results in separate estates being merged into one estate.

Because the question of the propriety of substantive consolidation is driven by factual determinations, there is usually a fact-intensive inquiry, with little opportunity to develop guidance other than through the mapping of clusters of cases. The following are factors that some courts have considered in determining whether substantive consolidation is appropriate.

- Whether prejudice resulting from consolidation is outweighed by greater prejudice posed by continued separation of the bankruptcy estates;

- Whether creditors perceived and/or treated the corporate group as one entity;

- The degree of difficulty in segregating individual corporate assets and liabilities, particularly the state of the records; whether records of transactions were kept along operational or legal entity lines; and whether such records may be disentangled and mapped along legal entity lines;

- The existence and extent of any commingling of assets and business functions and an indication as to whether any such commingling occurred pre-petition or post-petition;

- The existence of parent and intercompany guarantees on loans or any evidence of cross-collateralization, that is, contractual waivers of corporate separateness;

- The extent of the unity of ownership and interests between and among the various corporate entities;

- Whether transfers of assets have occurred without the observance of corporate formalities;

- The profitability of consolidation at a single physical location or as a single entity regardless of location;

- The assumption by the parent of contractual obligations of its subsidiaries;

- The sharing of overhead, management, accounting, and other related expenses among the different corporate entities;

- The failure to distinguish between properties of each entity;

- The shifting of funds from one company to another without observing corporate formalities;
- If the parent company was paying salaries to employees of subsidiaries;
- Whether the subsidiary has inadequate capital;
- The presence or absence of consolidated financial statements or separate financial statements;
- The parent owning all or a majority of the capital stock of the subsidiary;
- The parent, its affiliates, and subsidiaries having common directors or officers;
- The parent's or its affiliates' financing of the subsidiaries;
- The parent shifting people on and off the subsidiaries' board of directors;
- The subsidiaries having substantially no business except that with the parent or its affiliates or no assets except those conveyed to it by the parent or the affiliate;
- The parent referring to the subsidiary as a department or division;
- The directors of the subsidiary not acting independently in the interest of the subsidiary, but taking direction from the parent;
- The parent, its affiliates, and the subsidiary acting in the same business location.

# CHAPTER 18

# POST-CONFIRMATION ISSUES

Until the early 1990s, once a plan of reorganization was confirmed, there was relatively little judicial activity. At most, there were a few hearings on applications for final compensation of the professionals who were paid from the estate and a few tag-end hearings on objections to claims. Under the formal provisions of the Bankruptcy Code, the statutory language implied that the retention of post-confirmation jurisdiction was primarily intended to deal with any disputes over the construction of any provisions of the plan or the implementation of its provisions. This concept is partially embedded in the language of section 1123(b)(3):

> [A] plan may (3) provide for—
>
> (A) the settlement or adjustment of any claim or interest belonging to the debtor or to the estate; or
>
> (B) the retention and enforcement by the debtor, by the trustee, or by a representative of the estate appointed for such purpose, of any claim or interest.[1]

Perhaps the broadest implied post-confirmation jurisdiction under the catch-all provision under subsection 1123(b)(6):

---

1. 11 U.S.C. § 1123(b)(3).

include any other appropriate provision not inconsistent with the applicable provisions of [the Bankruptcy Code].[2]

Section 1142 does not appear to broaden the scope of postconfirmation jurisdiction except in the limited sense that under subsection (a), a party in interest may file a motion or an adversary proceeding compelling the reorganized debtor to "carry out the plan" and to "comply with any prior orders of the court," and under subsection (b), a party in interest may also file a motion or adversary proceeding to compel the reorganized debtor and any other necessary party to execute any instrument or effect a transfer dealt with under the plan or to perform any other act, including executing satisfactions of claims, to consummate the plan.[3]

Given the definition of the "substantial consummation" of a plan of reorganization under section 1102, once the initial distribution is made to creditors, the plan is substantially consummated, and the reorganized debtor then files a motion for the issuance of a final decree in the chapter 11 case. The debtor tends to be motivated to seek this decree because it terminates liability to the U.S. trustee for the quarterly surcharge based upon its cash flow.

Beginning in the early 1990s, plans of reorganization or liquidating plans began to establish litigation trusts in order to continue or, more often, to commence adversary proceedings that had not been addressed in the rush to confirmation. These litigation matters delayed the application for a final decree and the closing of the chapter 11 case. Further, in some instances, the litigation trusts also sought to bring non-bankruptcy-related causes of action, which raised the question of whether the jurisdiction to commence related proceedings survived the confirmation of a plan of reorganization.

---

2. 11 U.S.C. § 1123(b)(6).
3. Note that in some courts, much of this activity is done by filing a motion to show cause.

The jurisdictional predicate for both post-petition and post-confirmation jurisdiction is 28 U.S.C. § 1334(b), which vests original, but not exclusive, jurisdiction in the districts courts, and, by the general order of reference, the bankruptcy courts, of all civil proceedings arising under the Bankruptcy Code or arising in or related to a case under the Bankruptcy Code. Some courts have insisted that in any action brought by a non-debtor party against another non-debtor party after the plan is confirmed, the plaintiff identify the "nexus" between the plan of reorganization and the relief sought under the complaint, and the nexus must be close and material.

The court found a nexus where it had entered an order approving the assignment of a lease to a third party and also issued an injunction against filing any claims against the assignee for any rent owed by the estate, and the lessor sued the assignee in state court for the debtor's non-payment of rent during the administration of the chapter 11 case. The lessor also filed a request for the allowance and payment of the administrative expense against the reorganized debtor. Under these circumstances, the bankruptcy court issued an injunction against the lessor's proceeding against the assignee because the sale order was considered part of the plan.[4] Other courts have upheld "related proceedings" when their outcome would affect the distribution to creditors under the plan, but there is no uniform pattern and practice among the federal courts of appeal, with some clearly favoring limited post-confirmation jurisdiction.[5]

Notwithstanding the differences found by the appellate courts, the scope of "retained" or post-confirmation jurisdiction continues to expand in conjunction with the formation of litigation/liquidation trusts.

Because there tends to be a rush to sell substantially all of the assets and business operations or to push through pre-packaged or pre-negotiated chapter 11 plans, there is not

---

4. *See In re* Petrie Retail, Inc., 304 F.3d 223 (2d Cir. 2002).
5. *See* Zerand-Bernal Group, Inc. v. Cox, et al., 23 F.3d. 159 (7th Cir. 1994).

enough time for the debtor in possession to prepare and prosecute available causes of action. In fact, there may not even be enough time to schedule hearings to determine all of the pending objections to claims. Thus, the accelerated pace of the new breed of chapter 11 cases requires post-confirmation jurisdiction to maximize the distribution to creditors under a confirmed plan.

These accelerated cases also create a new category of professionals—the liquidating trustee. Naturally, questions surround this new category of professional. The first question is whether the appointment of a liquidation trustee can be grounded solely upon the provisions of the liquidating plan and order of confirmation, thus ignoring the statutory provisions for the appointment of a chapter 7 trustee and the standard of disinterestedness required for the retention of any professional person under sections 327 and 101(14). In addition, the standard order establishing the liquidation/litigation trusts often includes a provision stating that the compensation payable to the liquidation/litigation trustee and its professionals was not reviewable by the court or the U.S. trustee, raising the question of whether this position was a "bankruptcy professional."

There are other questions relating to the standing of the liquidation/litigation trustee to file adversary proceedings; and, if the trustee has standing, is he or she subject to the defenses that could be asserted against the debtor? This is of particular importance where there the defendant(s) to the trustee's complaint could raise the affirmative defense, commonly referred to as the *in pari materia* defense, that because the debtor and its officers, directors, or controlling persons equally or materially participated in the misconduct described in the trustee's complaint, the trustee as the representative of the debtor's bankruptcy estate has no "standing" to file that complaint.

In some ways, the very concept of post-confirmation or retained jurisdiction butts up against the normative principle of res judicata. It is easy to think of the confirmation of a plan of reorganization as the close equivalent of a final order of judgment closing litigation, which leads to the conclusion that all claims, counterclaims, or defenses that could have been, but were not, raised by the parties to that litigation are precluded from being raised in any subsequent litigation among the parties. Thus, for example, if, after confirmation of the plan, the reorganized debtor files a complaint alleging various claims of lender liability against the secured creditor that financed the pre-petition or pre-confirmation business of the debtor, it is entirely appropriate for the defendant to file a motion to dismiss for failure to state a claim under Fed. R. Civ. P. 12(b)(6) or to move for summary judgment of dismissal under Fed. R. Civ. P. 56.

The only exception to the principle of res judicata is a very specific reservation of jurisdiction under the plan to file a specific action. The question becomes, of course, how specific must the reservation be? One court held that a general reservation of rights to file complaints under Part 5 of the Bankruptcy Code, which includes the avoidance actions for fraudulent transfer and preferential transfers, was insufficient, and the court granted the defendant's motion to dismiss on res judicata grounds.[6]

---

6. *See In re* G-P Plastics, Inc., 320 B.R. 821 (E.D. Mich. 2001).

# CHAPTER 19

# CONCLUSION: ALTERNATIVES TO BANKRUPTCY RELIEF

In may appear odd that a book about the essentials of business bankruptcy ends with a discussion of alternatives to bankruptcy relief. Nonetheless, businesses confronting financial distress have several options available to them in attempting to work out their debt or manage their assets. These options include assignments for the benefit of creditors and receiverships. Each option has advantages and disadvantages that an attorney must be aware of to design a custom approach on behalf of a company seeking to chart the waters of financial distress. Creditor attorneys must also be aware of these procedures to ensure full protection of their clients' interests.

The Assignment for the Benefit of Creditors (ABC) is a transfer of legal and equitable title to all of the debtor's property to a trustee (assignee) with authority to liquidate the debtor's affairs and distribute proceeds equitably to creditors.[1] Functionally, an ABC appears to look similar to a chapter 7 bankruptcy case governed, however, by state, as opposed to federal, law, wherein the debtor generally assigns all of its property to an assignee for the benefit of its creditors. The

---

1. GARRARD GLENN & BAKER VOORHIS, THE LAW GOVERNING LIQUIDATION (1935).

consequence of the ABC is to place the property out of the reach of the debtor's creditors by direct enforcement action.

The ABC is a creature of state law. Thus, one must confront a mix of state laws to determine the scope, rights, and obligations associated with the use of ABC. These statutes are designed to effectuate the intent of ABCs, that is, the authority on the part of the debtor to make a general assignment of its assets to an assignee for the benefit of its creditors.[2]

The ABC is initiated by the issuance of a deed of assignment executed by the debtor/assignor to a named assignee/trustee. The deed transfers all of the debtor's assets to an assignee. Partial assignments are not authorized. Typically, the deed of assignment will include a list or inventory of assets transferred and a list of all creditors and their respective claims.

Upon the assignment and acceptance of the general assignment of assets, the assignee is required to provide public notice of the assignment to all listed creditors. As of the assignment, title to all property transferred vests in the assignee. The assignee has the power to transfer such assets, to sue on behalf of the estate, to collect accounts, and to settle and compromise all claims and disputes. In some jurisdictions, sales of property must be confirmed by a court.

The assignee generally has the authority to employ legal counsel and other relevant professional persons. In certain limited situations, usually with court approval, an assignee may also seek to operate the business for a limited time.

As a representative of the creditors, the assignee must act in their best interests and is subject to the panoply of fiduciary duties that regularly exist in this field. Furthermore, as the creditor's representative, an assignee may seek to

---

2. For an excellent source on ABCs, *see* GEOFFREY L. BERMAN, GENERAL ASSIGNMENTS FOR THE BENEFIT OF CREDITORS (American Bankruptcy Institute 2006).

enforce state fraudulent transfer law to rescind pre-assignment transfers as either actual or constructively fraudulent and, in some jurisdictions, seek to recover preferences, although the validity for bringing a preference action remains controversial.

Generally, an assignee must file a final accounting to close the case. At that time, an assignee will begin distributions to the creditors. Moreover, an assignee may seek permission to pay its professionals. An assignee is typically paid a commission based on a percentage of assets administered.

State law provides the distributional scheme in an ABC. First, secured creditors receive a return of their collateral or the value of their collateral. Second, administrative expenses are generally paid, including the expenses incurred in administering the estate. Third, various priority claims are paid, including taxes, wages, and other jurisdiction-specific claims. Finally, general unsecured claims are paid to the extent any proceeds from the monetization of assets remain.

The ABC provides many benefits. Among these are the following:

- Far less costly procedure than bankruptcy
- Greater flexibility than bankruptcy
- Expedited procedure
- Power to conduct investigations and examine and depose witnesses
- Limited power to operate the business post-assignment

The ABC does present several limitations and disadvantages, especially when compared to a bankruptcy law alternative. These include the following:

- Assignee may not sell property free and clear of liens
- Preference power does not exist in most states and is controversial in those states that do recognize it

- No recognition of equitable subordination
- Limited territorial jurisdiction
- No discharge
- Limited or no immunity to assignee

In addition to the ABC, jurisdictions also recognize the state court receivership. The state court receivership is governed by state law and generally requires the commencement of a civil action. Pursuant to the civil action, a state trial court orders the appointment of a receiver to take control of all the property of the defendant (debtor). The property is then considered in custodio legis. Thus, the property is no longer subject to direct enforcement action by the creditors.

The federal or state court receivership is an ancient remedy. Receiverships can be created based on the authority of many federal and state laws. Moreover, the general concept of an "equity receiver," that is, a party with full authority to operate the company during litigation, is an equitable remedy that exists in federal (and many states') common law, without the existence of a specific authorizing statute. As a result of this multiplicity of authority, both the blessing and the bane of receiverships is that they possess great flexibility. In large measure, they operate based solely on the authority granted by the court order that authorizes the receiver. Thus, it is critical that such an order be sufficiently broad and comprehensive to ensure that the receiver is granted the powers necessary to fully control the entity's assets and litigation. Such an order can, for instance, impose a stay on litigation that parallels the scope of the automatic stay in bankruptcy.

Essentially, a receiver is an individual appointed by the court with such powers as the court deems appropriate to take control of property of the defendant, usually to identify, marshal, and preserve the property, manage it, and, frequently, liquidate the property. Thus, a receiver can be appointed to take over the operation of a legitimate business that was being used to perpetrate a fraud or to locate assets stolen from the victims of a Ponzi scheme.

The receivership generally is commenced with the secured lender filing a complaint with the applicable state court as the plaintiff, setting forth the reason for the receivership, what it hopes to accomplish in the receivership, who it would like to have appointed as receiver, and how the receivership will operate mechanically. The receiver is appointed by, and periodically reports to, the judge and carries out the plan, most likely the disposition of assets.

If the disposition has not previously been approved, once the proceeds from the sale of assets have been collected, the receiver seeks the judge's approval for the distribution. The receivership is then wound down.

The receivership possesses many advantages, including the following:

- Receivers have essentially the same authority as bankruptcy trustees to bring actions to avoid fraudulent transfers.

- Receivers have tended to fare better than bankruptcy trustees in avoiding application of the in pari delicto defense when suing on behalf of the corporation.

- Receivers may enjoy immunity for actions within the scope of the receivership.

- Authority is flexible and may be tailored to the needs of the actual civil action.

- Receivership property is protected while in custodia legis.

- Receiver may displace incompetent or fraudulent management.

- Receiver may operate the business with greater flexibility.

- Receivership generally results in lower professional and administrative costs and, therefore, a higher amount of proceeds to be paid to the creditors.

- Because the receivership process generally is quicker than bankruptcy, a troubled company is less likely to fail because of cash shortages, fatigue, or the rigors of bankruptcy.

- Assets may be sold free and clear of liens.

The receivership does have several important limitations. These include the following:

- No preference power
- Limited jurisdiction
- No automatic stay
- Advisory opinion or guidance may not be permitted
- No discharge

Thus, in addition to the various bankruptcy alternatives discussed in prior chapters in this book, the practitioner must be cognizant of the increasing popularity of alternative procedures. Based on our collective knowledge, we are confident in one basic fact of bankruptcy life—one size does not fit all. There is sufficient variety in facts and circumstances to necessitate a careful, deliberate, and fresh look at each business distress context, ensuring that simple culture or habit does not drive counsel to a particular option when the facts and circumstances suggest another.

# Table of Cases

Ace Elec. Acquisition, LLC, *In re,* 342 B.R. 831, 833 (Bankr. M.D. Fla. 005); 196

Adwar v. Capgro Leasing Corp. (In re Adwar), 55 B.R. 111 (Bankr. E.D.N.Y. 1985); 160

Allegheny Int'l, Inc., *In re,* 136 B.R. 396, 402–03 (Bankr. W.D. Pa. 1991); 196

Am. Metrocomm Corp., *In re,* 274 B.R. 641 (Bankr. D. Del. 2002); 11

Anderson Industries, Inc. v. Anderson, 55 B.R. 922 (Bankr. W.D. Mich. 1985); 162

Andover Togs, Inc., *In re,* 231 B.R. 521, 545–46 (Bankr. S.D.N.Y. 1999); 196

A.W. Assoc., Inc., *In re,* 136 F.3d 1439 (11th Cir. 1998); 140

B.D.W. Assocs. Inc. v. Busy Beaver Bldg. Ctrs. Inc., 865 F.2d 65 (3d Cir. 1989); 41

B.Z. Corp. v. Continental Bank, N.A. (In re B.Z. Corp.), 34 B.R. 546 (Bankr. E.D. Pa. 1983); 156

Barnhill v. Johnson, 503, U.S. 393, 112 S. Ct. 1386 (1992); 156

Bellanca Aircraft Corp., *In re,* 850 F.2d 1275 (8th Cir. 1988); 138

BFP v. Resolution Trust Corp., 511 U.S. 531 (1994); 155, 159, 160, 163

Biggs v. Stovin (Luz Int'l, Ltd.), 219 B.R. 837 (9th Cir. B.A.P. 1998); 192

Bishop, Baldwin, Rewald, Dillingham & Wong, *In re,* 779 F.2d 471 (9th Cir. 1985); 42

Bluford v. First Fidelity Mtg. Co. (In re Bluford), 40 Bankr. 640 (Bankr. W.D. Mo. 1984); 154

Bob Schwermer & Assocs., Inc., *In re,* 27 B.R. 304 (Bankr. N.D. Ill. 1983); 157

Bob's Sea Ray Boats, Inc., *In re,* 143 B.R. 229, 231 (Bankr. D.N.D. 1992); 196

Bookbinder's Restaurant, Inc., *In re,* 2006 WL 3858020 (Bankr. E.D. Pa. Dec. 28, 2006); 189

Bozeck v. Danning, 486 U.S. 1056 (1988); 138

Brown & Cole Stores, LLC, *In re,* 375 B.R. 873 (9th Cir. B.A.P. 2007); 191

Bullion Reserve, *In re,* 836 F.2d 1214 (9th Cir.); 138

Burlingham v. Crouse, 228 U.S. 459 (1913); 21

Busick, *In re,* 831 F.2d 745 (7th Cir. 1987); 41

Calairo v. Pittsburgh Nat'l Bank (In re Ewing), 33 B.R. 288 (Bankr. W.D. Pa. 1983); 155

Campbell v. Macartie, 64 B.R. 335 (Bankr. W.D. Pa. 1986); 156

Carr v. Demusis (In re Carr), 34 Bankr. 653 (D. Conn. 1983); 154

Catapult Entm't, Inc., *In re,* 165 F.3d 747 (9th Cir. 1999); 122

Chicago Bd. of Trade v. Johnson, 264 U.S. 1 (1924); 79

CLFC, Inc., *In re,* 89 F.3d 673 (9th Cir. 1996); 121

Cooper v. Ashley Commc'ns, Inc. (In re Morris Commc'ns NC, Inc.), 75 B.R. 619, (Bankr. W.D.N.C. 1987); 162

Communicall Central, Inc., *In re,* 106 B.R. 540, 544 (Bankr. N.D. Ill. 1989); 197

Connectix Corp.., *In re,* 372 B.R. 488, 491–94 (Bankr. N.D. Cal. 2007); 196

D'Lites of Am., Inc., *In re,* 108 B.R. 352 (Bankr. N.D. Ga. 1989); 56

Dana Corp.., *In re,* 367 B.R. 409 (Bankr. S.D.N.Y. 2007); 188

Danning v. Progressive Pharma. Sys., Inc. (In re Western Adams Hosp. Corp.), 609 F.2d 929 (9th Cir. 1979); 161

Darby v. Atkinson (In re Ferris), 415 F. Supp. 33 (W.D. Okla. 1976); 156

Deer, *In re,* No. 06-02460, slip op. at 2 (Bankr. S.D. Miss. June 14, 2007); 191

Demusis v. Carr (In re Carr), 40 B.R. 1007 (D. Conn. 1984); 161

DePrizio, *In re,* 874 F.2d 1186 (7th Cir. 1989); 148

Durrett v. Washington Nat'l Ins. Co., 621 F.2d 201 (5th Cir. 1980); 155, 159

E.R. Fegert, Inc., *In re,* 887 F.2d 955 (9th Cir. 1989); 138

Eder v. Queen City Grain, Inc. (In re Queen City Grain, Inc.), 51 B.R. 722 (Bankr. S.D. Ohio 1985); 156

Edward Harvey Co., *In re,* 68 B.R. 851 (Bankr. D. Mass. 1987); 156

Ellenberg v. DeKalb County, Ga. (In re Maytag Sales and Serv., Inc.), 23 B.R. 384 (Bankr. N.D. Ga. 1982) (case under § 547(b)); 157

Elstead v. Nolden, 168 B.R. 226 (Bankr. N.D. Cal. 1994); 56

F&S Cent. Mfg. Corp., *In re,* 53 B.R. 842 (Bankr. E.D.N.Y. 1985); 138

Factory Tire Distribs., Inc., In re,64 B.R. 335 (Bankr. W.D. Pa. 1986); 156

FDIC v. Malin, 802 F.2d 12 (2d Cir. 1986); 157

Financial News Network, Inc., *In re,* 149 B.R. 348, 351 (Bankr. S.D.N.Y. 1993); 197

First Fed. Sav. & Loan Ass'n v. Hulm (In re Hulm), 738 F.2d 323 (8th Cir.); 155, 158

First Jersey Sec., *In re,* 180 F.3d 504 (3d Cir. 1999); 140

First NLC Financial Services, L.L.C., *In re,* 382 B.R. 547 (Bankr. S.D. Fla. 2008); 91

Foreman Indus., Inc., *In re,* 59 B.R. 145 (Bankr. S.D. Ohio 1986); 138

Frank v. Berlin (In re Frank), 39 B.R. 166 (Bankr. E.D.N.Y. 1984); 156, 158

Fretheim, *In re,* 102 B.R. 298 (Bankr. D. Conn. 1989); 56

Fuel Oil Supply & Terminaling, Inc., *In re,* 837 F.2d 224 (5th Cir. 1988); 138

Furedy v. Appleman (In re Vodco Volume Dev. Co.); 158

Gantos, Inc., *In re,* 176 B.R. 793, 795–96 (Bankr.W.D. Mich. 1995); 197

Georgetown Steel Co., LLC, In re; 318 B.R. 336 (Bankr. S.C. 2004); 135

Global Home Products, LLC, *In re,* 2006 WL 3791955 (Bankr. D. Del. Dec. 21, 2006); 188

Global Tissue, LLC v. E.B. Eddy Forest Products, Ltd., 302 B.R. 808 (D. Del. 2003); 140

Goodys' Family Clothing, Inc., *In re,* 2009 WL 294384 (Bankr. D. Del. 2009); 190, 191

G-P Plastics, Inc., *In re,* 320 B.R. 821 (E.D. Mich. 2001); 219

Granfinanciera S.A. v. Nordberg, 492 U.S. 33, 58, 109 S. Ct. 2782 (1989); 204

Image Worldwide, *In re,* 139 F.2d 574 (7th Cir. 1998); 164

*In re. See* name of party.

Inst. Pasteur v. Cambridge Biotech Corp., *In re,* 104 F.3d 489 (1st Cir. 1997); 122

Interstate Commerce Comm'n v. Holmes Transp., Inc., 931 F.2d 984 (1st Cir. 1991); 71

Iron-Oak Supply Corp.., *In re,* 169 B.R. 414, 419–20 (Bankr. E.D. Cal. 1994); 196

Jacoway v. Anderson (In re Ozark Restaurant Equip. Co.), 850 F.2d 342 (8th Cir. 1988); 159, 162

Johns-Manville Corp., *In re,* 60 B.R. 612 (Bankr. S.D.N.Y. 1986); 56

Join-In Int'l (U.S.A.) Ltd. v. N.Y. Wholesale Distribs. Corp. (In re Join-In Int'l (U.S.A.) Ltd.), 56 B.R. 555, 560 (Bankr. S.D.N.Y. 1986); 166

Kelley v. Horner (In re Kelley), 7 B.R. 384 (Bankr. D.S.D. 1980); 156

Key Mech Inc. v. BDC, 330 F.3d 111 (2d Cir. 2003); 41

Kjeldahl v. United States (In re Kjeldahl), 52 B.R. 926 (Bankr. D. Minn. 1985); 162

Klein v. Tabatchnick, 610 F.2d 1043 (2d Cir. 1979); 159

Kras, United States v., 409 U.S. 434 (1973); 25

Kupetz v. Continental Ill. Nat'l Bank & Trust Co., 77 B.R. 754 (C.D. Cal. 1987); 157

Kupetz v. Wolf, 845 F.2d 842 (9th Cir. 1988); 157

Lagenkamp v. Culp, 498 U.S. 42, 44, 111 S. Ct. 330 (1990); 204

Larrimer v. Feeney, 411 Pa. 604 192 A.2d 351, 353 (1963)158

Lawrence Paperboard Corp. v. Arlington Trust Co. (In re Lawrence Paperboard Corp.), 76 B.R. 866 (Bankr. D. Mass. 1987); 157

Lemley-Cabbiness Farms v. FDIC (In re Lemley Estate Business Trust), 65 B.R. 185 (Bankr. N.D. Tex. 1986); 157

Levit v. Ingersoll Rand Financial Corp., 874 F.2d 1186 (7th Cir. 1989); 148

Lough, *In re,* 57 B.R. 933 (Bankr. E.D. Mich. 1986); 41

Lovett v. Shuster, 633 F.2d 98 (8th Cir. 1980; 158

Luz Int'l, Ltd., *In re,* 219 B.R. 837 (9th Cir. B.A.P. 1998); 192

Madrid v. Lawyers Title Ins. Corp. (In re Madrid), 725 F.2d 1197 (9th Cir.); 155, 158

Magness, *In re,* 972 F.2d 689 (6th Cir. 1992); 121

Main v. Brim (In re Main), 75 B.R. 322 (Bankr. D. Ariz. 1987); 158

Mancuso v. Champion (In re Dondi Fin. Corp.), 119 Bankr. 106 (Bankr. N.D. Tex. 1990); 158

McKenzie v. Irving Trust Co., 323 U.S. 365 (1945); 158

Miller v. Florida Mining and Materials, 136 F.3d 1439 (11th Cir. 1998); 140, 148

Mitchell v. Travis (In re Jackson Sound Studios, Inc.), 473 F.2d 503 (5th Cir. 1973); 157

Moore v. Bay, 284 U.S. 4 (1931), 129

Murphy v. General Elec. Credit Corp. (In re Rodriguez), 77 B.R. 939 (Bankr. S.D. Fla. 1987); 154

Nemeti v. Seaway Nat'l Bank (In re Nemeti), 65 B.R. 391 (Bankr. N.D.N.Y. 1986); 154, 159

New Valley Corp.., *In re,* 2000 WL 1251858, at *11–12 (D.N.J. 2000); 196

On Tour LLC, *In re,* 276 B.R. 407 (Bankr. D. Md. 2002); 38

Ottaviano, *In re,* 63 B.R. 338 (Bankr. D. Conn. 1986); 156

Parkline Corp., *In re,* 185 B.R. 164 (Bankr. D.N.J. 1994); 140

Peters, *In re,* 2004 WL 1291125, at *6, n.20 (Bankr. E.D. Pa. 2004); 196

Petrides v. Park Hill Restaurant, Inc., 265 A.D. 509, 511, 39 N.Y.S.2d 645, 647 (1943); 157

Petrie Retail, Inc., *In re,* 304 F.3d 223 (2d Cir. 2002); 217

Phoenix Steel Corp., *In re,* 76 B.R. 373 (Bankr. D. Del. 1987); 138

Pioneer Ford Sales, Inc., *In re,* 729 F.2d 27 (1st Cir. 1984); 121

Plastech Engineered Products, Inc., et al. *In re,* (Plastech I), 394 B.R. 147 (Bankr. E.D. Mich. 2006); 188

Plastech Engineered Products, Inc., et al. *In re,* (Plastech II), 2008 WL 5223014; 190

Plastech Engineered Products, Inc., et al. *In re,* (Plastech III) , 397 B.R. 828 (Bankr. E.D. Mich. 2008); 190

Plymouth United Sav. Bank v. Lee, 278 Mich. 545, 270 N.W. 781, 782 (1936); 161

Prudential Lines, Inc., *In re,* 928 F.2d 565 (2d Cir. 1981); 80

Richardson Builders, Inc., *In re,* 123 B.R. 736 (Bankr. W.D. Va. 1990); 71

Riker Indus., Inc., *In re,* 122 B.R. 964 (Bankr. N.D. Ohio 1990); 56

Ristich, *In re,* 57 B.R. 568 (Bankr. N.D. Ill. 1986); 154

Roost v. Associates Home Equity Servs., Inc., 234 B.R. 801 (Bankr. D. Or. 1999); 149

Rubin v. Mfrs. Hanover Trust Co., 661 F.2d 979 (2d Cir. 1981); 157, 160

Rubin, *In re,* 769 F.2d 611 (9th Cir. 1985); 40

Sandoz v. Bennett (In re Emerald Oil Co.), 807 F.2d 1234 (5th Cir. 1987); 158

Schaefer v. Fisher, 137 Misc. 420 242 N.Y.S. 308, 314 (1930); 157

Schafer v. Hammond, 456 F.2d 15, 17 (10th Cir. 1972); 155

Schatzman v. Campo (In re Oesterle), 2 B.R. 122 (Bankr. S.D. Fla. 1979); 158

Service Mtg. Corp. v. Welson, 293 Mass. 410 200 N.E. 278, 279 (1936); 157

Sieling Assocs. Ltd. P'ship, *In re,* 128 B.R. 721 (Bankr. E.D. Va. 1991); 56

Sims, *In re,* 994 F.2d 210 (5th Cir. 1993); 40

Suppa v. Capalbo (In re Suppa), 8 B.R. 720 (Bankr. D.R.I. 1981) (case under § 547(b)); 157

T.B. Home Sewing Enters., Inc., *In re,* 173 B.R. 790 (Bankr. N.D. Ga. 1993); 140

Tabor Court Realty Corp., United States v., 803 F.2d 1288 (3d Cir. 1986); 157

Taylor & Assocs. LP, *In re,* 193 B.R. 465 (Bankr. E.D. Tenn. 1996); 40

That's Entmt't Mkt'g Group. Inc., *In re,* 168 B.R. 226 (Bankr. N.D. Cal. 1994); 56

Today's Woman of Fla., Inc., *In re,* 195 B.R. 506, 507–08 (Bankr. M.D. Fla. 1996); 197

United States v. *See* name of party,

Utility Stationery Stores, Inc. v. Am. Portfolio (In re Utility Stationery Stores, Inc.), 12 B.R. 170 (Bankr. N.D. Ill. 1981); 161

Vadnais Lumber Supply, Inc. v. Byrne (In re Vadnais Lumber Supply, Inc.), 100 B.R. 127 (Bankr. D. Mass. 1989); 167

Venice Western Motel, Ltd. v. Venice Motor Inn, Ltd. (In re Venice Western Motel, Ltd.), 67 B.R. 777 (Bankr. M.D. Fla. 1986); 155

Wieboldt Stores, Inc. v. Schottenstein, 94 B.R. 488 (N.D. Ill. 1988); 167

Williams, *In re,* 234 B.R. 801 (Bankr. D. Or. 1999); 149

Wilson v. Holub, 202 Iowa 549, 552, 210 N.W. 593 (1926); 157

Winshall Settlor's Trust, *In re,* 758 F.2d 1136 (6th Cir. 1985); 155

Zerand-Bernal Group, Inc. v. Cox, et al., 23 F.3d. 159 (7th Cir. 1994); 217

# Index

## A

automatic stays 71–77
  acts in violation of 72
    possible sanctions 72
    self-enforcing nature of stay 72
  civil actions, stoppage of 72
  debtor protection afforded 72
  exceptions to 73
    criminal actions 73
  filing requirements 74
  purposes of 71
  relief from 73–74
    criteria for obtaining 75
    reasons for granting 73
    reasons for seeking 74–75
  scope of 71–72
    duration of 71
  section 362 71
  termination of 77
avoidance powers 125–82
  avoidable preferences under section 547(b) 129–49
    avoidable preference, defined 129
    chapter 11, burden of proof 130
    chapter 7 liquidation 130
  bankruptcy case vs. state debt collection activity 125
  changes to fraudulent transfer law 171–75
    condemnation of certain asset-protection strategies 173–78
    insider employment contracts 172–78
    two-year reach-back period 171–78
  fraudulent transfers under section 548(a). *See also.*
  liability under section 550 181–82
  post-petition transfers under section 549(b) 175
  pre-petition property transfers 125
  purposes of 126
  setoff under section 553. *See also.*
  statutory lien avoidance under section 545 150
  trustee powers under section 544(b) 128–29
    applicable state law 129
    successful invocation of 129
    Uniform Fraudulent Transfer Act 129
  trustee strong-arm powers 126–28
    purchaser of debtor's real property 127
    section 544(A) 126–28
    Uniform Commercial Code, Article 9 127

## B

bankruptcy relief, alternatives to 221–26
  Assignment for the Benefit of Creditors 221–23
    benefits of 223
    chapter 7 case, similarity to 221
    defined 221
    final accounting, filing of 223

general assignment of assets 222
  initiation of 222
  limitations of 223
  state law provisions 222
state court receivership 224–26
  advantages of 225
  civil action 224
  commencement of 225
  equity receiver, defined 224
  flexibility of 224
  limitations of 226
  receiver, court appointment of 224
bankruptcies, types of 27–32
  chapter 11 28–29
    disclosure statement, approval of 29
    orderly liquidation 28
    plan confirmation 29
    rehabilitation 28
    section 365(b) sales 29
  chapter 12 29–30
    family farmers 29
    fishermen 29
  chapter 13 30
    individuals with regular income who meet certain debt limits 30
  chapter 15 30–32
    ancillary cases 31
    Bankruptcy Abuse Prevention and Consumer Protection Act 30
    foreign proceedings 31
    goals of 32
    Model Law on Cross-Border Insolvency 30
    objectives of 30
    purpose of 30
    United Nations Commission on International Trade Law 30
  chapter 7 27–28
    creditors, goal of 28
    individual debtor, goal of 28
    liquidation 27
  chapter 9 28
    insolvent municipalities 28
Bankruptcy Abuse Prevention and Consumer Protection Act 22–24, 30, 43–46, 101, 118, 123–24, 133, 139, 145–49
bankruptcy cases, professionals in 53–69
  application process 58–62
    application provisions 59–61
    Rule 2014 requirements 58
    timing 62
    verified statement requirements 61–62
  billing 62–64
    Lodestar Standard 62
  conflict/contact check 57–58
    disclosure failures 58
    entities checks should be run against 57
  fee application 64–69
    contents of 65–66
    fee considerations 66–69
    frequency 64–65
  ordinary course professionals 56–59
  retainees 53–57
    approval by bankruptcy court 53
    bankruptcy professionals 54
    chapter 11, professionals involved with 53
    ordinary course professionals 54
    special purpose professionals 54
  Section 327(a) professionals 54–55
    disinterest of 54
  Section 327(e) special counsel 55
bankruptcy debtors 49–51
  chapter 13 50
  chapter 7 49–50

duties of 50–51
   Bankruptcy Rule 4002 51
   cooperation with trustees or examiners 50
   disclosure obligations 50
   examination under oath 51
   failure to abide by 51
   surrender of property 50
   tax returns, filing of 51
exclusion of 49
identification of 49–51
residency requirement 49
bankruptcy estate 79–81
   limits to property of the estate 81
   scope of 79–80
      chapter 11 79
      chapter 13 79
      chapter 7 79
      post-petition earnings 79
      property of the estate, defined 79
      property of the estate, questions concerning 80
      property subject to exemption 80
bankruptcy law, history of 21–26
   Bankruptcy Abuse Prevention and Consumer Protection Act 22–24
   Bankruptcy Code 23–25
      chapters 23
      policies of 25
   bankruptcy relief 24
   business debtors 25–26
   individual debtors 25

## C

cash collateral 109–11
   debtor use of 110–12
      adequate protection 111
      section 363(c)(2) 110
      defined 110
      prohibition against usage 110
chapter 7
   avoidance powers 130
   bankruptcy debtors, identification of 49
   claims and distribution 184
   conversion of case from chapter 11 47
   executory contracts 114
   filing the petition 37
   individual debtor, goal of 28
   involuntary cases 38
   liquidation 27
   post-petition earnings 79
chapter 9
   insolvent municipalities 28
chapter 11 83–107
   avoidance powers 130
   bankruptcy debtors, identification of 50
   claim classification 94–95
      administrative priority expenses 94
      cram-down provisions 94
      importance of 94
      secured claims 94
      taxing authorities 94
      topic for litigation 94
   claims and distribution 184
   conversion of case to chapter 7 47
   core v. non-core 36
   creditors' committee, appointment of 84
   debtor in possession 83–84
      authority, limiting of 84
      court approval, need for 84
      options available to 83
      replacement of 84
   discharge under 106–07
      section 1141(d) 106
      section 1141(d), limits to 106
   disclosure statement, approval of 29

distribution to creditors 199
establishing and protecting claims 202
examiner, appointment of 85
executory contracts 114
filing the petition 37
first-day motions
    benefits of 89
    problems of 89
    Rule 6003. *See also.*
    types of 85–89
involuntary cases 38
Official Committee of Unsecured Creditors 84–85
plan and disclosure statements, contents of 93–94
plan confirmation 29
plan confirmation. *See* reorganization plan confirmation.
post-confirmation issues 218
professionals involved with 53
reorganization plan, acceptance and confirmation of 97–98
    absolute priority rule 98
    absolute priority rule, new value exception to 98
    class of claims, criteria for acceptance 97
    class of interests, criteria for acceptance 97
    court refusal of confirmation 98
    fair and equitable standard 98
reorganization plan, alternatives to 95–97
    avoidance powers 95–96
    equity infusions 97
    equity-for-debt swaps 97
    feasibility of plan 95
    future operations 97
    post-petition financing 96
    sale of assets 95
reorganization plan, filing of 92–93

reorganization plan confirmation, effect of 104–05
reorganization plan, modification of 105–06
    facilitation of 106
    procedure for 105
section 1115 79
section 365(b) sales 29
chapter 12
    family farmers 29
    fishermen 29
chapter 13 30
    bankruptcy debtors, identification of 50
    claims and distribution 185
    distribution to creditors 200
    individuals with regular income who meet certain debt limits 30
    section 1306 79
chapter 15 30–32
    Bankruptcy Abuse Prevention and Consumer Protection Act 30
    foreign proceedings 31
    goals of 32
    Model Law on Cross-Border Insolvency 30
    objectives of 30
    purpose of 30
    United Nations Commission on International Trade Law 30
claims and distribution 183–204
    Bankruptcy Code rules
        allowance, treatment, and satisfaction of claims 186
        priorities under 197–99
    chapter 11 case 184
        distribution to creditors 199
    chapter 13 case 185
        distribution to creditors 200
    chapter 7 Case 184
    characterization of claims 186
    claim, defined 202

claims for unexpired non-residential real property. *See also.*
establishing and Protecting Claims 202
establishing and protecting claims 202–03
  chapter 11 case 202
  proof of claim, importance of 203
proof of claim, filing 203
  failure to file 204
subordination of claims 201
  equitable subordination, defined 201
secured claims 192–93
suppliers of goods leading up to the bankruptcy. *See also.*
unsecured claims 193, 197
  categories of 197
claims for unexpired non-residential real property 194–97
  applying 502(b)(6)(A) 197
  Bankruptcy Code, priorities under unsecured claims, categories of 197
  Bankruptcy Code claim caps 194
  damages due to the breach, caps 194
  known factors 195
  questioned factor 196–97
client's perspective 1–13
  manufacturers 8–9
    disclosure and plan confirmation issues 9
    Pension Benefits Guaranty Corporation 9
    section 363 sales 9
  professional firms 9
    limited liability companies 9
  real estate developers 4–6
    Official Committee of Unsecured Creditors 5
    secured lender 5
    unsecured creditor 5
  retailers, national 8
    committee composition 8
    international relationships 8
    section 363 sales of assets 8
  retailers, small 6–8
    claims against 7
    secured lenders 7
    trade creditors 7
  single-asset real estate 2–4
  your firm 9–13
    charging or retention liens 12
    confidential privilege 12
    files and work product, turning over 10
    Official Committee of Unsecured Creditors 12
    pre-petition claims 13
    proof of claim 10
    retainer to secure payment 10
    section 361 protections 12
commencement 37–47
  eligibility 37–38
    requirements for establishing 37
  filing the petition 37–38
    chapter 11 37
    chapter 7 37
    filing date, importance of 37
    involuntary petition 37
    voluntary 37
    voluntary cases 38
  involuntary cases. *See also.*
  voluntary cases 38
    orders for relief 38
consolidation, substantive 211–13
  appropriateness of, consideration factors 211
  as equitable remedy 211
  question of the propriety 211

# D

debtor in possession 83–84
  authority, limiting of 84
  court approval, need for 84

options available to 83
replacement of 84
debtor transactions 111–12
  court approval, seeking 112
  ordinary course transaction, determining 111
  section 1108 111
  section 363 111
discharge 205–09
  as objective for bankruptcy filing 205
  effect of 206
  granting of 205
  non-discrimination provision 206–07
  Section 1141 207
    limits to 207
  Section 141
    reorganization plan, confirmation of 207
  tax claims 207
    false pretenses 208
    fraudulent taxes 208
    non-priority/non-dischargeable taxes 208
    qui tam claims 209

# E

equipment leases 123–24
  Bankruptcy Abuse Prevention and Consumer Protection Act 124
  additional burdens imposed by 123
  financing lease 123
  true or actual operating equipment leases 123
executory contracts 113–24
  assignment 116–17
  assumption or rejection, determination of 115
  assumption or rejection, timing of 114
  assumption, standard for 116
    court approval 116
    chapter 11 case 114
    chapter 7 case 114
  defined 113–14
    difficulty of defining 114
  rejection, consequences of 115–16
    anticipatory repudiation of the contract 115
    rejection damages 115
  rejection of 114
  special contract types
    assignments of interests in intellectual property 122
  special contract types 119–24
    equipment leases. *See also.*
    franchisees 120–21

# F

financial tool, bankruptcy as 33–34
fraudulent transfers under section 548(a) 150–71
  challenge transfers or obligations 151
  constructively fraudulent transfers 153–71
    insolvent or rendered insolvent 165–67
    lack of reasonably equivalent value 159–64
    left with an inability to pay debts 171–78
    left with unreasonably small capital 167–70
    statutorily defined financial distress 165
  transfer, defined 154
  types of fraudulent transfers 150

# G

Generally Accepted Accounting Principles 165

## I

information sources 15–20
  notices to creditors 16–17
    failure to receive notification 17
    information covered 16
    recipients of 16
    section 523 17
  plan and disclosure statements 20
  Rule 2004 examinations 19
    requests for 19
  schedules, statements filed with court 18–19
    proper claim listing 19
  Section 341 meeting of creditors 17–18
    creditor questions 18
involuntary cases 39–46
  answering the petition 39
  Bankruptcy Abuse Prevention and Consumer Protection Act 43
    abusive cases, curbing of 43
  bona fide disputes 40
    standard for determining 41
  chapter 11 38
  chapter 7 38
  contingent claims 40
    defined 40
  conversion to other chapters 45–47
    Bankruptcy Abuse Prevention and Consumer Protection Act 46
    chapter conversion sections 46
    means-testing requirement 46
  debtor in possession 42
  discovery 40
  dismissal of 45–47
    debtor abuse 46
    good-faith confirmation requirement 45
    non-statutory grounds for 45
    statutory grounds for relief 46
  entities exempt from 38
  failure to answer in timely manner 40
  fraudulent cases 43
    criminality of filing 44
    sealing of records, requirements for 43
  gap period 42
    defined 42
    operation of business during 43
  generally not paying debts, court determination of 41
  grounds for a denial of 39
  order for relief 40
  rareness of 44
  reasons for commencing 44
  relief, grounds for 40
  requisite creditor signatures 38
  summary judgment, motion for 40

## J

jurisdiction 35–47
  core v. non-core 35–37
    chapter 11 case 36
    core matter, defined 35
    distinction between, unclearness of 36
    general rule regarding 36
  district court 35
    assignment to bankruptcy court 35

## M

Model Law on Cross-Border Insolvency 30

## O

Official Committee of Unsecured Creditors 5, 12, 84–85

## P

Pension Benefits Guaranty Corporation  9
post-confirmation issues  215–19
  chapter 11 cases
    debtor causes of action  218
  liquidation/litigation trustee adversary proceedings  218
  litigation matters  216
  non-bankruptcy-related causes of action  216
  post-confirmation jurisdiction  215
    expansion of  217
    scope of  216
  principle of res judicata  218
    exception to  219
  substantial consummation  216

## R

real estate developers  4–6
  Official Committee of Unsecured Creditors  5
  unsecured creditor  5
real property, special cases of
  unexpired lease of non-residential real property  118
    debtor is lessee  118
reorganization plan confirmation  99–104
  Bankruptcy Abuse Prevention and Consumer Protection Act  101
  competing plans  104
  cram-down  103–04
    defined  103
    fair and equitable treatment  104
  means  99
  Section 1129(a)  99–101

  tax claims  101–03
    fraudulent taxes  103
    periodic payments of taxes  102
    standards for tax disclosures  102
Rule 6003  89–95
  20-day bar to the motions  90
  guidelines limiting relief  90
  importance of  90
  protections afforded  90
  provisions of  89
  slowing down the bankruptcy process  89
  standard for relief  91

## S

section 547(b), avoidable preferences under
  antecedent debt, for or on account of  131–32
    establishing when transfer takes place  131
  benefit of creditor, to or for  131
  debtor insolvency  133
  defenses  137–53
    Bankruptcy Abuse Prevention and Consumer Protection Act changes  146
    contemporaneous exchange  137–38
    enabling loans  143
    floating liens  144
    ordinary course of business payments  139–43
    payment of debt for domestic support obligations  145
    small business debt payments  146
    small consumer debt payments  145
    statutory liens  145
    subsequent advancement of unsecured credit  143–44

elements of 130–36
preferential effect 133–37
   Automatic Stay 136
   Bankruptcy Abuse Prevention and Consumer Protection Act 133
   property of the estate, defined 135
   reclamation claims 133
   section 362 136
   section 503(b)(9) 134
   section 541 135
   section 546(c) 134
   section 546(c)(2) 135
timing of transfer 132
   insider as transferee 132
transfer of debtor's property 130
transfer, defined 130
setoff under Section 553 177–82
  limitations on creditors 177–82
    calculation of possible recovery 178–79
  right to setoff 175–78
    debt netting 176
    existence under state law 176
    steps to effectuate 176
single-asset real estate 2–4
suppliers of goods leading up to the bankruptcy 187–92
  503(b)(9) administrative expenses 188–95
    502(d), inapplicability of 190
  reclamation rights 187–88
    section 546(c) provisions 187

assumption, standard for 116
  court approval 116
chapter 11 case 114
chapter 7 case 114
defined 113–14
  difficulty of defining 114
rejection, consequences of 115–16
  anticipatory repudiation of the contract 115
  rejection damages 115
rejection of 114
real property, non-residential, special cases of 117–19
  commercial leases in shopping centers 119
  debtor is lessee 118–19
  debtor is lessor 117–18
  time periods 118–24
Uniform Commercial Code 123, 127
Uniform Fraudulent Transfer Act 129
United Nations Commission on International Trade Law 30

# U

unexpired lease 113–24
  assignment 116–17
  assumption or rejection, determination of 115
  assumption or rejection, timing of 114

# About the Authors

**Stan Bernstein** served as a U.S. bankruptcy judge for more than 12 years, first from 1982 through 1984 in Flint and Detroit, Michigan, and from 1996 though 2007 on Long Island, New York, before retiring to teach full time as a law professor at Atlanta's John Marshall Law School. There he regularly offers courses on sales and secured transactions, bankruptcy, and equitable remedies. Recently, with co-authors Susan Seabury and Jack Williams, he has published two major Law Review articles on the application of the bankruptcy court's duties for admitting or rejecting testimony on financial matters in bankruptcy cases. Judge Bernstein was raised and educated in Boston, Massachusetts. He is a graduate of the Boston Latin School (founded in 1635), Brandeis University (B.A.), the University of Chicago (M.A., political science), Harvard University (Ph.D., political science), and Rutgers (J.D.) He was admitted to the bar of the states of Ohio, Michigan, California, Arizona, and Massachusetts, and focused primarily on business bankruptcy law and commercial finance for 35 years, including his federal judicial service.

**Susan Seabury** holds a bachelor's degree in economics from Vanderbilt University, an MBA from the Owen Graduate School of Management at Vanderbilt University, and a juris doctorate (cum laude) from Georgia State University College of Law. She is a member of the Georgia Bar, several federal bars, the Atlanta Bar, the American Bankruptcy Institute, the Association of Insolvency and Restructuring Advisors, and the International Women in Restructuring Confederation. Ms. Seabury is the author of several books and articles, and often speaks on business bankruptcy topics. She practices law, concentrating on commercial bankruptcy-related issues, and provides financial advisory services in bankruptcy and insolvency matters. Ms. Seabury is a director and special counsel with BDO Seidman, LLP's Business Restructuring Services.

**Jack Williams** is a professor of law at Georgia State University where he teaches and conducts research in numerous areas, including bankruptcy, business, and commercial law, and taxation. His honors include induction as a Fellow in the American College of Bankruptcy; resident scholar, Association of Insolvency and Restructuring Advisors; and Robert M. Zinman Scholar in Residence, American Bankruptcy Institute. He has served as a commentator or drafter of several foreign bankruptcy and taxation codes and as the tax adviser to the National Bankruptcy Review Commission. Professor Williams has written seven books and more than 150 articles and papers. He is a member of the Texas and Pennsylvania bars, several federal bars, and the Native American Bar Association. He is also a member of the American Bankruptcy Institute, the Association of Insolvency and Restructuring Advisors, the American Statistical Association, and the American Bar Association. He is a certified insolvency and r estructuring advisor and holds the certification in distress business valuations. Professor Williams holds a bachelor's degree in economics from the University of Oklahoma and a law degree from the George Washington University National Law School, where he graduated with high honors and was elected to the Order of the Coif. He is a Ph.D. candidate in archaeology and ancient history at the University of Leicester, Leicester, United Kingdom. Professor Williams is also a managing director with BDO Seidman, LLP.